Data Structure for 'C' Programming

DATA STRUCTURE FOR 'C' PROGRAMMING

[For DOEACC, IGNOU, BCA, MCA, B.Sc. (IT), B.E., B.Tech. and Other Courses in Computing]

By

AJAY KUMAR

B.Sc. (Computer Science), MCA

C.C.S. Daksh eServices Pvt. Ltd.

FIREWALL MEDIA

(An Imprint of Laxmi Publications Pvt. Ltd.)

BANGALORE • CHENNAI • COCHIN • GUWAHATI • HYDERABAD
JALANDHAR • KOLKATA • LUCKNOW • MUMBAI • PATNA
NEW DELHI

Published by :
FIREWALL MEDIA
(An Imprint of Laxmi Publications Pvt. Ltd.)
113, Golden House, Daryaganj,
New Delhi-110002

Phone : 011-43 53 25 00
Fax : 011-43 53 25 28

www.laxmipublications.com
info@laxmipublications.com

First Edition : 2002, *Second Revised Edition* : 2004
Reprint : 2005, 2006, 2007, 2008, 2009, 2012

OFFICES

✆ **Bangalore**	080-26 75 69 30	✆ **Chennai**	044-24 34 47 26
✆ **Cochin**	0484-237 70 04, 405 13 03	✆ **Guwahati**	0361-251 36 69, 251 38 81
✆ **Hyderabad**	040-24 65 23 33	✆ **Jalandhar**	0181-222 12 72
✆ **Kolkata**	033-22 27 43 84	✆ **Lucknow**	0522-220 99 16
✆ **Mumbai**	022-24 91 54 15, 24 92 78 69	✆ **Patna**	0612-230 00 97
✆ **Ranchi**	0651-221 47 64		

FDA–2717–210–DATA STRUCTURE FOR 'C' PROG **C—071/09/05**

Typeset at : ABRO Enterprises, Delhi. Printed at: Repro Knowledgecast Limited, Thane

PREFACE

(Second Edition)

Information Technology, the acronym of which is **IT**, has come a long way to stay for ever in our midst.

It is said : "One month of IT is equivalent to one social year". The domains of IT are expanding by each passing day, month and year. Every day, newer application softwares are being developed, with programming as the base, which itself has its essentials in Data Structure and File Structure. A good programmer is expected to know both these skills. Standard softwares like Customer Relationship Management and ERP, which need Data Structure are in great demand. Even search engine programming needs Data Structure.

Though Data Structure can be learned through any programming language, 'C' language renders the learning much easier and worthwhile.

Students of various universities like IGNOU, MDU, KU, DU and others, and those preparing for different courses such as MCA, BCA, PGDCA, B.Tech will find that their syllabuses are fully covered in this book.

Those having the working knowledge of C programming and who have at least understood the pointers will be able to comprehend the complete programs and algorithms.

Needless to say, these programs have been duly tested and algorithms have been written in a very simple form.

I am sure the book is bound to improve your programming skills and program analysis.

Suggestions for further improvement of the book will be welcome. Also your problems vis-a-vis programming will receive our prompt attention.

You can mail your suggestions and problems at ds_cp@rediffmail.com for a sure and prompt reply.

—Author

FOREWORD

The book 'Data Structure for 'C' Programming' is the result of Ajay Kumar's persistent effort. The stamp of his earlier work on Web Site Development and 15 Live Projects in C language is, at once, visible.

He has got certification *Brain Bench (USA)* in C Programming and Data Structure, which must have lent him both encouragement and strength in pursuing the subject. He has developed many new programs and algorithms for data structure which may not be found in other books.

His book is written in easy language. This work is intended to be a structured reference book and arrangement of subject-matter of the book is according to the examination point of view.

Even average students stand to perform well by using this book.

Moreover, the book covers the courses of IGNOU, MDU, KU, DU for BCA, MCA, PGDCA, B.Tech exams.

He has a passion for programming and love for meditation.

I hope more useful books will be forthcoming from Mr. Ajay Kumar in the coming years.

Jennifer Tabako
Aetna US Health Care,
U.S.A.

CONTENTS

Chapter 5

C STRUCTURES 77–90

Chapter 6

LISTS 91–138

Chapter 7

STACK AND QUEUES **139–170**

Chapter 8

GRAPHS **171–203**

Dedication

This book is dedicated to my grandfather Late Shri. C.R. Sharma. He was a well known poet, mathematician, accountant and intellectual person.

1

BASIC CONCEPTS OF DATA REPRESENTATION

1.1 INTRODUCTION

Data representation deals with the generalization of data in terms of **type.** A **type** is a set, and the elements of the set are called the **value** of the type. We may think that type *integer* represents the set of all integers, type *real* represents the set of all real numbers. C defines some built-in data types. C type *int*, for example, is not the set of all integers rather it is a subset of a set integer with a maximum range INT_MAX. Similarly, the C type *double* generally means a certain set of floating point numbers that is only a small subset of the set of all real numbers. C provides tools such as arrays, files and pointers with which we can build new types called structured types. We will discuss structured type in detail in due course.

Data structure is a representation of the logical relationship among individual elements of data. There are some classic data structures that form the building blocks for more sophisticated structures. A scalar item is the simplest of all data structures. A scalar item represents a single element of information that may be addressed by an identifier, *e.g. integer, float, char* etc. When scalar items are organized as a list or continuous group, an array is formed.

An array is the most common of all data structures and supports variable indexing of information. An array can have 1, 2. . .n dimensions.

String are also considered as classic data structures. Difference between a *char array* and a *string* lies in the form that a *string* is an *array* of characters with NULL character at the end of the array. Structure type data are used for grouping of items. Array is an example of structured structure type data. Other two structure type data are *Struct template* and *file.* We will discuss both of them in forthcoming chapters.

A **node** is the basic building block of data structure. We can picture the node as a box that is capable of holding a value drown from same basic or composition data type. Data structures are created by giving names to aggregates of nodes and (optionally) interpreting the values of some nodes as representing connection (*e.g.* pointers) among nodes.

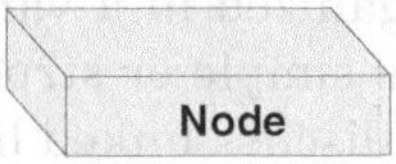

Fig. 1.1

1.2 CONCEPTUAL VIEW OF RAM

Computer uses *random-access memory* (RAM) to store information while it is operating. RAM is located in integrated circuits, or *chips*, inside your computer. RAM is *volatile*, which means it is erased and replaced with new information as often as needed. Being volatile also means that RAM 'remembers' only while the computer is turned on and loses its information when you turn off the computer. Each computer has a certain amount of

RAM installed. The amount of RAM in a system is usually specified in kilobytes (K), or megabytes (MB). One kilobyte of memory consists of 1,024 bytes. Thus, a system with 640K of memory actually has 640 times 1,024, or 655,360 bytes of RAM. One megabyte is 1,024 kilobytes.

Note. *A* ***byte*** *is the fundamental unit of computer data storage.*

Data	Bytes Required
The letter *x*	1
The number *100*	2
The number *120.145*	4
String *"New Delhi"*	10

Table 1.1. Memory space required to store data

The RAM in your computer is organized sequentially, one byte following another. Each byte of memory has a unique *address* by which it is identified, an address that also distinguishes it from all other bytes in memory. Addresses are assigned to memory locations in order, starting at 0 and increasing to the system limit. For now, you need not to worry about adresses; it is all handled automatically for you by the C compiler.

1.2.1 Usage of RAM

What is your computer's RAM used for ? It has several uses, but only one, *data storage*, need concern you as a programmer. *Data* means the information with which your C program works. Whether your program is maintaining an address list, monitoring the stock market, keeping a household budget, or tracking the healthcare services, the information (names, stock prices, expense amounts, or healthcare services) is kept in your computer's RAM while the program is running.

Now that you understand a little about the nuts and bolts of memory storage, you can get back to data structure and how C uses memory to store information.

1.3 ABSTRACT AND SYSTEM DEFINED DATA TYPES

Simple and structured data can be organized in a variety of formats. A linked list is a data structure that organizes noncontiguous simple or structured items in a manner that enables them to be processed as a list. We will discuss linked list in coming chapters. Data structures can be represented at different levels of abstraction. For example, a stack is a conceptual model of a data structure that can be implemented as an array or linked as an array or a linked list. We will discuss about stacks in forthcoming chapters, some other data structure models are queues, trees and graphs. All of these topics are thoroughly covered in the course.

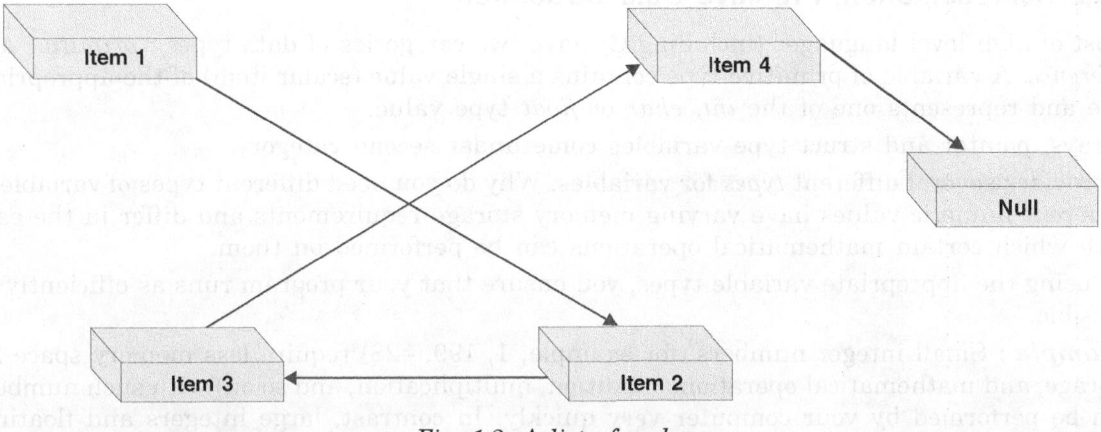

Fig. 1.2. A list of nodes

1.3.1 Abstract Data Type

Abstract data type is defined as a mathematical model with a collection of operations defined on that model. Sets of integers, together with the operations of UNION, INTERSECTION and SET DIFFERENCE form a simple example of an ADT. Some examples of ADT are LIST, STACK GRAPH, TREE, QUEUE etc. You may think ADT as a *class* in a object-oriented language.

1.3.1.1 Properties of ADT

There are two properties of **abstract data types.**

(A) Generalization

ADT's are generalizations of primitive data types, *e.g.,* int, float, char.

(B) Encapsulation

The ADT encapsulates a data type in the sense of the **type** and all operations on that **type** can be localized to one section of the program. Hence it is easy to make changes in the implementation of an ADT's by program. Moreover outside the section in which the ADT's operation are defined, we can treat the ADT as a primitive type.

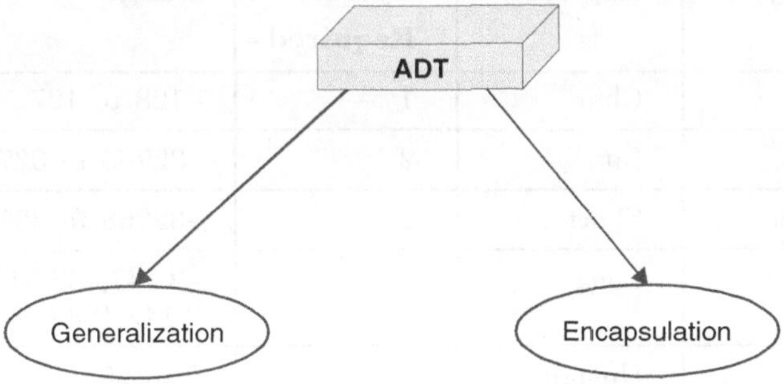

Fig. 1.3

1.3.2 Representation, Primitive Data Structures

Most of high level languages (including C) have two categories of data types : *primitive* and *reference.* A variable of primitive type contains a single value (scalar item) of the appropriate size and represents one of the *int, char* or *float* type value.

Arrays, pointer and struct type variables come under second category.

C provides several different *types* for variables. Why do you need different types of variables ? Different numeric values have varying memory storage requirements and differ in the ease with which certain mathematical operations can be performed on them.

By using the appropriate variable types, you ensure that your program runs as efficiently as possible.

Example : Small integer numbers (for example, 1, 199, –28) require less memory space for storage, and mathematical operations (addition, multiplication, and so on) with such numbers can be performed by your computer very quickly. In contrast, large integers and floating-point values (417,000,000 or 0.000000961250, for example) require more storage space and more time for mathematical operations.

1.3.3 Variables

A *variable* is a named data storage location in your computer's memory. By using a variable's name in your program, you are, in effect, referring to the data stored there.

1.3.3.1 Numeric Variable Categories

C's numeric variables fall into the following two main categories :

- *Integer variables* hold values that have no fractional part (that is, whole numbers only). Integer variables come in two flavours : signed integer variables can hold positive or negative values, whereas unsigned integer variables can hold only positive values (and 0, of course).
- *Floating-point variables* hold values that have a fractional part (that is, real numbers).

Within each of these categories are two or more specific variable types. These are summarized here, which also shows the amount of memory, in bytes, required to hold a single variable of each type when you use a microcomputer with 16-bit architecture.

Variable Types	**Keyword**	**Bytes Required**	**Range**
character	Char	1	–128 to 127
integer	Int	2	–32768 to 32767
short integer	Short	2	–32768 to 32767
long integer	Long	4	–2,147,483,648 to 2,147,483,648
unsigned character	Unsigned char	1	0 to 255
unsigned integer	Unsigned int	2	0 to 65535
unsigned short integer	Unsigned short	2	0 to 65535

unsigned long integer	Unsigned long	4	0 to 4,294,967,295
single-precision floating point	Float	4	1.2E–38 to 3.4E38 Approximate range; precision = 7 digits.
Double-precision floating-point	Double	8	2.2E–308 to 1.8E308 Approximate range; precision = 19 digits.

Table 1.2. C's numeric data types

1.3.3.2 Approximate Range

Approximate range means the highest and lowest values a given variable can hold. (Space limitations prohibit listing exact ranges for the values of these variables.)

1.3.3.3 Precision

Precision means the accuracy with which the variable is stored. (For example, if you evaluate 1/3, the answer is 0.33333 . . . with 3s going to infinity. A variable with a precision of 7 stores seven 3s).

1.3.3.4 int Versus short

Looking at Table 1.2, you may notice that the variable types int and short are identical. Why then have two different types ? The int and short variable types are indeed identical on 16-bit IBM PC-compatible system, but they may be different on other types of hardware. On a VAX system, a short and an int are not the same size. Instead, a short is 2 bytes, whereas an int is 4. Remember that C is a flexible, portable language, so it provides different keywords for the two types. If you are working on a PC, you can use int and short interchangeably.

1.3.3.5 Integer Variables : Signed by Default

No special keyword is needed to make an integer variable signed; integer variables are signed by default. You can, however, include the signed keyword if you wish.
Listing 1.1 will help you determine the size of variables on your particular computer.

LISTING 1.1

```
/*  data  types  */
/*  Program  to  tell  the  size  of  the  C  */
/*  variable  type  in  bytes  */

#include  <stdio.h>
int  main  (void)
{
   printf  ("\nA  char      is  %d  bytes",
            sizeof  (char));
   printf  ("\nAn  int      is  %d  bytes",
            sizeof  (int));
   printf  ("\nA  short     is  %d  bytes",
            sizeof  (short));
   printf  ("\nA  long      is  %d  bytes",
            sizeof  (long));
```

```
    printf ("\nAn unsigned char         is %d bytes",
            sizeof (unsigned char));
    printf ("\nAn unsigned int          is %d bytes",
            sizeof (unsigned int));
    printf ("\nAn unsigned short        is %d bytes",
            sizeof (unsigned short));
    printf ("\nAn unsigned long         is %d bytes",
            sizeof (unsigned long));
    printf ("\nA float     is %d bytes",
            sizeof (float));
    printf ("\nA double    is %d bytes",
            sizeof (double));
    return 0;
}
```

Output

```
A char           is 1 bytes
An int           is 2 bytes
A short          is 2 bytes
A long           is 4 bytes
An unsigned char    is 1 bytes
An unsigned int     is 2 bytes
An unsigned short   is 2 bytes
An unsigned long    is 4 bytes
A float          is 4 bytes
A double         is 8 bytes
```

1.3.3.6 The Size of Variables

- The size of a char is 1 byte.
- The size of a short is less than or equal to the size of int.
- The size of an int is less than or equal to the size of a long.
- The size of an unsigned int is equal to the size of an int.
- The size of a float is less than or equal to the size of a double.

CONCEPTUAL PROBLEM

Problem 1.1 : *For a Banking software consider the following facts : Tracking of the customer account, Total number of transitions in a week. Point out at least four variables and their types from these facts.*

Solution :

Variables	*Types*
Cust_name	char
Account_id	int
T_week	long int

KEY POINTS

- A **type** is a set, and the elements of the set are called the **value** of the type.
- Data structure is a representation of the logical relationship among individual elements of data.
- A scalar item is the simplest of all data structures.
- Difference between a *char array* and a *string* lies in the form that a *string* is an *array* of characters with NULL character the end of the array.
- Each byte of memory has a unique *address* by which it is identified, an address that also distinguishes it from all other bytes in memory.
- Abstract data type is defined as a mathematical model with a collection of operations defined on that model. Sets of integers, together with the operations of union, intersection and set difference form a simple example of an ADT.
- A *variable* is a named data storage location in your computer's memory.

EXERCISE

1. In what variable type would you best store the following values ?
   (*a*) A person's weight in pounds.
   (*b*) Your annual salary.
   (*c*) The temperature.
   (*d*) A person's net worth.

2. Write the value return by sizeof() function for the following statements :
   (*a*) sizeof(char) ....
   (*b*) sizeof(int) ....
   (*c*) sizeof(200) ....
   (*d*) sizeof(2.5) ....
   (*e*) sizeof(void) ....
   (*f*) sizeof("DATA STRUCTURE") ....

3. What are the two properties of ADT ?

4. Define the term static variable and dynamic variable.

5. What is a pointer ?

6. What are atomic and structured types ?

2

INTRODUCTION TO ALGORITHM DESIGN AND DATA STRUCTURE

2.1 INTRODUCTION

Software engineering methods are used to solve a complex real life problem. Problem definition is the first step to solve a problem. Algorithm design is the second step to solve a problem. We will discuss algorithm design and analysis for an algorithm in following sections. There are two approaches for algorithm design, we will study both top down and bottom up approaches for algorithm design. There is always a time-space trade off in the algorithm implementation. The study of complexity measures in terms of time and space is very important for algorithm analysis. Finally, structured approach to programming is discussed in this chapter.

2.2 ALGORITHM

The algorithm is the basic step in designing phase to find a solution of a problem, **an** algorithm is defined as *the finite sequence of instructions, each of which has a clear meaning and can be performed with a finite amount of effort in a finite length of time.* We can write algorithms using a pseudo-language that is a combination of the constructs of a programming language together with informal English statements. For any input, an algorithm terminates after executing a finite number of instructions.

2.3 ALGORITHM DESIGN

Writing and executing programs and then optimizing them may be effective for small programs. Optimization of a program is directly concerned with algorithm design. But for a large program, each part of the program must be well organized before writing the program. In very large projects, difficulties usually do not arise from the inability to find the solution but it is due to the fact that there can be so many different methods and algorithms that might work.

2.3.1 Top Down Design

Top down design is the incremental approach to construction of program structure. Modules are integrated by moving downward through the control hierarchy. Starting module is the main program.

Bottom-up approach works in opposite direction. Starting with specific modules and build them into more complex structures, ending at the top.

Being a structured language, C programs are designed by Top-Down approach.

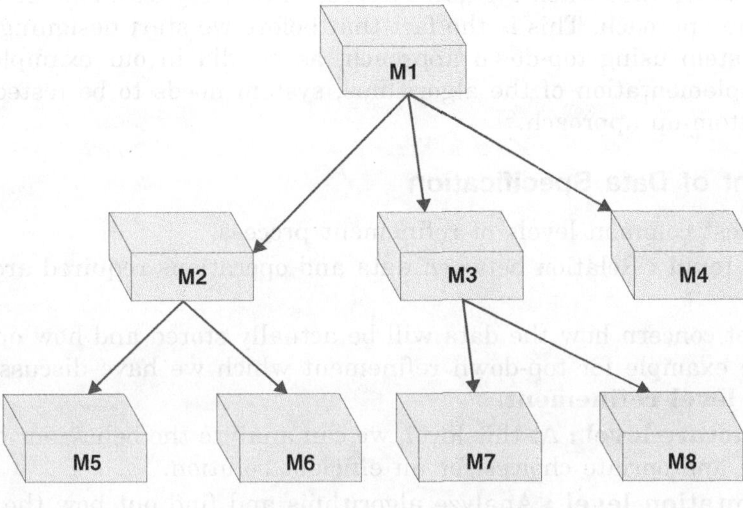

Fig. 2.1. Top-down design

Let us consider an example, design view of an ERP system of **"New Transport Organisation". NTO** is using a system called NTO Session Manager (NSM). NSM works as the main program. There are four subsystems Enterprise Customer Database (ECD), Inventory System (IS), Logistic Control (LC), Strategic Price (SP) respectively. Further IS is refined in two subsystems Transferred Goods (TG) and Moving Goods (MG). Further, MG is refined into Goods on Stock (GS) and Goods on Vehicle (GV). LC System is refined in HV, LV stands for high and light vehicles respectively. SP system is used to calculate freight charges. The subsystems are further refined up to many levels in actual implementation. These subsystems are commonly known as modules. Each module can easily be implemented as a function during coding. This system is designed on the top-down approach. Top-down makes your life easy, a complex system can be refined to simple and small systems. The entire project is represented by following top-down model diagram.

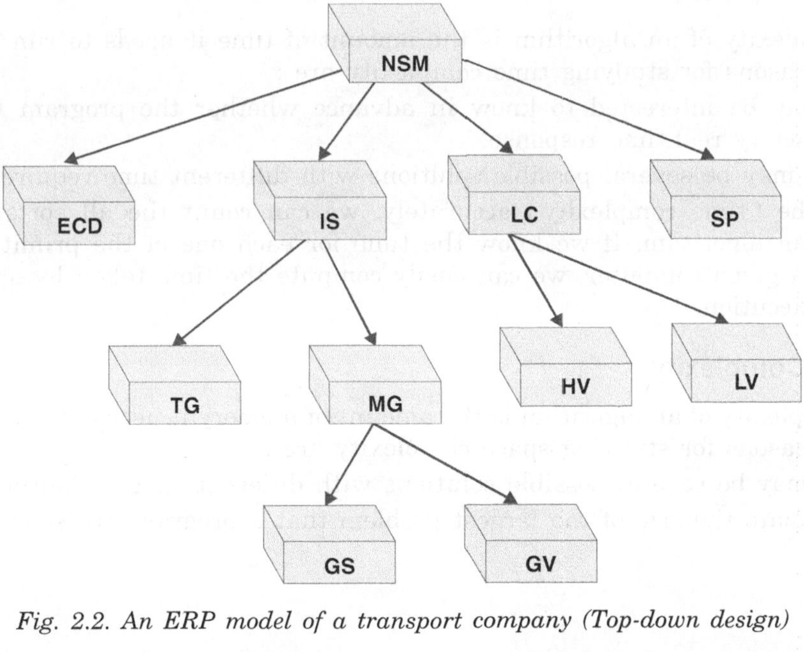

Fig. 2.2. An ERP model of a transport company (Top-down design)

Here is a good question that when top-down approach is really excellent then why and when we need bottom-up approach. This is the fact that before we start designing our algorithms, we design our system using top-down approach, as we did in our example. But after the designing and implementation of the algorithms, system needs to be tested. In the testing phase we use bottom-up approach.

2.3.2 Refinement of Data Specification

There are four most common levels of refinement process.

1. **Abstruct level :** Relation between data and operations required are defined at this level.

   We are not concern how the data will be actually stored and how operations will be done. The example for top-down refinement which we have discussed comes under **abstruct level refinement.**
2. **Data structure level :** At this level, we can analyze the behaviour of the operations and make appropriate choices for an efficient solution.
3. **Implementation level :** Analyze algorithms and find out how the data structures will be represented in memory.
4. **Application level :** Attributes of an application are assigned and interaction between two more applications is done. This level consists of coding in a high level or low level language.

2.4 ALGORITHM COMPLEXITY

An algorithm is a sequence of steps to solve a problem; there may be more than one algorithm to solve a problem. The choice of a particular algorithm depends on following considerations :

1. *Time complexity*
2. *Space complexity.*

2.4.1 Time Complexity

The time complexity of an algorithm is the amount of time it needs to run to completion. Some of the reasons for studying time complexity are :

- We may be interested to know in advance whether the program will provide a satistactory real-time response.
- There may be several possible solutions with diffterent time requirements.

To measure the (time complexity) accurately, we can count the all sorts of operations performed in an algorithm. If we know the time for each one of the primitive operations performed on a given computer, we can easily compute the time taken by an algorithm to complete its execution.

2.4.2 Space Complexity

The space complexity of an algorithm is the amount of memory it needs to run to completion. Some of the reasons for studying space complexity are :

- There may be several possible solutions with different space requirements.
- To estimate the size of the largest problem that a program can solve.

The total space needed by a program can be divided in two parts :

1. A fixed part that is independent of a particular problem, and includes instruction space, space for constants.
   Simple variables and fixed size structured variables.
2. A variable part that includes structured variables whose size depends on the particular problem being solved, dynamically allocated space and the recursion stack space.

2.5 TIME-SPACE TRADE-OFF

There may be more than one approach to solve a problem. One such approach may require more space but takes less time to complete its execution. The second approach may require less space but takes more time to compute its execution. We have to choose the first approach if time is a constraint. And if space is our constraint, then we have to choose the second approach.

2.6 BIG OH NOTATION

Big Oh is a characterization scheme that allows us to measure properties of algorithms. There is a complexity function f (n) of an algorithm which increases as *n* increases. It is the rate of increase of f (n) which we want to examine.
Let f(n) and g(n) be two functions, for all n > 0 .
Then function f(n) = O [g(n)],
Read as "f of n is big oh of g of n", or as "f(n) is of the order of g(n)."
If there exists a positive constant K and C, such that

```
f(n)  <=  K  *  g(n),  for  all  k>=C
```

Based on Big Oh notation, the algorithms can be categorized as follows :

1. **Constant Time (O(1)) Algorithm**
   If the algorithm is independent of problem size, the complexity in time and space, *i.e.*, O (1).
2. **Logarithmic Time Algorithms**
   (*i*) O ($\log_2$n). If the problem size doubles and the algorithm takes one more step, we relate the number of steps to the problem size by

   $$O\ (\log_2 n)$$

   It is read as **order** of $\log_2$n.
   (*ii*) O (n $\log_2$n). If the problem size doubles and algorithm takes more than twice as many steps *i.e.*, the number of steps required grows faster than the problem size, we use the following expression

   $$O\ n \log_2 n$$

3. **Linear Time [O(n)] Algorithm**
   If the problem size doubles and the algorithm takes twice as many steps.
4. **Polynomial Time [O(nk)] ∀ k >1 Algorithm**
   If the number of steps used is proportional to the kth power of the problem size.

2.7 STRUCTURED PROGRAMMING

In 1960s, Dijkstra proposed the use of constrained logical constructs from which any program could be formed. The constructs emphasized "maintenance of functional domain". That is, each construct had a predictable logical structure, which is entered at the top and exited at the bottom. Such a programming which gives exact readability and procedural flow to reader is called structured programming.

There are three structured constructs :

1. **Sequence :** It indicates processing steps that are essential in the specification of any algorithm.

   Example :

```
printf("enter a number");
scanf("%d",&n);
```

2. **Condition :** Condition provides the facility for selected processing based on some logical fact. For example, IF condition in C.

   Example :

```
if(n%2==0)
printf("Number is Even");
else
printf("Number is odd");
```

3. **Repetition :** When a set of instructions are executed number of times. For example,

```
for (i=1;i<=10;i++)
{
printf("\n%d",n*i);
}
```

These three constructs are the essential components of structured programming.

Core objective of the structured programming is to improve the execution speed of a program. In traditional programming GOTO statements were used in common. A GOTO statement slow downs the execution of a program. A fully structured program does not contains any GOTO statement.

Let us take an example of complete structured program.

2.8 DATA STRUCTURE

A data structure is a logical model of a particular organization of data. The programs have to follow certain rules to access and process the structured data. Therefore data structure is represented as:

Data structure = Organized Data + Allowed Operations

The study of data structures deals with the following:

(*i*) Logical description of the data structure
(*ii*) Implementation of the data structure
(*iii*) Quantitative analysis of the data structure.

There are two types of data structures :

2.8.1 Linear Data Structure

The elements form a sequence, *i.e.* linear list. Examples of linear data structures are *arrays, linked lists, stacks* and *queues*.

2.8.2 Non Linear Data Structure

The elements do not form a sequence. Examples of non-linear data structures are trees and graphs.

2.9 MEMORY ALLOCATION

Memory blocks are allocated for program entities during execution phase. Allocation of memory blocks is done randomly inside the RAM.

Memory allocation is of two types :

(1) *Static memory allocation.*

(2) *Dynamic memory allocation.*

2.9.1 Static Memory Allocation

Memory is allocated to the entities by the Operating System. Once the memory blocks are allocated to the entities, they remain reserved till the end of the program. Such a memory allocation for arrays is called *static memory allocation*.

2.9.2 Dynamic Memory Allocation

Memory is allocated dynamically to the entities of the program. Programmer has freedom to allocate and free the memory for the program entities. Such a memory allocation is called *dynamic memory allocation.*

CONCEPTUAL PROBLEM

Problem 2.1 : *Show that any sorting algorithm that moves elements only one position at a time must have time complexity of at least $O(n^2)$ where 'n' is the number of elements.*

(MCA December, 2001)

Solution : Time complexity is least when given array of elements is already in sorted form. In such a case for n elements, first pass requires n–1 comparisons and second pass requires n–2 comparisons and so on. Therefore, total number of comparisons are :

$$f(n) = (n-1) + (n-2) + \ldots + 3 + 2 + 1.$$
$$= n(n-1)/2$$
$$= O(n^2).$$

KEY POINTS

- An algorithm is defined as *the finite sequence of instructions, each of which has a clear meaning and can be performed with a finite amount of effort in a finite length of time.*
- Top-down and Bottom-up approaches are used to design a solution of a problem.
- Top-down design is the incremental approach to construction of program structure. Modules are integrated by moving downward through the control hierarchy. Starting module is the main program.
- There are four most common levels of refinement process.
  1. Abstraction level
  2. Data structure level
  3. Implementation level
  4. Application level.
- There exist a time-space complexity to select an algorithm.
- Big Oh is a characterization scheme that allows us to measure properties of algorithms.
- There are three structured constructs in a structured programming.
  1. Sequence
  2. Control
  3. Repetition.

EXERCISE

1. Name four levels of refinement of data specification.
2. Arrange the following functions into increasing order; that is, f(n) should come before g(n) in your list if and only if f(n) and O(g(n)).

1000000	nlog n	$(\log n)^3$	2^n
n^4-100n^3	n+log n	log log n	n^2

3. Give, using "bog oh" notation, the worst case running times of the following procedure as a function of n.

```
void function1 (int n)
{
int  i,j,k;
for(i=0;i<n;i++)
for(j=0;j<n;j++)
for(k=0;k<n;k++)
//some  statements  requiring  O(1)  time.
}
```

3

ARRAYS

3.1 INTRODUCTION

An *array* is a collection of data storage locations, each having the same data type and the same name. Each storage location in an array is called an *array element.*

Why do you need arrays in your programs ? This question can be answered with an example given below.

Figure 3.1 illustrates the difference between using individual variables and an array. If you are keeping track of your business expenses for the current financial year, and filing your receipts by month, you could have a separate folder for each month's receipts, but it would be more convenient to have a single folder with twelve compartments. Extend this example to computer programming. Imagine that you are designing a program to keep track of your business expense totals. The program could declare twelve separate variables, one for each month's expense total. This approach is analogous to having twelve separate folders for your receipts. Good programming practice, however, would utilize an array with twelve elements, storing each month's total in the corresponding array element. This approach is comparable to filing your receipts in a single folder with twelve compartments.

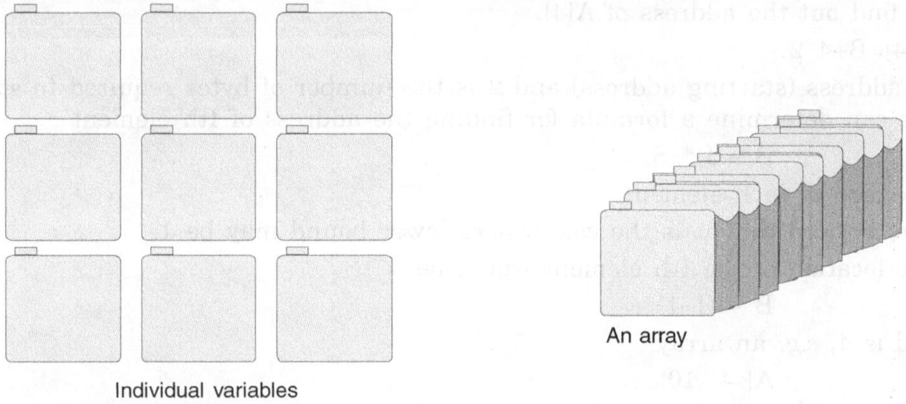

Fig. 3.1. Variables are like individual folders, whereas an array is like a single folder with many compartments

3.2 SINGLE-DIMENSIONAL ARRAYS

A *single-dimensional* array is an array that has only a single subscript. A *subscript* is a number in brackets following an array's name. This number can identify the number of individual elements in the array. All of C's data types can be used for arrays. C arrays elements are always numbered starting at 0.

Example :

> For the business expenses program, you could use the program line
>
> ```
> float  expenses  [12];
> ```
>
> to declare an array of type float. The array is named expenses, and contains twelve elements. Each of the twelve elements is the exact equivalent of a single float variable. The twelve elements of expenses are numbered 0–11.

3.2.1 Storage of Arrays in Main Memory

When you declare an array, the compiler sets aside a block of memory large enough to hold the entire array. Individual array elements are stored in sequential memory locations, as illustrated in Figure 3.2.

One dimensional array can be mapped onto the memory cells in a one-to-one correspondence manner. However, the address of first entry of the array is random. Let us see it through an example. Consider an array of 5 elements as follows :

A={10,20,30,40,50}

A[0] A[4]

If we have to find out the address of A[4].

Address of A[4]=B+4*2

B is the base address (starting address) and 2 is the number of bytes required to store an integer. So we can determine a formula for finding the address of Ith element :

$$B + I * S \qquad \text{...(1)}$$

where S is the size of each element.

You must have noticed that it is the case where lower bound may be 1.

In such a case location of the Ith element would be

$$B + (I-1) \qquad \text{...(2)}$$

If lower bound is 4, *e.g.* an array :

A[4...10].

Location of Ith element

$$= \quad B + (I-4) \qquad \text{...(3)}$$

From eqs. (1), (2), (3), we can conclude that for location of Ith element, following general equation can be used :

$$B + (I-L) \qquad \text{...(4)}$$

where L is the lower bound on subscript. It may be positive, negative or zero.

For example,

```
int array[10];
```

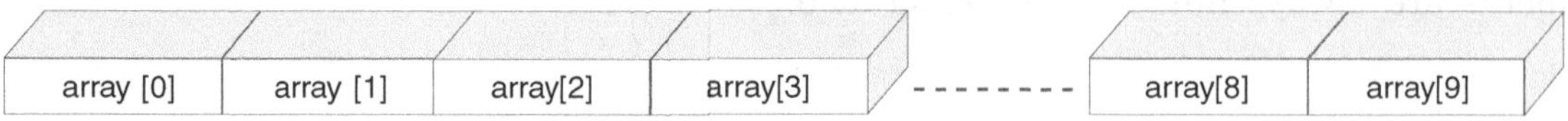

Fig. 3.2. Array elements are stored in sequential memory locations

3.2.2 Use of Array Elements

An array element can be used in your program anywhere. A nonarray variable of the same type can be used. Individual elements of the array are accessed by using the array name followed by the element subscript enclosed in square brackets.

Example :

The statement

```
expenses[1] = 50.99;
```

stores the value 50.99 in the second array element. (Remember, the first array element is expenses[0], not expenses[1].) Likewise, the statement

```
expenses[10] = expenses[11];
```

assigns the value that is stored in array element expenses[11] to array element expenses[10].

3.2.3 Types of Array Subscripts

When you refer to an array element, the array subscript can be a literal constant, as in `expenses[1]`. Your programs may, however, frequently use a subscript that is a C integer variable or expression, or even another array element. Refer to Example (*a*).

3.2.4 Allowable Subscripts

When you use arrays, keep the element numbering scheme in mind. In an array of n elements, the allowable subscripts range from 0 to n–1. If you use the subscript value n, you may get program errors. The C compiler does not recognize whether your program uses an array subscript that is out of bounds. Your program compiles and links, but out-of-range subscripts generally produce erroneous results. Sometimes you might want to treat an array of n elements as if its elements were numbered 1–n. Refer to Example (b).

Example (a) :

Here are some examples :

```
float expenses[100];
int a[10];
/* additional statements go here */
expenses[i] = 100;          /* i is an integer
variable */
expenses[2 + 3] = 100;  /* equivalent to
expenses[5] */
expenses[a[2]] = 100; /* a[] is an integer array */
```

That last example may need an explanation. Say, for instance, you have an integer array named a[ ] and that the value 8 is stored in element a[2]. Then, writing

```
expenses[a[2]]
```

has the same effect as writing

```
expenses[8];
```

Example (b) :

For instance, in the previous example of a program to keep track of business expense totals, January's expense total would be stored in expenses[0], February's in expenses[1], and so on. A more natural method might be to store January's expense total in expenses[1], February's in expenses[2], and so on. The simplest way to do this is to declare the array with one more element than needed, and ignore element 0. In this case, you would declare the array

```
float expenses[13];
```

You also could store some related data in element 0 (the yearly expense total, perhaps).

3.2.5 Example Program

The Listing 3.1 demonstrates the use of an array. This is a simple program with no real practical use; its for demonstration purposes only.

LISTING 3.1

```
/* month_expenses.c arrays */
/* use of an array */

#include <stdio.h>

/* Declare an array to hold expenses, and a */
/* counter variale. */

float expenses[13];
int count;

int main(void) {
    /* Input data from keyboard into array. */
    for (count = 1; count < 13; count++) {
       printf("Enter expenses for month %d;", count);
       scanf("%f", &expenses[count]);
    }
    /* Print array contents. */

    for (count = 1; count < 13; count++) {
       printf("\nMonth %d = Rs. %.2f", count,
           expenses[count]);
    }
    return 0;
}
```

Output

```
Enter   expenses   for   month   1:    2000
Enter   expenses   for   month   2:    3000.25
Enter   expenses   for   month   3:    4500.50
Enter   expenses   for   month   4:   20000
Enter   expenses   for   month   5:    1500.50
Enter   expenses   for   month   6:    1490.25
Enter   expenses   for   month   7:     550.25
Enter   expenses   for   month   8:    2050.00
Enter   expenses   for   month   9:    1330.25
Enter   expenses   for   month  10:    1210.25
Enter   expenses   for   month  11:    2320.25
Enter   expenses   for   month  12:    1300.00

Month   1 = Rs.  2000.00
Month   2 = Rs.  3000.25
Month   3 = Rs.  4500.50
Month   4 = Rs. 20000.00
Month   5 = Rs.  1500.50
Month   6 = Rs.  1490.25
Month   7 = Rs.   550.25
Month   8 = Rs.  2050.00
Month   9 = Rs.  1330.45
Month  10 = Rs.  1220.25
Month  11 = Rs.  2320.25
Month  12 = Rs.  1300.00
```

3.3 MULTIDIMENSIONAL ARRAY

A multidimensional array has more than one subscript. A *two-dimensional array* has two subscripts, a *three-dimensional array* has three subscripts, and so on. There is no limit to the number of dimensions a C array can have. (But there is a limit on total array size.) The structure of this two-dimensional array is illustrated in Figure 3.3.

> You might write a program that plays checkers. The checkerboard contains 64 squares aranged in eight rows and eight columns. Your program could represent the board as a two-dimensional array, as follows :
>
> `int checker[8][8];`
>
> The resulting array has 64 elements : checker[0][0], checker[0][1], checker[0][2] ... checker[7][6], checker[7][7].

```
int checker [8] [8] :
```

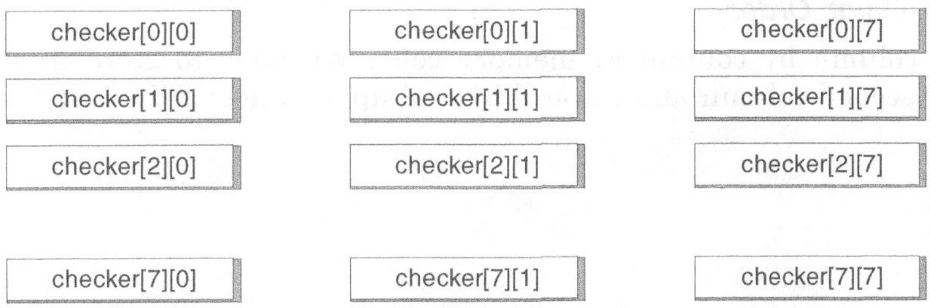

Fig. 3.3

3.3.1 Representing Two-Dimensional Array in Memory

Two-dimensional arrays are called matrices in mathematics. A two-dimensional m*n array is shown below :

$$\begin{array}{ccccc} a_{00} & a_{01} & a_{02} & \cdots & a_{0n} \\ a_{10} & a_{11} & a_{12} & \cdots & a_{1n} \\ a_{20} & a_{21} & a_{22} & \cdots & a_{2n} \\ a_{30} & a_{31} & a_{32} & \cdots & a_{3n} \\ . & & & & \\ . & & & & \\ . & & & & \\ a_{m0} & a_{m1} & a_{m2} & \cdots & a_{mn} \end{array}$$

Fig 3.4 Array a[m,n]

This array is represented in memory by a block of m*n sequential memory locations. However, the elements can be stored in two different ways.

3.3.1.1 Row Major Order

Data is stored row by row in memory cells. It means we store first the first row of the array, then the second row of the array and then the next and so on.

For example, the array defined by A which logically appears as given in Fig. 3.5 appears physically as given in Fig. 3.6. Such a storage scheme is called row major order.

int A[3][3]

A[0][0]	A[0][1]	A[0][2]
A[1][0]	A[1][1]	A[1][2]
A[2][0]	A[2][1]	A[2][2]

Fig. 3.5 Logical representation

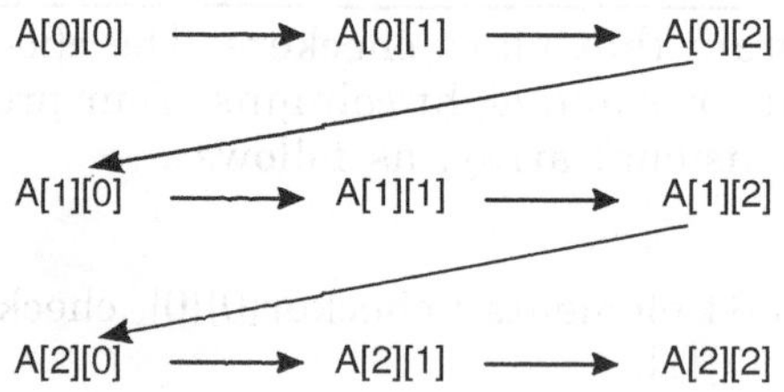

Fig. 3.6 Row major representation

3.3.1.2 Column Major Order

Data is stored column by column in memory cells. We have to store first column of the array, then the second column and so on. Physical appearance of the last example is shown in Fig. 3.7

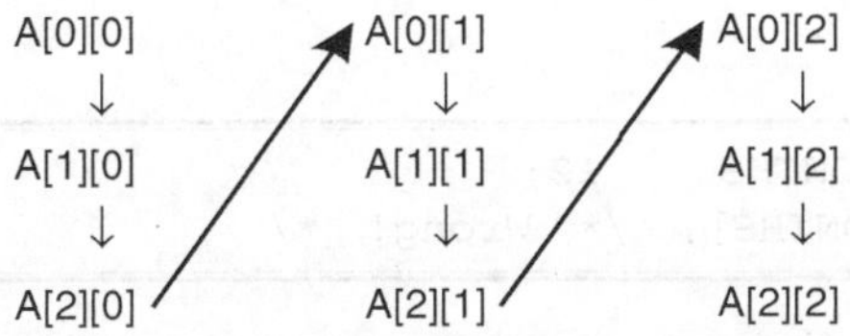

Fig. 3.7 Column major representation

In all implementations of C the Storage Allocation Scheme used is the row major order.

Addressing an element in a 2-Dim. Array :

Let's consider the following 2 dim. Array :

```
A[L1..U1,L2..U2]
```

where L1 and L2 are lower bounds of the two subscript ranges and U1 and U2 are the upper bounds of the two subscript ranges.

The location of an element A(I,J) for such an array would be

```
B  +  (I-L1)*(U2-L2+1)*S+(J-L2)*S
```

3.3.2 Three- or Four-Dimensional Arrays

A three-dimensional array could be thought of as a cube. Four-dimensional arrays (and higher) are probably best left to your imagination. All arrays, no matter how many dimensions they have, are stored sequentially in memory.

3.4 NAMING ARRAYS

The rules for assigning names to arrays are the same as for variable names. An array name must be unique. It cannot be used for another array or for any other identifier (variable, constant, and so on). As you have probably realized, array declarations follow the same form as declarations of nonarray variables, except that the number of elements in the array must be enclosed in square brackets immediately after the array name.

3.5 DECLARING ARRAYS

When you declare an array, you can specify the number of elements with a literal constant (as was done in the earlier examples) or with a symbolic constant created with the #define directive. Refer to Example (*c*).

With most compilers, however, you cannot declare an array's elements with a symbolic constant created with the const keyword. Refer to Example (*d*).

Example (c) :

```
#define MONTHS 12
int array[MONTHS];
```

is equivalent to

```
int array[12];
```

Example (d) :

```
const int MONTHS = 12;
int array[MONTHS]; /* Wrong! */
```

Example Program

Listing 3.2, students_grades.c, is another program demonstrating the use of a single-dimensional array. student_grades.c uses an array to store 10 grades.

LISTING 3.2

```
/* array */
/* student_grades.c Example program with array */
/* Get 10 grades and then average them. */

#include <stdio.h>

#define MAX_GRADE 100
#define STUDENTS 10

int grades[STUDENTS];

int idx;
int total = 0; /* Used for average. */

int main(void) {
    for (idx = 0; idx < STUDENTS; idx++) {
        printf("Enter Person %d's grade: ", idx +1);
        scanf("%d", &grades[idx]);
        while (grades[idx] > MAX_GRADE) {
            printf("\nThe highest grade possible is %d",
                MAX_GRADE);
            printf("\nEnter correct grade: ");
            scanf("%d", &grades[idx]);
        }

        total += grades[idx];
    }

    printf ("\n\nThe average score is %d",
        (total / STUDENTS));

    return 0;
}
```

Output

```
Enter Person 1's grade: 85
Enter Person 2's grade: 75
Enter Person 3's grade: 145
The highest grade possible is 100
Enter correct grade: 67
Enter Person 4's grade: 87
Enter Person 5's grade: 99
Enter Person 6's grade: 76
```

```
Enter Person 7's grade: 45
Enter Person 8's grade: 90
Enter Person 9's grade: 100
Enter Person 10's grade: 78
The average score is 80
```

3.6 INITIALIZING SINGLE-DIMENSIONAL ARRAYS

You can initialize all or part of an array when you first declare it. Follow the array declaration with an equal sign and a list of values enclosed in braces and separated by commas. The listed values are assigned in order to array elements starting at number 0.

If you omit the array size, the compiler creates an array just large enough to hold the initialization values.

You can, however, include too few initialization values.

See some Examples below :

```
int array[4] = { 2, 4, 6, 8 };
```

assigns the value 2 to array[0], 4 to array[1], 6 to array[2], and 8 to array[3].

Thus, the statement

```
int array[] = { 2, 4, 6, 8 };
```

would have exactly the same effect as the pevious array declaration statement, *i.e.* it assigns the value 2 to array[0], 4 to array[1], 6 to array[2], and 8 to array[3].

```
int array[10] = { 3, 6, 9 };
```

If you do not explicitly initialize an array element, you cannot be sure what value it holds when the program runs. If you include too many initializers (more initializers than array elements), the compiler detects an error.

3.7 INITIALIZING MULTIDIMENSIONAL ARRAYS

Multidimensional arrays also can be initialized. The list of initialization values is assigned to array elements in order, with the last array subscript changing first.

One Format

For example,

int array[4][3] = {1, 2, 3, 4, 5, 6, 7, 8, 9, 10, 11, 12} ;

results in the following assignments :

array[0][0] is equal to 1
array[0][1] is equal to 2
array[0][2] is equal to 3
array[1][0] is equal to 4
array[1][1] is equal to 5
array[1][2] is equal to 6
...
array[3][1] is equal to 11
array[3][2] is equal to 12

A Clearer Format

When you initialize multidimensional arrays, you can make your source code clearer by using extra braces to group the initializatoin values and also by spreading them over several lines. The following initialization is equivalent to the one given previously :

```
int array[4][3] = {{1, 2, 3}, {4, 5, 6},
                   {7, 8, 9}, {10, 11, 12}};
```

Remember, initialization values must be separated by a comma—even when there is a brace between them. Also, be sure to use braces in pairs—a closing brace for every opening brace—or the compiler becomes confused.

Example Program

Now look at an example that demonstrates the advantages of array. The program in Listing 3.3, **rundom_number.c**, creates a 1000-element, three-dimensional array and fills it with random numbers. The program then displays the array elements on the screen. Imagine how many lines of source code you would need to perform the same task with nonarray variables.

You see a new library function, getchar(), in this program. The getchar() function reads a single character from the keyboard. In Listing 3.3, getchar() pauses the program until the user presses ENTER.

LISTING 3.3 : **rundom_number.c**

```
/* array */
/* random_number.c -- Demonstrates using a */
/* multidimensional array */

#include <stdio.h>
#include <stdlib.h>

/* Declare a three-dimensional array with 1000 */
/* elements. */

int random[10] [10] [10];
int a, b, c;

int main(void) {
    /* Fill the array with random numbers. The C*/
    /* library function rand() returns a random */
    /* number. Use one for loop for each array */
    /* subscript. */

    for (a=0; a < 10; a++) {
        for (b=0; b < 10; b++) {
            for (c=0; c < 10; c++) {
                random[a] [b] [c] = rand();
            }
        }
    }
    /* Display the array elements 10 at a time. */
    for (a=0; a < 10; a++) {
        for (b=0; b < 10; b++) {
```

```
            for (c=0; c < 10; c++) {
                printf("\nrandom[%d][%d][%d] =",
                    a, b, c);
                printf("%d", random[a][b][c]);
            }
            printf("\nPress ENTER to continue,"
                "CTRL-C to quit.");
            getchar();
        }
    }
    return 0;
}
```

Output

```
random[0][0][0] = 400
random[0][0][1] = 253
random[0][0][2] = 10082
random[0][0][3] = 1190
random[0][0][4] = 12345
random[0][0][5] = 7896
random[0][0][6] = 29595
random[0][0][7] = 7415
random[0][0][8] = 22948
random[0][0][9] = 31126
Press ENTER to continue, CTRL-C to quit.
random[0][0][0] = 8884
random[0][0][1] = 24588
random[0][0][2] = 3576
random[0][0][3] = 22549
random[0][0][4] = 18476
random[0][0][5] = 3460
random[0][0][6] = 5412
random[0][0][7] = 68721
random[0][0][8] = 34463
random[0][0][9] = 12047
Press ENTER to continue, CTRL-C to quit
    ...           ...
random[9][8][0] = 2387
random[9][8][1] = 56957
random[9][8][2] = 7830
random[9][8][3] = 89171
random[9][8][4] = 4551
random[9][8][5] = 313
random[9][8][6] = 2433
random[9][8][7] = 2973
random[9][8][8] = 3502
random[9][8][9] = 3896
Press ENTER to continue, CTRL-C to quit.
```

This program has two for loops nested. Before you look at the for statements in detail, note that lines 11 and 12 declare 4 variables. The first is an array named random, used to hold random numbers. Random is a three-dimensional type int array that is 10 by 10 by 10 giving a total of 1,000 type int elements (10×10×10). Imagine coming up with 1,000 unique variable names if you couldn't use arrays. Line 12 then declares three variables, a, b and c, used to control the for loops.

This program also includes a new header file, STDLIB.H (for standard library), in line 6. This is included to provide the prototype for the rand() function used on line 23.

3.8 64K OF DATA VARIABLES

Because of the way memory models work, you should not try to create more than 64K of data variables for now. An explanation of this limitation is beyond the scope of this course, but there's no need to worry; none of the programs in this course exceed this limitation. To understand more, or to get around this limitation, consult your compiler manuals. Generally, 64K is enough data space for programs, particularly the relatively simple programs you write as you work through this course. A single array can take up the entire 64K of data storage if your program uses no other variables. Otherwise, you need to apportion the available data space as needed.

3.9 TO CALCULATE THE STORAGE SPACE REQUIRED

The size of an array in bytes depends on the number of elements it has, as well as each element's size. Element size depends on the data type of the array. The sizes for each numeric data type are shown in table 3.1 for your convenience. To calculate the storage space required for an array, you multiply the number of elements in the array by the element size. For example, a 500-element array of type float requires (500) * (4) = 2000 bytes of storage space.

Data Type	Size (Bytes)
Int	2
Short	2
Long	4
Float	4
Double	8

Table 3.1. Storage space requirements for numeric data types for most PCs.

3.9.1 Sizeof() Operator

Storage space can be determined within a program by using C's sizeof() operator; sizeof() is a unary operator and not a function. It takes as its argument a variable name or the name of a data type and returns the size, in bytes, of its argument.

The use of sizeof() is illustrated in Listing 3.4.

LISTING 3.4

```
/* array */
/* Demonstrates the sizeof() operator. */

#include <stdio.h>

/* Declare several 100 element arrays. */
```

```
int  intarray[100];
float  floatarray[100];
double  doublearray[100];

int main(void)  {
   /* Display the sizes of numeric data types. */

   printf("\n\nSize of int = %d bytes",
      sizeof(int));
   printf("\nSize of short = %d bytes",
      sizeof(short));
   printf("\nSize of long = %d bytes",
      sizeof(long));
   printf("\nSize of float = %d bytes",
      sizeof(float));
   printf("\nSize of double = %d bytes",
      sizeof(double));

   /* Display the sizes of the three arrays. */

   printf("\nSize of intarray = %d bytes",
      sizeof(intarray));
   printf("\nSize of floatarray = %d bytes",
      sizeof(floatarray));
   printf("\nSize of doublearray = %d bytes",
      sizeof(doublearray));
   return 0;
}
```

3.10 ARRAYS Vs. POINTERS

An array is a collection of homogeneous elements stored in adjacent memory locations, whereas a pointer is a reference of a memory location. There are following differences between arrays and pointers.

Pointers	Arrays
1. Pointer is a reference object.	1. Array is a collection and reference object.
2. Memory can be dynamically assigned to a pointer.	2. Only static memory allocation is possible.
3. A pointer may not be an array.	3. An array variable is a pointer to its first element.
4. Statement like ptr++, ptr– – and *ptr++, *ptr– – are possible.	4. Statements like arr++, arr– – are not possible but arr[n]++ is possible.

Table 3.2

An array is actually a pointer to the 0th element of the array. Dereferencing the array name will give the 0th element. This gives us a range of equivalent notations for array access. In the following examples, arr is an array.

Array Access	Pointer Equivalent
arr[0]	*arr
arr[1]	*(arr+1)
arr[n]	*(arr+n)

Table 3.3

The array is treated as a constant in the function where it is declared. This means that we can modify the values in the array, but not the array itself, so statements like `arr++` are illegal, but `arr[n]++` is legal.

Since an array is like a pointer, we can pass an array to a function, and modify elements of that array without having to worry about referencing and de-referencing. Since the array is implemented as a hidden pointer, all the difficult stuff gets done automatically.

3.10.1 Using a Pointer for One Dimensional Array

Once we assign the address of first variable to a pointer then traversing in array by the pointer becomes much faster. Let n[ ]={5, 3, 6, 4, 7} be the array of 5 elements and let *head* be a pointer to int type data. Following listing sorts given array by a pointer *head.*

LISTING 3.5

```
#include<conio.h>
#include<stdio.h>
void main()
    {
        int  a[]={5,3,6,4,7};
        int  *head;
        int  i,j,temp;
    clrscr();
        head=&a[0];
        for(j=4;j>0;j--)
        {
            for  (i=1;i<j+1;i++)
            {
            if(*head<*(head+i))
                {
                temp=*head;
                *head=*(head+i);
                *(head+i)=temp;
                }
            }
            head=head+1;
        }
            for(i=0;i<5;1++)
            printf("%d\n",a[i]);
    }
```

Listing 3.5 sorts the given array in the descending order. In this listing total numbers to be sorted are declared in the beginning of the program. But if total numbers of elements are to be given at run time by the user then following listing serves our purpose.

LISTING 3.6

```
#include<conio.h>
#include>stdio.h>
void  main()
    {
        int*ptr,*head;
        inti,j,temp,n;
        clrscr();
        printf("enter  total  number  of  integers  to  be  sort");
        scanf("%d",&n);
        for(i=0;i<n;i++)
        scanf("%d",&(*(ptr+i));
        head=ptr;
        for(j=n-1;j>0;j--)
        {
            for(i=1;i<j+1;i++)
            {
            if  (*ptr<*(ptr+i))
                {
                temp=*ptr;
                *ptr=*(ptr+i);
                *(ptr+i)=temp;
                }
            }
            ptr=ptr+1;
        }
        clrscr();
        for(i=0;i<n;i++)
        {
        printf("\t%d",*(head+i));
        }
    }
```

There are two pointers named *ptr* and *head* in listing 3.6 Refer to line 12 (head=ptr)ptr is assigned to head because after the execution of nested *for loop*, ptr will point to the next to the last element entered at run time. Now retrieve the sorted numbers *head* is used which points to the first element.

Following figure makes thing much clear.

Let following four numbers are entered at run time.

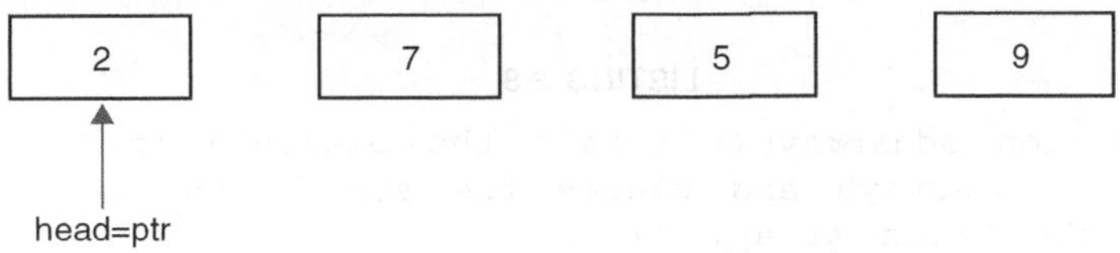

Fig. 3.8. Elements before sorting

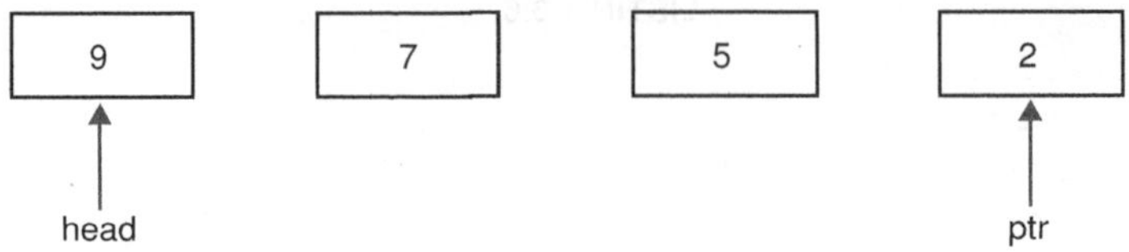

Fig. 3.9. Elements after sorting.

SOLVED EXAMPLE LISTINGS ON ARRAY

LISTING 3.7

```
/* random_number.c using a single dimensional array */

#include<stdio.h>
#include<stdlib.h>
/* Declare a single-dimensional array with 500 elements. */

int random[500];
int a,b,c;
long total = 0;

int main(void) {
/* Fill the array with random numbers. The C library */
/* function rand() returns a random number. Use one */
/* for loop for each array subscript */

for (a=0; a<500; a++) {
    random[a] = rand();
    total +=random[a];
}
/* Now display the array elements 10 at a time. */

for (a=0; a<500; a++) {
    printf("\nrandom[%d]=", a);
printf("%d", random[a]);

if (a%10=0&&a > 0) {
    printf("\nPress ENTER to continue, CTRL-C to quit.");
    getchar();
    }
}
printf("\n\nAverage is:%d",total/500);
}
```

LISTING 3.8

```
/* Function addarrays() totals the elements in the */
/* first 2 arrays and places the sum in the elements */
/* of the third array. */

void addarrays(int x[], int y[], int totarray[],
              int arrsize)}
int count;
```

```
for (count=0; count<arrsize; count++)
   totarray[count]=x[cout] + y[count];
return;
}
```

LISTING 3.9

```
/* Combine the attendance of boys and girls in several */
/* classes to determine the total attendance of each class */

#include<stdio.h>
#define MAX 100

int boys[10] = {7, 10, 5, 8, 13, 7, 13, 9, 11, 9};
int girls[10] = {8, 9, 12, 16, 7, 10, 11, 13, 10, 9};
int attend[10];
int count;
int *addarrays(int x[], int y[], int z[], int arrsize);
int *arrptr;

int main(void) {
   arrptr = addarrays(boys, girls, attend, MAX);
/* Print totals for each class. */
printf("Totals per Class\n");
printf("Class#\tBoys\tGirls\tTotal\n");
for (count=0; count<10; count++) {
   printf("%d\t %d\t %d\t %d\n",
      (count + 1), boys[count], gils[count],
      *(arrptr + count));
   }
   return 0;
}
/* Function addarrays() totals the elements in the */
/* first 2 arrays and places the sum in the elements */
/* of the third array. The function returns a */
/* pointer to the array containing the totals */
int *addarrays (int x[], int y[], int totarray[], int arrsize) {
   int count;
   for (count=0; count<arrsize; count++)
      totarray[count]=x[count] + y[count];
return (totarray);
}
```

LISTING 3.10

```
/* Reads numbers from keyboard, sorts them and displays list */

#include <stdio.h>
#include <string.h>

#define MAXLINES 10

int getlines(char *lines[]);
void sort(char *p[], int n);
void printstr(char *p[], int n);
int comp(char buff1[], char buff2[]);
```

```
char *lines [MAXLINES];
int numlines;

int main(void) {
/* Read in lines from the keyboard */
numlines = getlines(lines);

if (numlines < 0)
{
   puts ("Memory allocation error");
   exit(-1);
}
sort (lines, numlines);
printstr (lines, numlines);
return 0;
}
int getlines (char *lines[]) {
   int n = 0;
   char buffer[80];

   puts ("Enter one number at a time; enter a blank when done.");
   while ((n<MAXLINES) &&(gets(buffer)!=0) &&(buffer[0]!='\0')) {
      if ((lines[n] = (char *)malloc (strlen(buffer)+1)) == NULL)
         return -1;
      strcpy (ines[n++], buffer);
   }
   return n;
   }
   void sort(char *p[n], int n) {
      int a, b;
      char *x;
      for (a=1; a<n; a++) {
         for (b=0; b<n-1; b++) {
         if (comp(p[b], p[b + 1]) > 0) {
      x = p[b];
      p[b] = p[b + 1];
      p[b + 1] = x;
         }
      }
   }
}
void printstr(char *p[], int n) {
   int count;
   for (count=0; count<n; count++)
      printf("\n%s", p[count]);
}
/* Compare return positive number if 1st num>2nd num. */
int comp(char buff1[], char buff2[]) {
   unsigned int num1, num2, x, retcode;

/*Convert ASCII to integer */
num1 = (unsigned char)buff1[0]-0x30;
```

```
        for  (x=1;  buff1[x]!='\0';  x++)
            num1  =  (num1  *10) + ((unsigned  char)  buff1[x] - 0x30);

        num2  =  (unsigned  char)buff2[0]-0x30;
        for  (x=1;  buff2[x]!='\0';  x++)
            num2  =  (num2  *10) + ((unsigned  char)  buff2[x] - 0x30);

        if(num1>num2)
            retcode  =  1;
        else
            retcode  =  0;
        return  retcode;
        }
```

CONCEPTUAL PROBLEMS

Problem 3.1 : *What happens if I use a subscript on an array that is larger than number of elements in the array ?*

Answer : If you use a subscript that is out of bounds from the array declaration, the program will probably compile and even run. However, the results from such a mistake can be unpredictable. This can be a difficult error to find once it starts causing problems, so make sure you are careful when initializing and accessing array elements.

Problem 3.2 : *What happens if I use an array without initializing ?*

Answer : This mistake does not produce a compiler error. If you do not initialize an array, there can be any value in the array elements. You may get unpredictable results. You should always initialize variables and arrays so that you know exactly what is in them.

Problem 3.3 : *How many dimensions can an array have ?*

Answer : As stated in the unit, you can have as many dimensions as you want. As you add more dimensions, you use more data storage space. You should declare an array only as large as you need to avoid wasting storage space.

KEY POINTS

- An *array* is a collection of data storage locations, each having the same data type and the same name.
- A *single-dimensional* array is an array that has only a single subscript.
- Storage space can be determined within a program by using C's sizeof() operator; sizeof() is a unary operator and not a function.
- An array is actually a pointer to the 0th element of the array. Dereferencing the array name will give the 0th element.
- if arr is a array variable then statements like arr++, arr– – are not possible but arr[n]++ is possible.

EXERCISE

1. Why is it better to use an array instead of individual variables ?
2. Write a C program line that would declare three one-dimensional integer arrays, named one, two, and three, with 1,000 elements each.
3. Write the statement that would declare a 10-element integer array and initialize all its elements to 1.
4. What is wrong with the following code fragment ?

```
int x, y;
int array[10][3];
int main(void) {
     for (x=0; x<3; x++)
          for (y=0; y<10; y++)
               array[x][y]=0;
}
```

5. What is wrong with the following ?

```
int array[10];
int x=1;

int main(void) {
     for (x=1; x<=10; x++)
          array[x]=99;
}
```

6. Write a program that puts random numbers into a two-dimensional array that is 5 by 4. Print the values in columns on the screen. (Hint: use the rand() function from Listing 3.3).
7. Write a program to print multiplication of two matrices.

4

APPLICATION OF ARRAYS

4.1 INTRODUCTION

Arrays are most frequently used in programming. Mathematical problems like matrix algebra can be easily handled by arrays. Sparse array is another important application of arrays. Main objective of using arrays is to minimize the space requirement and improving the execution speed of a program. Arrays are also known as vectors. Arrays are widely used in scientific applications.

4.2 SPARSE ARRAYS

Sparse arrays are the special case of simple arrays. An array is said to be sparse array if such array has majority of zero elements. A two-dimensional sparse array is called *sparse matrix*. Special algorithms have to be followed while storing a sparse array in RAM. We will use both the terms sparse matrix and sparse array and *vice versa*.
There are two types of sparse matrices.
A spreadsheet is a classic example of sparse array. The following two terms are very important for sparse arrays implementation :

1. **Logical array.** A spreadsheet matrix of 26 columns and 1000 rows will required a logical array of 26*1000=26000 dimensions.
2. **Physical array.** The elements of a spreadsheet matrix which are actually exists in computer memory. For example, if 10 elements are in use then physical array will be of size 10 * (elements base size). For 10 integers physical array will be of size 10*2=20 bytes.

4.2.1 Structured Non-Zero Region Matrices

The sparse matrices in which all the non-zero elements are arranged in a particular structure are called *structured non-zero region matrices*. Diagonal matrix and Tridiagonal matrix are examples of such matrices.
Non-zero elements of such matrix are stored in one dimensional array. If we store all the elements of a sparse matrix, then there will be a wastage of the memory space because most of the space will be occupied by zero elements of the array. Therefore we try to store only non-zero elements.

$$\begin{matrix} 1 & 0 & 0 & 0 \\ 0 & 2 & 0 & 0 \\ 0 & 0 & 5 & 0 \\ 0 & 0 & 0 & 3 \end{matrix}$$

Fig 4.1. Diagonal matrix

We will discuss more about this type of matrices in coming sections.

4.2.2 Unstructured Non-Zero Region Matrices

The matrices having irregular non-zero elements are called *unstructured non-zero region matrices*. Fig. 4.2 shows a 7 × 7 sparse matrix.

0	0	0	0	0	1	0
0	0	0	0	1	0	0
0	0	0	0	0	0	0
0	0	0	0	3	0	0
0	2	0	0	0	0	0
0	0	0	0	4	0	0
0	0	0	0	2	0	0

Fig. 4.2 Sparse array (unstructured non-zero)

We will try to store only non-zero elements because storing all the elements of this matrix will be wasting of memory space. There are two alternative representations that will store explicitly only the non-zero elements.

1. *Vector representation*
2. *Linked list representation.*

We shall discuss only the first representation in this unit. The linked list representation shall be discussed in a later unit. Only the non-zero elements are stored in another array of the form

```
A(0...n,1..3)
```

where n is number of non-zero elements.

The sparse array given in Fig. 4.2 may be stored in the array A(0..6,1..3) as shown in Fig. 4.3.

	1	2	3
0	7	7	6
1	1	6	1
2	2	5	1
3	4	5	3
4	5	2	2
5	6	5	4
6	7	5	2

Fig 4.3 Sparse array representation

The element A(0,1) and A(0,2) contains the number of rows and columns of the sparse array. A(0,3) contains the number of non-zero elements of sparse array.

> ***Note.*** *Each non-zero element in a 2-dim. array is represented as a triplet with the format (row, col, element). It must be very much clear to you that we will store only non-zero elements of any sparse matrix in our own data type which must be equivalent to the triplet (row, col, element).*

How can we create our own data type?

You will get a detailed discussion on this question in Chapter 5.

But if you have studied structures in C language, you can create your own data type to store Sparse matrices. Let us create our own data type by the name triplet.

```
typedef struct sparse matrix
      {
            int row;
            int col;
            int element;
      }triplet;
```

We are giving a listing (you may not find it in any other book) to store and retrieve elements of the sparse matrix.

LISTING 4.1

```
#include<stdio.h>
#include<conio.h>
typedef struct sparse
{
   int i;
   int j;
   int n;
}triplet;
void createsparsematrix(triplet **s,int row1,int col1,int nz1)
{
       int ele,l,m;
       int nz=0;
       triplet *k;            //k is used for constant position
       k=*s;
       for(l=0;l<row1;l++)
       for(m=0;m<col1;m++)
  {
            printf("enter %d%d element",l,m);
            scanf("%d",&ele);
            if( ele!=0)
            {
                  if(nz==nz1)
                  printf("you have already entered all non-zero
                  elements\n");
                  else
                  {
                        nz++;
                        (*s)->i=l;
                        (*s)->j=m;
                        (*s)->n=ele;
                        (*s)++;
                  }
            }
       }
       *s=k;                  //set s to first position

}
void traverse(triplet *s,int row1,int col1,int nz1)
{
int x=1,z;
int l,m;
triplet *k;
```

```
        k=s;
           clrscr();
           for(l=0;l<row1;l++)
                {
                 printf("\n");
                 for(m=0;m<col1;m++)
                 {
                 s=k;
                 for(z=0;z<nz1;z++)
                 {
                      if(s->i==l&&s->j==m)
                      {
                      printf("%d\t",s->n);
                      x=1;
                             break;
                      }
                      else
                             x=0;
                             s++;
                 }
                      if(x==0)
                      printf("0\t");
                }
        }
}
int  retrieval(triplet  *s,int  rowlocation,int  collocation,int  row1,int
col1,int  nz1)
  {

           int  z;
           if(rowlocation>(row1-1)||collocation>(col1-1))
           {
                printf("subscript  is  out  of  range");
                return  0;
           }
           else
           {
                for(z=0;z<nz1;z++)
                {
                             if(s->i==rowlocation&&s->j==collocation)
                                     {
                               return  (s->n);
                                     }
                                     else
                                     s++;
                     }
                               return  0;

                }
          }
```

```
void main()
{
        triplet *s,*k;          //k is used for constant position

        int choice,rowlocation,collocation;
        int row1,col1,nz1,retele;
        k=s;
        while(1)
        {

        clrscr();
        s=k;                    //set s to first position
        printf("1.create sparse matrix\n");
        printf("2.view all elements of sparse matrix\n");
        printf("3.retrieve the element\n");
        printf("4.exit\n");
        printf("enter your choice\n");
        scanf("%d",&choice);
        switch(choice)
        {
      case 1:
            printf("Enter no. of row of matrix a ");
            scanf("%d",&row1);
            printf("Enter no. of colof matrix a");
            scanf("%d",&col1);
            printf("enter no. of non-zero ele.of matrix a");
            scanf("%d",&nz1);
                createsparsematrix(&s,row1,col1,nz1);
            break;
      case 2:
            traverse(s,row1,col1,nz1);
            getch();
            break;
      case 3:
            printf("enter row no.\n");
            scanf("%d",&rowlocation);
            printf("enter col no.\n");
            scanf("%d",&collocation);
      retele=retrieval(s,rowlocation,collocation,row1,col1,nz1);
            printf("\nelement at \[%d\]\[%d\] is %d",rowlocation,
   collocation,retele);
            getch();
        break;
   case 4:
        exit();
        }

      }
}
```

When you will run this program you will get the output as follows :

```
1. create sparse matrix
2. view all elements of sparse matrix
3. retrieve the element
4. exit
enter your choice
```

Output

If you enter 1, then createsparsematrix() function will be executed. If you enter 2, then traverse() function is executed. If you enter 3, then retrieval ()function is executed. And if you enter 4, then program will be terminated.

Note. *"You must follow the sequence while entering your choice. You should not enter 2 or 3 before 1. When matrix is not created how a program can show its elements?"*

Algorithm 4.1 : *To store elements of a sparse matrix*

```
START
          Void createsparsematrix(triplet **s,int row,int col,int non-zeroele)
STEP 1
          Declare ele,l,m,z ,nz of type int
          Declare *k of type triplet.
          Initialise nz=0
STEP 2
          Assign *s to k
STEP 3
          Loop for l=0;l<row;l++
          Loop for m=0;m<col;m++
STEP 4    Read number in ele at the position l, m
          If ele not equal to 0
          If nz==nonzeroele
          Output "you have already entered all non-zero elements"
STEP 5
          Else
           nz++
          (*s)->i=l;
          (*s)->j=m;
          (*s)->n=ele;
          (*s)++;
          end if
          end if
STEP 6
          end loop
STEP 7
          *s=k
```

STEP 8

end loop

STOP

Algorithm 4.2 : *To retrieve of elements from a sparse matrix*

START

int retrieval(triplet *s,int rowlocation,int collocation,int row,int col,int non-zeroele)

STEP 1

Declare z of integer type.

STEP 2

If rowlocation>(row-1)||collocation>(col-1)
Output "subscript is out of range"
return;

STEP 3

Loop for z=0; z<non ozeroele; z++
If s->i == rowlocation AND s->j == collocation

Return s->n
End if

STEP 4

Else
s++

STEP 5

End loop

STEP 6

Return 0

STOP

Algorithm for traverse function is left as an exercise for you.

4.2.3 Operations on Sparse Matrices

1. Addition of two sparse matrices.
2. Transpose of a sparse matrix.
3. Multiplication of two sparse matrices.

4.2.3.1 Addition of Two Sparse Matrices

Addition of two sparse matrices is possible if and only if order of two matrices are equal. We are giving the listing of a Menu driven program for the addition of two sparse matrices.

LISTING 4.2

```
#include<stdio.h>
#include<conio.h>
typedef  struct  sprarse
{
   int  i;
```

```
    int j;
    int n;
}triplet;
void createsparsematrix(triplet **s,int row1,int col1,int nz1)
{
        int ele,l,m,z;
        triplet *k;
        int nz=0;

        k=*s;
        for(l=0;l<row1;l++)
        for(m=0;m<col1;m++)
{
              printf("enter %d%d element",l,m);
              scanf("%d",&ele);

                if( ele!=0)
                {
                      if(nz==nz1)
                      printf("you have already entered all non-zero
                      elements\n");
                      else
                        {
                              nz++;
                              (*s)->i=l;
                              (*s)->j=m;
                              (*s)->n=ele;
                              (*s)++;
                        }
                }
        }
        *s=k;
}
void traverse(triplet *s,int row1,int col1,int nz1)
{
  int x=1,z;
  triplet *k;
  int l,m;

  k=s;
        clrscr();
        for(l=0;l<row1;l++)
              {
                printf("\n");
                for(m=0;m<col1;m++)
                {
                s=k;
                for(z=0;z<nz1;z++)
                {
                      if(s->i==l&&s->j==m)
                      {
                      printf("%d\t",s->n);
                      x=1;
```

```
                    break;
                    }
                    else
                    x=0;
                    s++;
                }
                    if(x==0)
                    printf("0\t");
                 }
          }
}
void  sumofmatrix(triplet  *s1,triplet  *s2,int  row1,int  col1,int
row2,int  col2,int  nz1,int  nz2)
{
        triplet  *sum,*sk,*k1,*k2;
        int  y1=0,y2=0;
        int  l,m,z,sumnz=0;
            sk=sum;
        k1=s1;
        k2=s2;
            if(row1!=row2||col1!=col2)
            {
                    printf("Order  of  matrices  are  not  same :  sum  is
                    not possible\n");
                    getch();
                    return;
            }
            for(l=0;l<row1;l++)
            for(m=0;m<col1;m++)
            {
                    s1=k1;
                    s2=k2;
                    for(z=0;z<nz1;z++)
                    {
                          if(s1->i==l&&s1->j==m)
                          {
                          y1=1;
                          break;

                          }
                          s1++;

                    }

                    for(z=0;z<nz2;z++)
                    {

                          if(s2->i==l&&s2->j==m)
                          {
                                y2=1;
                                break;
                          }
```

```
                            s2++;
                    }

                                    if(y1&&y2)
                                    {
                                    sum->i=l;
                                    sum->j=m;
                                    sum->n=s1->n + s2->n;
                                    sum++;
                                    sumnz++;
                                    }
                        if(y1&&!y2)
                        {
                        sum->i=l;
                        sum->j=m;
                        sum->n=s1->n;
                        sum++;
                        sumnz++;
                        }
                        if(!y1&&y2)
                        {
                        sum->i=l;
                        sum->j=m;
                        sum->n=s2->n;
                        sum++;
                        sumnz++;
                        }
                        y1=0;
                        y2=0;
                    }
                    sum=sk;
                    traverse(sum,row1,col1,sumnz);
                    getch();
            }
void main()
{
        triplet *s1,*k1,*s2,*k2;
              int choice;
        int row1,col1,nz1,row2,col2,nz2;
        k1=s1;
    k2=s2;
    while(1)
        {
    clrscr();
      s1=k1;
s2=k2;
     printf("1.craete sparse matrix A\n");
     printf("2.view all elements of sparse matrix A\n");
     printf("3.create sparse matrix B\n");
     printf("4.view all elements of sparse matrix B\n");
     printf("5.Sum of A and B\n");
     printf("6.exit\n");
     printf("enter your choice\n");
```

```
        scanf("%d",&choice);
        switch(choice)
        {
      case 1:
      printf("Enter no. of row of matix A ");
      scanf("%d",&row1);
      printf("Enter no. of colof matix A");
      scanf("%d",&col1);
      printf("enter no. of non-zero ele.of matix A");
      scanf("%d",&nz1);
      createsparsematrix(&s1,row1,col1,nz1);
   break;
   case 2:
      traverse(s1,row1,col1,nz1);

      getch();
      break;
   case 3:
      printf("Enter no. of row of matrix B\n");
      scanf("%d",&row2);
      printf("Enter no. of column of matrix B\n");
           scanf("%d",&col2);
           printf("Enter no of non-zero elements of matrix B\n");
           scanf("%d",&nz2);
           createsparsematrix(&s2,row2,col2,nz2);
      break;
   case 4:
                 traverse(s2,row2,col2,nz2);
                 getch();
      break;
   case 5:
           sumofmatrix(s1,s2,row1,col1,row2,col2,nz1,nz2);
           break;
   case 6:
      exit();

      }
      }
}
```

Algorithm 4.3 : *To find sum of two sparse matrices*

START

void sumofmatrix(triplet *s1,triplet *s2,int row1,int col1,int row2,int col2,int non-zero1,int nonezero2)

STEP 1

Declare ele,l,m,z ,nz of type int
Declare *sum,*sk ,*k1,*k2 of type triplet.
Declare l,m,z,y1,y2 ,sumnz of type int
Initialize y1=y2=0,sumnz=0

STEP 2

```
sk=sum;
k1=s1;
k2=s2;
```

STEP 3

```
If row1 != row2 AND col1 != col2 then
Output "order of two matrices are not equal : sum is not possible"
Return
```

STEP 4

```
Loop for l=0;l<row1; l++
Loop for m=0; m<col1; m++
      s1=k1
      s2=k2
[k1 and k2 have the first state of s1 and s2 respectively]
```

STEP 5

```
Loop for z=0; z<non-zeroele;z++
```

STEP 6

```
If s1->i==l AND s1->j=m then
y1=1
break
end if
s1++
end loop
```

STEP 7

```
Loop for z=0;z<non-zeroele;z++
```

STEP 8

```
If s2->i==l AND s2->j=m then
y2=1
break
end if
s2++
end loop
```

STEP 9

```
If y1==1 AND y2==1 then
      sum->i=l;
      sum->j=m;
      sum->n=s1->n + s2->n;
      sum++;
      sumnz++;
end if
```

STEP 10

If y1==1 AND y2==0 then
sum->i=l;
sum->j=m;
sum->n=s1->n;
sum++;
sumnz++;

end if

STEP 11

if y1==0 AND y2=1 then
sum->i=l;
sum->j=m;
sum->n=s2->n;
sum++;
sumnz++;
end if

STEP 12

Set y1=y2=0

STEP 13

Endloop
End loop

STEP 14

Sum=sk

STEP 15

Call traverse(sum,sk,row1,col1,nz1) function to print sum of two matrices.

STOP

4.2.3.2 Transpose of a Sparse Matrix

LISTING 4.3

```
#include<stdio.h>
#include<conio.h>
typedef  struct  sprarse
{
  int  i;
  int  j;
  int  n;
}triplet;
void  createsparsematrix(triplet  **s,int  row1,int  col1,int  nz1)
{
    int  ele,l,m,z;
    triplet  *k;
    int  nz=0;
    k=*s;
```

```
    for(l=0;l<row1;l++)
    for(m=0;m<col1;m++)
{

        printf("enter %d%d element",l,m);
        scanf("%d",&ele);

        if( ele!=0)
        {
            if(nz==nz1)
            printf("you have already entered all non-zero
            elements\n");
            else
            {
                nz++;
                (*s)->i=l;
                (*s)->j=m;
                (*s)->n=ele;
                (*s)++;
            }
        }
    }
    *s=k;

}
void traverse(triplet *s,int row1,int col1,int nz1)
{
  int x=1,z;
  triplet *k;
  int l,m;

k=s;
    clrscr();
    for(l=0;l<row1;l++)
    {
        printf("\n");
        for(m=0;m<col1;m++)
            {
            s=k;
            for(z=0;z<nz1;z++)
            {
                if(s->i==l&&s->j==m)
                {
                printf("%d\t",s->n);
                x=1;
                break;
                }
                else
                x=0;
                s++;
                }
                        if(x==0)
```

```
                        printf("0\t");
                    }
                }
            }
        void transpose(triplet *s,int row,int col, int nz)
        {
            triplet *t,*tk,*k;
            int l,m,z;
                k=s;
                tk=t;

                    for(l=0;l<row;l++)
                    for(m=0;m<col;m++)
                    {  s=k;
                        for(z=0;z<nz;z++)
                        {
                        if(s->i==l&&s->j==m)
                        {
                        t->j=l;
                        t->i=m;
                        t->n=s->n;
                        t++;
                        break;
                        }
                        s++;
                        }
                    }
                    t=tk;
                    traverse(t,col,row,nz);
                    getch();
                }
            void main()
            {
                triplet *s,*k;

                int choice;
                int row,col,nz;
                k=s;
            while(1)
                  {
                clrscr();
                        s=k;
                printf("1.create sparse matrix A\n");
                printf("2.view all elements of sparse matrix A\n");
                printf("3.Transpose of matrix A\n");
                printf("4.exit\n");
                printf("enter your choice\n");
                scanf("%d",&choice);
                switch(choice)
                {
                case 1:
                printf("Enter no. of row of matix A ");
                scanf("%d",&row);
```

```
            printf("Enter no. of colof matix A");
            scanf("%d",&col);
            printf("enter no. of non-zero ele.of matix A");
            scanf("%d",&nz);
            createsparsematrix(&s,row,col,nz);
            break;
            case 2:
            traverse(s,row,col,nz);
            getch();
            break;
            case 3:

                        transpose(s,row,col,nz);
            break;
            case 4:
            exit();

             }
        }
    }
```

Algorithm 4.4 : *To transpose a sparse matrix*

START

transpose (triplet *s,int row,int col,int non-zeroele)

STEP 1

Declare *t,* tk ,*k of type triplet
Declare l,m,z of type int

STEP 2

Assign t to tk

STEP 3

Loop for l=0;l<row,l++
Loop for m=0;m<col;m++

STEP 4

s=k

STEP 5

loop z=0;z<non-zeroele;z++

STEP 6

If s->l==l AND s->j==m then
    t->j=l
    t->i=m
    t->n=s->
    t++
    break

STEP 7

s++

STEP 8

End loop
End loop
End loop

STEP 9

t=tk

STEP 10

traverse(t,tk,col,row,non-zeroele)

STOP

4.2.3.3 Multiplication of Matrix

Multiplication program and algorithm is left as an exercise for you.

4.3 ALGEBRA OF MATRICES

Matrix definition : A collection of numbers arranged in the form of an ordered rectangular array is called *a matrix.* If any rectangular arrangement A of numbers has m rows and n columns, then A is called *an m*n matrix.*
Or a matrix of the type m*n.

$$A = \begin{matrix} A_{11} & A_{12} \text{ - - - - } & A_{1n} \\ A_{21} & A_{22} \text{ - -- - } & A_{2n} \\ A_{31} & A_{32} \text{ -- -- -- } & A_{3n} \\ \ldots & \ldots & \\ \ldots & \ldots & \\ A_{m1} & A_{m2} & A_{mn} \end{matrix}$$

*Fig. 4.4. Represents a convenient notation for a general m*n matrix A*

Note. *You may take first rows A_{00} A_{01}, ... A_{on}*
An entry occupying in the ith row (from the left) is called (i, j)th entry and is denoted by A_{ij}.

The entry

$$(A_{11}, A_{22}, A_{33} \text{ - - - - - -}, A_{nm})$$

itself is called the principal diagonal of the matrix A. Let's consider an example. Following matrix represents an 4*3 matrix A :

$$A = \begin{matrix} 2 & 3 & 5 \\ 7 & 9 & 11 \\ 13 & 15 & 17 \\ 17 & 21 & 23 \end{matrix}$$

Fig. 4.5

Principal diagonal of matrix shown in Fig. 4.5 is (2, 9, 17).

SPECIAL TYPES OF MATRICES

4.3.1 Square Matrices

A matrix *a* in which the number of rows is equal to the number of columns is called a *square matrix*, otherwise it is called a *rectangular matrix.*

Example :

1	2
2	4

*Fig. 4.6. A 2*2 matrix*

4.3.2. Row Matrix

A matrix consisting of a single row like :

$$A=[a_{ij}]_{1*n}=[a_{11},\ a_{12},\ a_{13}.........a_{1n}]$$

Fig. 4.7

This matrix is called *a rows matrix* or *a rows vector column matrix.* A matrix having a single column is called a column matrix or a *column vector.*

$$B=[b_{ij}]_{m*1} = \begin{matrix} b_{11} \\ b_{21} \\ b_{31} \\ . \\ . \\ b_{m1} \end{matrix}$$

Fig. 4.8. Column vector

4.3.3 Zero Matrix

A matrix in which all the entries are zero is called a *zero matrix.*

e.g.

0	0	0
0	0	0

Fig. 4.9

is a zero matrix of type 2*3.

4.3.4 Diagonal Matrix

A square matrix in which all non-diagonal elements are zero is called a *diagonal matrix.*
A matrix A =$[a_{ij}]$, where
A_{ij}=(where (i=! j) is called a *diagonal matrix.*

Note. *The diagonal elements may or may not be zero.*

Example : A =

5	0
0	8

Fig. 4.10(a)

B =

2	0	0
0	8	0
0	5	0

Fig. 4.10(b)

$$C = \begin{matrix} 2 & 0 & 0 & 0 \\ 0 & 8 & 0 & 0 \\ 0 & 0 & -3 & 0 \\ 0 & 0 & 0 & -1 \end{matrix}$$

Fig. 4.10(c)

Diagonal matrices come in the category of sparse matrices. So we must represent diagonal matrix in memory with special care. We must not assign any memory location for non-diagonal elements. We can represent a diagonal matrix D in a one dimensional array d. Let us represent following diagonal matrix in one dimensional array :

$$D = \begin{matrix} a_{00} & a_{01} & a_{02} & a_{03} \\ a_{10} & a_{11} & a_{12} & a_{13} \\ a_{20} & a_{21} & a_{22} & a_{23} \\ a_{30} & a_{31} & a_{32} & a_{33} \end{matrix} \qquad d = \begin{matrix} 2 & 0 & 0 & 0 \\ 0 & 4 & 0 & 0 \\ 0 & 0 & 6 & 0 \\ 0 & 0 & 0 & 8 \end{matrix}$$

Fig. 4.11

The following code shows the implementation of addElement() function.

LISTING 4.4

```
Void addelement(int *d,int n,int i,int j,int element)
{
        if(i<0||j<0||i>n-1||j>n-1)
        {
        printf("Array index out of limits\n");
        return;
        }
        else if((i!=j)&&(element!=0))
        {
        printf("\nElement must be zero");
        return;
        }
        else
        d[i]=element;
}
```

Following function shows the retrieval from array d.

LISTING 4.5

```
int retrieval(int *d,int n,int i,int j)
{
        if(i<0||j<0||i>n-1||j>n-1)
        {
              printf("Index out of bounds");
              exit();
        }
else if(i!=j)
{
return 0;
else
return d[i];
}
}
```

4.3.5 Scalar Matrix

The diagonal matrix, in which the diagonal elements are all equal to a number say, *c* is called a *scalar matrix*.

e.g.

5	0
0	5

Fig. 4.12(a)

2	0	0
0	2	0
0	0	2

Fig. 4.12(b)

Following listing shows the implementation of function addElement() to store all non-zero elements in one dimensional array d.

LISTING 4.6

```
void addElement(int *d,n,element)
{
        int i=0;
        if(element!=0)
        {
              for(i=0;I<n;i++)
              {
                     d[i]=element;
              }
        }
}
```

Suppose at runtime we have passed n=3 and element =2 then function listed above will place 2 in one dimensional array d. Now memory picture for d will be:

d

2	2	2

Fig. 4.13

Hence you can see there is a wastage of memory space as same element is stored n times.

So, a better approach to store a scalar matrix is listed below:

LISTING 4.7

```
void addElement(int *d,int n,int I,int j,int element)
{
        if(i<0||j<0||i>n-1||j>n-1)
        {
              printf("Array index out of bounds");
              return;
        }
    else if ((i!=j)&&(element!=0))
    {
              printf("\nElement must be zero");
              return;
    }
    else if (!(*d))
              {
                     *d=element;
              }
```

```
        else  if(*d)
                      {
                            if(*d!=element)
                      printf("Diagonal elements of scalar matrix must be same");
                      }
    }
```

In the above listing *d holds the reference of a variable declared in main() function.

You must initialize this variable with zero in main function or you may declare such variable as static type.

Function for retrieval of elements is left as an exercise for the readers.

4.3.6 Identity Matrix or Unit Matrix

A scalar matrix, in which the value of the scalar c=1 is called an *identity matrix or unit matrix* and is denoted by I_n , where *n* is its order.

e.g.

$$I_2 = \begin{matrix} 1 & 0 \\ 0 & 1 \end{matrix} , \qquad I_3 = \begin{matrix} 1 & 0 & 0 \\ 0 & 1 & 0 \\ 0 & 0 & 1 \end{matrix}$$

Fig. 4.14 *Fig. 4.15*

4.3.7 Lower Triangular Matrix

A square matrix A, in which entries above the main diagonal are all zero is called a *lower triangular matrix*. In symbols $A=[a_{ij}]m \times n$ is a lower triangular matrix if $a_{ij} = 0$, when i<j.

e.g.

$$A = \begin{matrix} 1 & 0 & 0 \\ 2 & 2 & 0 \\ -4 & 1 & -3 \end{matrix}$$

Fig. 4.16

where the entries above the main diagonal are all zero, is an example of *lower triangular matrix*.

You may or may not consider this type of matrix as a sparse matrix. But here we want to store all elements of matrix A excluding the entries above the main diagonal. But before writing listing to store elements of lower triangular matrix A, row 1 has one non-zero element, row 2 has 2 and row n has n.Total number of non-zero elements is n(n+1)/2.

This matrix can be represented using an one dimentional array d[] of size n(n+1)/2. The element can be mapped by rows or by columns. If the lower triangular matrix of Fig. 4.16 is mapped by rows then d[ ]={1, 2, 2, –4, 1, –3} The columnwise mapping is given by d[ ] = {1, 2, –4, 2, 1, –3}. The total no. of elements that precede it in a rowwise mapping is i(i–1)/2+j–1.

The following listing shows the implementation of addElement() function.

LISTING 4.8

```
void addElement(int *d,int n,int i,int j,int element)
{
        if(i<0||j<0||i>n-1||j>n-1)
        {
                printf("\nArray index out of bounds");
        return;
        }
        else    if(i>=j)
                d[i*(i-1)/2+j]=element;
        else
                printf("\n Element must be zero");
}
```

The following listing shows retrieval of element of a lower triangular matrix.

```
int retrieval(int *d,int n,int i,int j)
{
        if(i<0||j<0||i>n-1||j>n-1)
        {
                printf("\nArray index out of bounds");
                exit();
        }
        else if(i>=j)
        return d[i*(i-1)/2+j];
        else
           return 0;
}
```

4.3.8 Upper Triangular Matrix

A square matrix in which the entries below the main diagonal are all zero is called *an upper triangular matrix.*

In Symbols a matrix B =$[b_{ij}]n \times n$ will be an upper triangular matrix if $b_{ij}=0$ when i>j *e.g.* the matrix

$$B = \begin{matrix} -15 & 7 & 8 \\ 0 & 2 & 5 \\ 0 & 0 & -1 \end{matrix}$$

Fig. 4.17. Upper triangular matrix

We can store and retrieve the elements of upper triangular matrix in the same manner as we did in lower triangular matrices. But you must interchange i and j inside both the functions.

addElement() and retrieval().

Following is the listing of addElement () function.

LISTING 4.9 (*a*)

```
Void addElement(int *d,int n,int I,int j,int element)
{
```

```
        int  k;
        if(i<0||j<0||i>n-1||j>n-1)
        {
              printf("\nArray  index  out  of  bounds");
              return;
        }

        else  if(i<=j)
        {
              k=i;
              i=j;
              J=k;
              d[i*(i-1)/2+j]=element;
        }
   else
        printf("\nElement  must  be  zero");
   }
```

Following listing shows retrieval of elements of a upper triangular matrix.

LISTING 4.9 (*b*)

```
int  retrieval(int  *d,int  n,int  I,int  j)
{

        int  k;
        if(i<0||j<0||i>n-1||j>n-1)
        {
              printf("\nArray  index  out  of  bounds");
              return;
        }

        else  if(i<=j)
        {
              k=i;
              i=j;
              J=k;

              return(d[i*(i-1)/2+j]);
        }

   else
        return  0;
}
```

4.3.9 Triangular Matrix

A matrix which is either an upper triangular matrix or a lower triangular matrix is called *a triangular matrix.*

Remarks. In the article above, we have defined diagonal matrices, a lower triangular or an upper triangular matrix only for square matrices. However, we can extend these definitions even to rectangular matrices as given below :

Let $A = [a_{ij}]m \times n$ then the entries
a11,a22,a35...aqq, where q = min(m,n).
Above elements are called diagonal entries.
$A = [a_{ij}]m \times n$ is called a diagonal matrix if $a_{ij} = 0$ whenever i! = j
It is a lower triangular matrix if $a_{ij} = 0$ whenever i<j.
It is an upper triangular matrix if $a_{ij} = 0$,whenever i>j.

4.3.10 Tridiagonal Matrix

In a n × n Tridiagonal matrix T, the non-zero elements lie on one of the three diagonals.
1. Main diagonal for which i = j. It has n elements.
2. Diagonal below main diagonal for which i = j+1. It has n–1 elements.
3. Diagonal above main diagonal, for which i = j–1. It also has n–1 elements.
Hence, an n × n Tridiagonal matrix T has 3n–2 non-zero elements
e.g.

$$T = \begin{matrix} 1 & 2 & 0 & 0 \\ 3 & 4 & 5 & 0 \\ 0 & 6 & 7 & 8 \\ 0 & 0 & 9 & 10 \end{matrix}$$

Fig. 4.18. Tridiagonal matrix

The following listing shows the implementation of addElement() function :

LISTING 4.10

```
void addElement(int *d,int n,int I,int j,int element)
{
        if(i<0||j<0||i>n-1||j>n-1)
        {
              printf("\nArray index out of bounds");
        }
        switch(i-j)
        {
        case 1: d[i-2]=element;
                break;
        case0:  d[n+i-2]=element;
                break;
        case -1:
                d[2*n+1-2]=element;
                break;
        default:
                printf("\n Element should be 0");
        }
}
```

The following listing shows the implementation of retrieval ()function.
Int retrieval(int *d,int n,int i,int j)

```
{
        if(I<0||j<0||I>n-1||j>n-1)
        {
```

```
                printf("\nArray index out of bounds");
                exit();
        }
        else
        {
                switch(i-j)
                {
                    case 1:
                            return d[i-2];
                            break;
                    case 0:
                            return d[n+I-2];
                    case-1:
                            return d[2*n+1-2];
                    default: return 0;
                }
        }

}
```

CONCEPTUAL PROBLEMS

Problem 4.1 : *Let A and B be two lower triangular matrices, each with 'n' rows. The total number of elements in both the matrices is n(n + 1). Devise a scheme to present both the triangular matrices in one array C(1..n, 1..n+1).* (MCA, June 2001)

(**Hint.** Represent the triangle of A as lower triangle of C and the transpose of B as the upper triangle of C. Write algorithms to determine the value of A[i,j], B[i,j], 1<=i, j<=n from the array C.)

Solution : Before writing the algorithm/program let us discuss the problem.

Total Elements of A = n(n+1)

rows of A = n

columns of A = n+1.

Similarly rows of B = n

columns of B = n + 1

Both A and B are rectangle matrices.

For example,

Let A and B are of order 2 × 3

$$A = \begin{matrix} 2 & 0 & 5 \\ 2 & 2 & 6 \end{matrix}$$

$$B = \begin{matrix} 1 & 0 & 3 \\ 3 & 5 & 4 \end{matrix}$$

$$C = \begin{matrix} 0 & 0 & 0 \\ 0 & 0 & 0 \end{matrix}$$

To find the principle diagonal in A and B, q = Min (n, n+1)
that is q=n.
(note A (q × q) and B (q × q) are lower triangular refer to remark under section 4.3.9).
We need not to retrieve last column as given in hint.
Retrieve A[i][j], B[i][j] where 1<=i, j<=n
If we start indexing from 0 instead of 1 then condition becomes
Retrieve A[i][j], B[i][j] where 0<=i, j<=n–1
Add C and A as follows :
if i>j then
C[i][j]+=a[i][j]
Similarly
Add C and B
if i>=j
then
C[j][i+1]+=B[i][j]
Finally, we get

$$C = \begin{matrix} 2 & 1 & 3 \\ 2 & 2 & 5 \end{matrix}$$

You can retrieve elements of A and B by following algorithm :

Algorithm :

```
        int Retrieve(int C[N][N+1], int row, int col, char matrix_name)
Start Function
        IF row<col THEN
        Return 0
        END IF
        IF matrix_name='A'
        return C[row][col]
        END IF
        IF matrix_name='B'
        return C[col][row+1];
        END IF.
End Function.
```

Following C program is the complete solution for our problem.

LISTING 4.11

```
#include<stdio.h>
#include<conio.h>
#define N 2
int retrieve (int c[N][N+1], int row, int col, char matrix_name)
   {
   if (row<col)
        return 0;
        else
```

```
            {
                if  (matrix_name=='a'||matrix_name=='A')
                return  (c[row][col]);
                if  (matrix_name=='b'||matrix_name=='B')
                return  (c[col][row+1]);
            }
        return 0;
        }

    void main()
    {
        int a[N][N+1], b[N][N+1], c[N][N+1];
        int i,j,value;
        char matrix_name,ch;

        clrscr();
        for(i=0;j<N;i++)
        for(j=0;j<N+1;j++)
        {
            c[i][j]=0
            if(i>=j)
            {
                printf("\nEnter a[%d][%d] element:",i,j);
                scanf("%d", &a[i][j]);
                printf("\nEnter b[%d][%d]",i,j);
                scanf("%d", &b[][j]);
            }
            else
            {
                a[i][j]=0;
                b[i][j]=0;
            }
        }
    clrscr();
        for(i=0;i<N;i++)
            for(j=0;j<N+1;j++)
            if(i>=j)
        {
            c[i][j]+=a[i][j];
        c[j[i+1]+=b[i][j];
        }
    printf("\nMatrix C=");
    for(i=0;i<N;i++)
    {
        printf("\n");
        for(j=0;j<N+1;j++)
        printf("\t%d",c[i][j]);
    }

    while(1)
    {
        printf("\nenter Matrix name A/B to retrieve the element");
```

```
            matrix_name=getche();
            printf("\nenter Row number in the range of 0 to %d", N-1);
            scanf("%d",&i);
            printf("\nenter Column number in the range of 0 to %d",N-1);
            scanf("%d",&j);
            if(i>=N||j>=N)
            continue;
         if (matrix_name)!='A'&&matrix_name!='a'&&matrix_name!
            ='b'&&matrix_name!='B')
            continue;
            value=retrieve(c,i,j,matrix_name);
            printf("Value of %c[%d][%d]=%d", matrix_name,i,j,value);
            printf("\nSearch other values Y/N");
            ch=getch();
            if(ch=='y'||ch=='Y')
            {
            clrscr();
            continue;
            }
         break;
         }
   }
```

Problem 4.2 : *Write a complete program in C-language to reverse the characters in a string from starting position to end position recursively. The program must have a function rev_strg(string,start,end).* (PGDCA June, 1997)

Solution :

```
#include<stdio.h>
#include<conio.h>
#define MAX 10
void rev_str(char name[],int s,int e)
{
        if(s!=e)
        {
        char c;
        c=name[s];
        name[s]=name[e];
        name[e]=c;
        rev_str(name,++s,—e);
        }
        else
        printf("%s",name);

}
void main()
{
        int s,e;
        char name[MAX];
        printf("\nEnter the name");
        gets(name);
        printf("enter the starting position");
        scanf("%d",&s);
        printf("enter the end position");
```

```
        scanf("%d",&e);
        fflush(stdin);
        rev_str(name,s,e);
    }
```

Problem 4.3 : *(a) Show through appropriate data structure the representation of the following 4 × 4 sparse matrix :* (MCA June, 1997)

0	0	11	0
12	0	0	0
0	–4	0	0
0	0	0	–25

Fig. 4.19

(b) Write an algorithm to create the matrix C=A+B where A and B are two sparse matrices. Your algorithm should leave the matrices unchanged and set up new matrix in accordance with this data representation.

Solution (*a*) : We use Vector representation to store non-zero elements of this matrix. This matrix can be stored in the array A(0..n,1..3) where n is number of non-zero elements. Vector representation of this matrix is shown as follows :

	1	2	3
0	4	4	4
1	1	3	11
2	2	1	12
3	3	2	–4
4	4	4	–25

Fig. 4.20

Solution (*b*) :

Let order of Matrix A and Matrix B be m × n. Following algorithm can be used to solve this problem.

Algorithm :

START

STEP 1

Declare a two dim. Array C[m][n] of int type
Declare A [m][n]and B [m][n]of int type and assign the values.

STEP 2

Assign all entries of C equal to zero.

STEP 3

Loop for i=0;i<m;i++
Loop for j=0;j<n;j++
C[i][j]=A[i][j]+B[i][j]

STOP

Problem 4.4 : *Write a function in C to implement transposition of a sparse matrix.*

(MCA June, 2001)

Solution :

```
void transpose(triplet *s,int row,int col, int nz)
{
triplet *t,*tk,*k;

int l,m,z;
        k=s;
        tk=t;

        for(l=0;l<row;l++)
        for(m=0;m<col;m++)
        { s=k;
              for(z=0;z<nz;z++)
              {
                    if(s->i==l&&s->j==m)
                    {

                    t->j=l;
                    t->i=m;
                    t->n=s->n;
                    t++;
                    break;
                    }
                    s++;
              }
        }
        t=tk;

        traverse(t,col,row,nz);
        getch();
}
```

KEY POINTS

- An array in which not all the elements of the array are not actually in use, present or needed is called **sparse array.**
- A sparse matrix can be a structured non-zero or unstructured non-zero matrix.
- The matrices having irregular non-zero elements are called unstructured non-zero region matrices.
- A sparse matrix is implemented using vector representation or by linked list representation.
- A matrix in which the number of rows is equal the number of columns is called a square matrix, otherwise it is called a rectangular matrix.
- A matrix consisting a single row is called a row matrix or row vector.
- A matrix in which all the entries are zero is called a zero matrix.
- A square matrix in which all non-diagonal elements are zero is called a diagonal matrix. Refer listings 4.4 and 4.5.
- The diagonal matrix in which the diagonal elements are all equal to a number say c, is called a scalar matrix. Refer listings 4.6 and 4.7.

- A square matrix A, in which entries above the main diagonal are all zero is called a lower triangular matrix. Refer listing 4.8 to implement lower triangular matrix in C.
- A square matrix in which the entries below the main diagonal are all zero is called an upper triangular matrix.
- Triangular matrix can also be rectangular matrices. Refer to remark under section 4.3.9.

EXERCISE

1. How would a m × n array A[1..m,1..n] be stored in Column Major Order.

2. Write an algorithm to create the matrix C=A+B where A & B are two sparse matrices. Your algorithm should leave the matrices unchanged and set up new matrix in accordance with this data representation.

3. Implement transpose of a sparse matrix in C.

4. Write a program to perform the following operations on the sparse matrices (using arrays).

(*i*) Read and Display the sparse matrix.

(*ii*) Add two sparse matrices.

(*iii*) Find transpose of a matrix.

5. A complex valued matrix X is represented by a pair of matrices (A, B) where A contains real values and B contains imaginary part. Write a program to compute product of two complex valued matrices X and Y.

6. Write a function that will read the entries of a lower triangular matrix.

5

C STRUCTURES

5.1 INTRODUCTION

Many real life projects are coded in "C" language. When we work on a real life project, then there is a need to define some entities and their attributes.

Entities are called objects in Object Oriented Programming. Let us consider an example of real life project, "The University Management System". Certainly, this system will keep all information of the university students.

In such a project students would be an entity set and a particular student is called an entity. Now the student name, age, roll number etc. are attributes of the student. So when we have to develop a software for this system, then student should be declared with its attributes in memory. And this is possible in C language to declare such entities and attributes using structures.

A structure is referred by a keyword *struct* in C. Hence a *struct* is a user defined data type. This chapter focuses on struct and its properties.

5.2 DECLARING A *STRUCT*

The syntax for declaring a structure is

```
struct [ Tag name ]
{
        Data  type      var1;
        Data  type      var2;
        -------------------
        -------------------
        Data  type      varn;

} ;  ____________________
```

Whereas struct is a keyword to define a structure, *tagname* is the name given to structure and this name is optional. Data type may be built in *viz*. integer, Float, char etc. or user defined.

Consider the example of student record. Our *struct* declaration is as following.

```
strcut   Student
{
        char name [ 10 ] ;
        int age ;
        int roll_no ;
} ;
```

The position of the structure definition enclosed in curly braces is known as *structure template*. Here we have declared a struct, but no memory allocation is done for variables inside template. The memory allocation will be done when we declare a variable of *"struct student"* type.

5.3 DECLARING VARIABLES OF STRUCT TYPE

Method 1 :

Syntax :
struct tagname var1, var2, ...
For example,

```
struct student stud;
```

Declares a variable *stud* of struct student type
And at this time the memory is allocated for name, age, roll_no.

Method 2 :

We can also declare the variables of the structure type along with the structure declaration. Let us see declarations of stud in this method.

```
struct  student
{
        char name [10];
        int age;
        int roll_ no;
} stud;
```

Consider the memory map of above declaration.

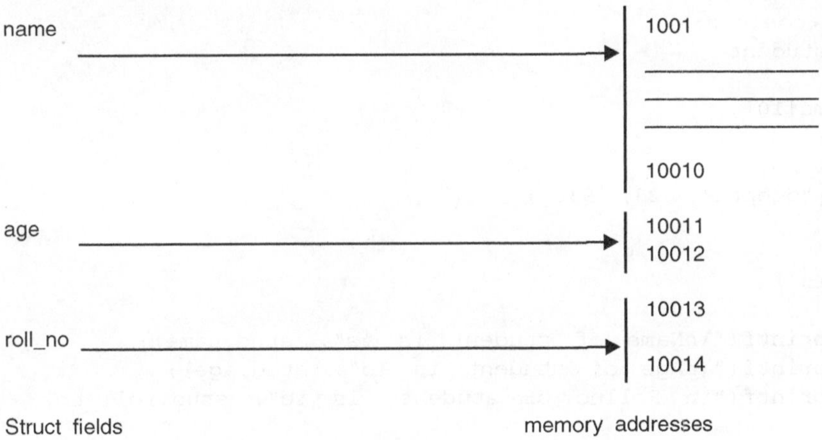

Fig. 5.1 Memory map for struct fields

5.4 INITIALIZING STRUCTURE

Consider the following example :

LISTING 5.1

```
#include<stdio.h>
struct student
{
```

```
    char  name="deepti";
    int  age=23;
    int  roll_no=938;
};
void  main()
   {
    struct  student  stud;
   printf("\nName  of  Student  is  %s",  stud.name);
   printf("\nAge  of  student  is  %d",  stud.age);
   printf("\nRoll  no  of  student  is  %d",  stud.roll_no);
   }
```

In this listing, we have tried to access the elements by *stud variable*. We can assign the values through stud in the same way.

But this program has errors. Let us compile this program and you will see the following output :

Compiling listing1.c

Error	c:\listing.c	4:Declaration missing ;
Error	c:\listing.c	5:Declaration missing ;
Error	c:\listing.c	6:Declaration missing ;

Numbers 4, 5, 6 in error messages represent line number of the program statements which are incorrect.

Now, let us modify our programs.

LISTING 5.2

```
#include<stdio.h>
#include<conio.h>
struct  student
{
char  name[10];
int  age;
int  roll_no;
}  stud={"deepti",  23,  938};


void  main()
{
       printf("\nName  of  student  is  %s",  stud.name);
       printf("\nAge  of  student  is  %d",  stud.age);
       printf("\n  Rollno  of  students  is  %d",  stud.roll_no);
}
```

Now compile this program and run.

Output

Name of student is deepti
Age of student is 23
Rollno of student is 938

You can do the same example as follows :

LISTING 5.3

```
#include<stdio.h>
#include<conio.h>
struct student
{
   char name[10];
   int age;
   int roll_no;
};
void main()
{
   struct student stud;
   printf("\nEnter the name");
   gets(stud.name);
   printf("\nEnter the age");
   scanf("%d", &stud.age);
   printf("\nEnter Rollno");
   scanf("%d", &stud.roll_no);
   clrscr();
        printf("\nName of student is %s", stud.name);
        printf("\nAge of student is %d", stud.age);
        printf("\n Rollno of student s is %d", stud.roll_no);
        getch();
}
```

5.4.1 Struct Alias

You have seen that we declare a *struct* variable as follows:

struct tag name var;

This declaration would be much better if we use struct alias that is a nick name of "struct tag name". We can give an alias name to any struct as follows.

```
typedef struct tag name
    {
        data type   ver;
        ............................
        ............................

    }   alias name;
```

Now you can declare any variable of *struct* tagname type as follows :

Alias name var:

Let us take an example.

LISTING 5.4

```
# include <stdio.h>
#include<conio.h>
typedef struct student
{
        char name[10];
        int age;
        int roll_no;
```

```
}st;
void main()
{
        st stud;
        printf("\nEnter the name");
        gets(stud.name);
        printf("\nEnter the age");
        scanf("%d", &stud.age);
        printf("\nEnter Rollno");
        scanf(("%d", &roll_no);
}
```

In above listing st is used in place of "struct student".

5.5 FEATURES OF STRUCT

1. Assignment of two struct variables.
2. Struct can be used with pointers.
3. A struct variable can be passed to a function.
4. A struct variable can be returned by a function.
5. Array of struct variable is possible.
6. Nested struct.
7. Self referential struct.

We will discuss the above-cited seven features of *struct* one by one with the help of examples.

To understand first feature of *struct* consider the following example :

LISTING 5.5

```
#include<stdio.h>
#include<conio.h>
typedef struct employee
{
     char name[10];
     int age;
     int sal;
}emp;

void main()
     {
          emp e1, e2;
          printf("\n Enter name of employee");
                 gets(e1.name);
          printf("\nEnter age of employee");
          scanf("%d", &e1.age);
          printf("\nEnter salary of employee");
          scanf("%d", &e1.sal);
          e2=e1;
          printf("%s\t%d\t%d", e2.name, e2.age, e2.sal);
          getch();
     }
```

Listing 5.5 shows that we can assign two struct variables.Second feature of struct is pointer. A *struct* variable can be of *struct* pointer type. Consider the following listing:

LISTING 5.6

```
#include<stdio.h>
#include<conio.h>
   struct student
   {
   char name;
   int rollno;
   int age;
   };
   void main()
   {
         struct student st, *st1;
         printf("enter name of student\n");
              scanf("%s", st.name);
              printf(" enter rollno\n");
              scanf("%d", &st.rollno);
              printf("enter age of student\n");
              scanf("%d", &st.age);
              st1=&st;
              clrscr();
              gotoxy(25, 2);
              printf("NAME\tAGE\tROLLNO\n");
              gotoxy(25, 3);
              printf("———————\n");
              gotoxy(25, 4);
              printf("%s\t%d\t%d\n", st1->name, st1->age, st1-
              >rollno);
              getch();
   }
```

In the example listed above, we have assigned the address of variable st to a pointer st1. By a rule, data type of st and st1 must be same. We can access the variables of a *struct* using pointers, but we can't access the variable like *st1.name because C compiler will evaluate (st1.name) which is wrong. So either we can write (*st1).name or we can use an arrow operator '->'.Hence we have used st1->name in our listing. Third feature can be well understood by the following example:

LISTING 5.7

```
#include<stdio.h>
#include<conio.h>
typedef struct employee
   {
        char name[10];
        int age;
        int sal;
   }emp;

void display(emp);
void main()
```

```
    {
        emp e1;
        printf("\nEnter name of employee");
        gets(e1.name);
        printf("\n Enter your age");
        scanf("%d", &e1.age);
        printf("\nEnter Salary");
        scanf("%d", &e1.sal);
        display(e1);
    }

void display(emp e2)
    {
        clrscr();
        printf("\nName  is %s", e2.name);
        printf("\nAge is %d", e2.age);
        printf("\nSalary is %d", e2.sal);
    }
```

In this example, we have entered the data of an employee through e1 and we have access through e2. Here you must note that when this program calls display() function then contents of e1 are copied into a runtime stack of function display().This is because we are passing the parameter by value. We can also pass the parameter e1 by reference. Next listing explain this.

LISTING 5.8

```
#include<stdio.h>
#include<conio.h>
typedef struct employee
{
   char name[10];
   int age;
   int sal;
}emp;

void display(emp *);
        void main()
        {
            emp e1;

            printf("\n Enter name of employee");
            gets(e1.name);
            printf("\nEnter age");
            scanf("%d", &e1.age);
            printf("\nEnter salary");
            scanf("%d", &e1.sal);
            display(&e1);
        }

void display(emp *ptr)
        {
            clrscr();
```

```
                printf("\n Name is %s", ptr->name);
                printf("\nAge is %d", ptr->age);
                printf("\nSalary is %d", ptr->sal);
            }
```

In the above listing, only a reference to struct template is put inside the runtime stack of function display. (You will learn about stacks in Chapter 7).

Fourth feature states that a function can return a struct variable. Now the returning variable may be simple struct variable or it may be a pointer to struct. We will do a program in which an insert () function accepts values and returns a pointer to main(). A program of returning a simple variable by a function is left as an exercise for the readers.

LISTING 5.9

```
#include<stdio.h>
#include<conio.h>
typedef struct employee
   {
      char name[10];
      int age;
      int sal;
   }emp;

emp* insert(void);

void main()
   {

      emp *ptr;
      ptr=insert();
      clrscr();
      printf("\nName of employee is %s", ptr->name);
      printf("\nAge of employee is %d", ptr->age);
      printf("\nSalary of employee is %d", ptr->sal);
   }

emp* insert()
{
   emp *loc;
   printf("\nEnter name");
   gets(loc->name);
   printf("\nEnter age");
   scanf("%d", &(loc->age));
   printf("\nEnter Salary");
   scanf("%d", &(loc->sal));
   return loc;
}
```

Fifth feature can be explained by the following listing.

LISTING 5.10

```
#include<stdio.h>
#include<conio.h>

typedef struct student
{
      char name[10];
      int age;
      int roll_no;
}stud;

void display(stud*);
void main()
{
      int i ;
      stud st[5];
      for(i=0;i<5;i++)
      {
            printf("\nEnter name of %d student", i);
            gets(st[i].name);
            printf("\nenter age of %d  student", i);
            scanf("%d", &st[i].age);
            printf("\n Enter Salary of %d student", I);
            scanf("%d", & st[i].sal);
            clrscr();
      }
      display(&st);
}

void display(stud *ptr)
{
      int i;
      for(i=0;i<5;i++)
      {
            printf("%d\t", ptr->name);
            printf("%d\t", ptr->age);
            printf("%dit", ptr->sal);
            printf("\n");
            ptr++;
      }
}
```

In the above listing we have created an array of 5 stud type variables.

It means we want to store records of 5 students. This store records of 5 students. This program accepts data in main(), and display 5 records in display function. Here *ptr holds the address of first element of st. Hence we have incremented ptr to access next record. Sixth feature is nested struct by which you can declare a struct variable inside another struct template.

Following example will make it more clear.

LISTING 5.11

```
#include<stdio.h>
#include<conio.h>
typedef struct dateofbirth
{
  int dd;
  int mm;
  int yy;
}date;
typedef struct employe
{
    char name[10];
    int sal;
    date d;
}emp;
void main()
{
    emp e;
    printf("enter name, sal, day of birth , month of birth and
    year of birth of employee\n");
    scanf("%s%d%d%d%d", e.name, &e.sal, &e.d.dd, &e.d.mm, &e.d.yy);
    clrscr();
    printf("%s\t%d\t%d\t%d\t%d", e.name, e.sal, e.d.dd, e.d.mm,
    e.d.yy);
    getch();
}
```

There is an alternate method to declare nested struct.

```
typedef struct employe
{
    char name[10];
    int sal;
    struct dateofbirth
    {
        int dd;
        int mm;
        int yy;
    }d;

}emp;
```

Now the seventh feature of the struct comes in focus, it is the most important feature of struct as it is used in making complex data structures such as linked lists, trees and graphs. The self-referential structures are the structures that include an element which is a pointer to another structure of same type, for example, declaration of self-referential structures is given below :

```
typedef struct linked_list
{
    int info;
    struct linked_list *next;
} node;
```

This template has one integer value and an address of node type (self-referential) variable. Self-referential structure will become much clearer in the next chapter.

CONCEPTUAL PROBLEM

Problem 5.1 : *A healthcare company requires a software to manage its members data. A member record have a unique ssn number, Date of birth, Depends information, employer's Id. Write C structures to implement initial design of our problem.*

(**Hint.** Use nested structures)

Solution :

```
typedef  struct  dateofbirth
{
   int  dd;
   int  mm;
   int  yy;
}birth;
typedef  struct  dependentsdata
{
   int  total_dep;
   char spous_name[10];
}dependent;
typedef  struct  memberdata
{
   long  int        ssn_no;
   birth            d_o_b;
   dependent        dep;
   int              emp_id;
}member;
```

KEY POINTS

- A structure is referred by a keyword ***struct*** in C.
- typedef is used to give an alias name to your structure template.
- Nested struct is a struct inside another structure.
- Self-referential structure uses a pointer of its own type.
- Structures templates are the building blocks of complex data structures like linked lists, trees, graphs, stack, queues etc.

EXERCISE

1. Write steps to create your own data type ?
2. How is a structure different from array ?
3. What is a structure template ?
4. Where self-referential structures are used ?
5. A medical hospital wants a software which keeps records of all patients with following fields. Name, age, address, diseases, date of last visit

Write a C program to create a data type named patient which accepts 10 records and displays them.

6. Define a structure for a student having name, roll number and marks obtained in six subjects. Assume that "all students" is an array of students. Write 'C' functions to Print the name and roll number of the students who have secured highest marks in each subject.

6

LISTS

6.1 INTRODUCTION

One of the needs of writing algorithms in data structure is to use computer memory efficiently. When we have to write an algorithm to solve a problem then it is a good strategy to categorise logically related data and to store such data as a *collection object* inside memory. Such a *collection object* can store homogeneous set of elements or objects. The *collection object* which stores homogeneous elements inside it is called a *list*.

6.2 IMPLEMENTATION OF LISTS

A *list* can be implemented statically or dynamically using an array index or pointer respectively.

6.2.1 Static Implementation of Lists

It is the simplest implementation; its size is fixed and allocated at compilation time. A list can be implemented as an array as follows :

```
Data type arrayvariable[size];
```

As you know arrays are the collection of homogeneous elements. An equivalent definition for list is also valid.

Now we will see as to why we need the dynamic implementation of lists. We will see the drawbacks of static implementation through following examples.

LISTING 6.1

```
#include<stdio.h>
#include<conio.h>
void main()
{
   int i,even_no[5]={2,6,8,10,12};
   printf("First five even nos.are \n");
   for(i=0;i<5;i++)
   {
   printf("%d\n",even_no[i]);
   }
}
```

Output

2

6

8

10

12

Looking at the output we come to know that we have missed the number 4 which should appear in between 2 and 6.Now if a restriction is imposed on this program that declaration should not modify then how can we insert 4 in between 2 and 6 ? To better understand, let us see the memory diagram of array variable :

1002	1004	1006	1008	1010
2	6	8	10	12
even_no[0]	even_no[1]	even_no[2]	even_no[3]	even_no[4]

Fig. 6.1

Looking at the above figure address of the first element is 1002(this address is randomly assigned). And addresses of successive elements are continuous. Difference of 2 between addresses is due to the reasons that every integer is stored in two bytes. Now we want to insert 4 between 2 and 6, so we have to shift 6 to column 1006, 8 to column 1008 and 10 to column 1010. Now we can insert 4 at 1004.

Following listing performs the above task.

LISTING 6.2

```
#include<stdio.h>
#include<conio.h>
void main()
{
        int i,even_no[5]={2,6,8,10,12}
        for(i=4;i>1;i--)
           even_no[i]=even_no[i-1];
           even_no[1]=4;
           clrscr();
           printf("\nFirst five even nos. are");
           for(i=0;i<5;i++)
           printf("%d\n"even_no[i]);
}
```

Output

2
4
6
8
10

In the above example, to shift the elements we have put a *for* loop that is running three times. But if the list is long (may be 10000 numbers), then we have to shift thousands of numbers that will slow down the execution of program. Secondly, if we want to insert number 14 after number 12 then it is certainly not possible because the size of this even numbers array is fixed up to 5 elements. Well, this problem can be solved by increasing the size of array but now we will discuss the problem which cannot be handled by the programmer if we use static implementation of list.

Let us suppose that there are some other programs already running in RAM so, when we compile our program and run it then a runtime error would be generated due to insufficient space inside RAM.

Such kinds of problem may arise when RAM does not have continuous free blocks to hold all array elements. Let's focus on following RAM map :

B1 xxxxxxxxx	B2	B3	B4	B5 xxxxxxxxx	B6 xxxxxxxxx
B7 xxxxxxxxx	B8 xxxxxxxxx	B9 xxxxxxxxx	B10 xxxxxxxxx	B11 xxxxxxxx	B12 xxxxxxxxx
B13	B14	B15 xxxxxxxxx	B16 xxxxxxxxx	B17 xxxxxxxxx	B18 xxxxxxxxx

Fig. 6.2

Suppose there are 18 blocks in our RAM (1 block = 2 bytes). B2, B3, B4, B13, B14 are free blocks and all others are filled blocks. Now, because we do not have 5 consecutive free blocks, we cannot store 5 array elements. To overcome all these drawbacks of static memory allocation, we prefer dynamic implementation of lists.

6.2.2 Dynamic Implementation of Lists

As we have discussed, the lists are a collection of homogeneous elements. For the dynamic implementation of lists, we can link all elements of lists using pointers. Also, we need not assign the size of the list. Now the list becomes dynamic in nature. The structure of such a list may be as shown next :

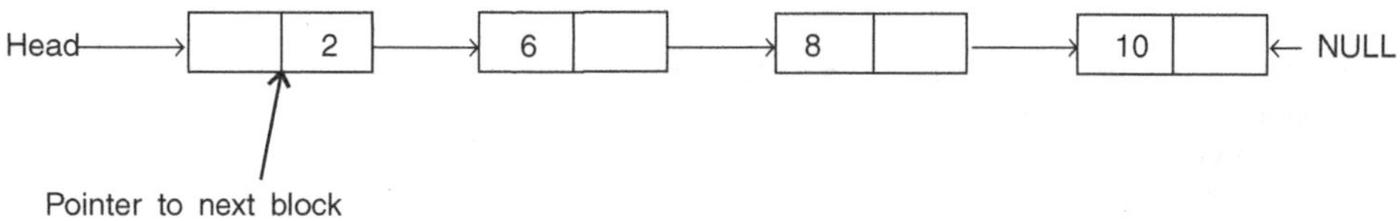

Fig. 6.3 A linked list

A linked list is a linear collection of data element called *nodes*. All nodes are *linked* by pointers. A linked list can be of the following types :

(1) *Linear linked list or one way list*

(2) *Doubly linked list*

(3) *Circular linked list.*

6.2.2.1 Linear Linked List

In a linear linked list, each node is divided in two parts.

- Data item
- Pointer to next node

A pointer variable is used that contains the address of the first element of the list. The last elements of the linked list have NULL value in the next pointer field. Now, let's see the structure declaration to represent a node of linked list.

```
typedef struct linked_list
{
   int info;
   struct linked_list *next;
}node;
```

[Remember that *node* becomes an alias or nickname for *struct linked_list*]

The *struct* declared above can store integer value. We can declare a *struct* in which we can store *char* type value or we can store another *struct* variable(nested struct).
We will discuss two examples on linear linked list. In first example, list will be of integer and in second example, list will be of struct (nested struct) elements. But before taking examples, let us focus on some basic operations on lists.

(1) Creating empty list.
(2) Adding a node at the end of list
(3) Traversing (In order)
(4) Traversing (Reverse order).
(5) Adding a node at the beginning of the list
(6) Search for an element in a list
(7) Inserting a node after a location or a specified node
(8) Deleting a list
(9) Deleting a node at the end
(10) Deleting a node at the beginning

Now let us do our first example to store a list of integers. The following listing implements first three operations only.

LISTING 6.3

```
#include<stdio.h>
#include<conio.h>
#include<alloc.h>
typedef struct int_list
      {
           int info;
           struct int_list *next;
      }node;

void create_empty(node **head)
      {
           *head=(node *)NULL;
      }

void add_at_end(node** head,int item)
{
      node* ptr, *loc;
      ptr=(node*)malloc(sizeof(node));
      ptr->info=item;
      ptr->next=(node*)NULL;
      if(*head==(node*)NULL)
           *head=ptr;
      else
      {
            loc=*head;
            while(loc->next!=(node*)NULL)
            loc=loc->next;
            loc->next=ptr;
      }

}
```

```
void traverse(node *head)
{
        while(head!=(node*)NULL)
        {
             printf("%d\n",head->info);
             head=head->next;
        }
}

void main()
{
        node *head;
        int item,choice;
        create_empty(&head);

        while(1)
        {
             clrscr();
             printf("1.Add new element in list\n");
             printf("2.Traverse the list\n");
             printf("3.Exit\n");
             printf("\nEnter your choice");
             scanf("%d",&choice);
             switch(choice)
             {
                 case 1:
                               printf("\nEnter a no");
                               scanf("%d",&item);
                               add_at_end(&head,item);
                               break;
                 case 2:
                               traverse(head);
                               getch();
                               break;
                 case 3:
                               exit();
             }
        }
}
```

Let us analyze the above *listing*. First of all, we see the *struct* declaration inside the node template. There are two fields, first is *int* type and second is *self-referential* pointer.

You may have done some C programs using pointer variables. For example, you might have declared an int pointer like :

```
int* ptr ;
```

Then, after this declaration, you can store address of any *int* type variable inside ptr. In other words, ptr is a variable of type (*int**), which means it is a variable that can hold address of any *int* type variable. Similarly in our linked list next is a pointer variable which can hold address of any *struct int_list* type variable. As you have gone through the last chapters, you can understand of the usage of *typedef* keyword. Here the *typedef* is used for renaming the struct int_list to *node*.

In further statements when we were required to declare a variable of struct int_list type, then instead of declaring :

```
struct_intlist variable name
```

we have used :

```
node variable name
```

Look at the first statement inside main() function, that is :

```
node *head;
```

It can also be declared as struct int_list *head;

Both statements are valid but the first statement is simple to use. Second statement inside main() is the declaration of two *int* type variables. Third statement is :

```
create_empty(&head);
```

This statement calls a function create_empty(node **head) which accepts the address of *head*(which is a pointer type variable). So this function accepts address of a *pointer* type variable in a **head variable. To create an empty list just assign *head=NULL but NULL needs typecast, hence right statement is :

```
head=(node*)NULL;
```

Fourth statement inside main() is infinite *while* loop. While(1) is always true and when first five statements inside *while loop* are executed, you will see the output as

```
1. Add new element in list
2. Traverse in list
3. Exit.

Enter your choice
```

Now, if you enter 1 then Case 1 inside switch is executed. If you enter 2, then Case 2 is executed. If you enter 3, Case 3 of switch is executed. When Case 1 or Case 2 is executed completely, control comes back to the while loop and you will see the output shown above again and again. But if Case 3 is executed, then a statement *exit()*; is encountered and this statement terminates the program. Inside Case 2 *add_at_end(node **head,int item)*function is called. In this function **head holds address of &head. First statement of this function is declaration of *ptr and *loc of type node. Now, by second statement ptr holds the reference of memory area required for node template. Size of memory area is calculated by the sizeof() function. And the memory of the referenced size is allocated to ptr by the function malloc().The prototype of this function is declared inside<alloc.h>.In some IDE it is also inside <stdio.h>but it is better to include<alloc.h>.

Now by the statement:

ptr=(node) malloc(sizeof(node *)).

ptr becomes a pointer to a *node* type template where the template area is allocated inside memory. Now you can logically think ptr as a box of two cells shown as below :

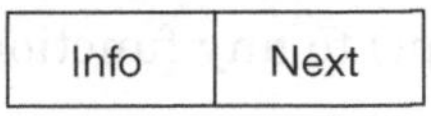

Ptr

Fig. 6.4

Clearly, ptr has two fields, Info and next. And now we have to assign values inside these two fields. Third statement assigns a value to info and fourth statement assigns a value to *next. As you have studied in the previous chapter, you can understand why –> operator is used with *ptr*. As you know, in a linear linked list the last node is NULL. And because we are adding a node at the end of linked list, so ptr–>next should be NULL. Hence the fourth statement inside add_at_end() function is :

```
ptr->next=(node *)NULL.
```

If you write this statement as

```
ptr->next=NULL;
```

C compiler will not give an error but a C++ compiler will not take it so kindly. Then type cast will be required so that it is always better to typecast the NULL with (node*). After the assignment of two fields (info,next) ptr is ready for joining the linked list. There are two possibilities, first is that list is empty and second is that list is not empty. First case can be checked by the statement if (*head==(node*)NULL)

If list is empty then *head must be equal to NULL because we have assigned *head=NULL inside the create_empty(node **head) function. So if the list is empty then ptr will be the first node, and head should point to the first node, hence we need to set *head=ptr.

If the list is containing nodes (list is not empty), then we have to find out the last node of the list and then add ptr after last node. Look at the *else* block inside add_at_end()function. First statement inside the else is loc=*head; It means loc is now holding the first node. Then by the while loop we have to move loc until

```
loc->next==NULL.
```

When loc->next==NULL we have just written a statement :

```
loc->next=ptr;
```

In this way ptr is added at the end of the list. You must notice that loc is moved forward by the statement

```
loc=loc->next.
```

Do you know why we have used loc pointer variable while we could do the same task without using loc, by the following statements:

```
While((*head)->next!=(node *)NULL)
        {
            *head=(*head)->next;
        }
            (*head)->next=ptr;
```

But if we use above three statements, then head is moved and comes at the end of the list. Since head must be at the beginning of the list, so we have declared a pointer loc of node type and incrementing in loc does not affect the *head. Before exploring the traverse() function you must note down the following points :

1. When we pass &head from main() to any function, then that function will accept address of head in **head.
2. When we pass head from main() to any function, then that function will accept value of head in *head.

3. When a function accepts address of head in **head, then whenever we have to use head inside our function body, it should be referred by *head.
   For example,

```
loc=*head;
```

4. When a function accepts address of head in **head, then whenever we assign any value to*head then actual value of head inside main() is changed. That is why, we have used loc in our add_at_end()function.
5. &head is passed to the function if function is inserting a node at any position in a list or if function is deleting any node from list or if function is to create an empty list.
6. head is passed to the function if function is used to search node or traverse a list.
   Let's come on Case 2 of our program, there are three statements inside Case 2.

```
traverse(head);
getch();
break;
```

traverse(node *head) function reads the entire list and prints the list. Inside traverse function, we have to check that if head is not equal to NULL, then we should print the value inside head–>info and increment the head by head–>next.You must notice that we are not using *head inside the traverse function as we have done in add_at_end() function. You must very clearly understand that whenever a function accepts address of head in ***head,* then we use **head* inside the body of that function and if a function accepts *head* in **head,* then we should write head instead of *head. Now in the case of traverse(node *head) this function will use head(node *head) inside its body.

Note. *[Function body represents the statements between {...}]*

traverse() function of our program reads data from beginning of the list to end of the list. Such an operation is called *In order traversal*. If a function reads the data from end of list to beginning of the list, then such an operation is called *Reverse order traversal*. We are giving a recursive function for *Reverse order traversal*.

void traverse_reverseorder(node *head)

```
{
    if (head->next!=(node *)NULL)
    traverse_reverseorder(haed->next);
    print("%d\n",head->info);
}
```

You may have studied recursion in C programming. We will discuss recursion in following chapters. We are listing algorithms of following operations :

1. Traverse in order
2. Traverse reverse order
3. Insert an element at end.

We have already discussed all above operations. Now, let's write algorithms of these operations.

Algorithm 6.1 : *To traverse in order*

START
    traverse_inorder(node *head)
STEP 1
    Repeat while head != NULL
STEP 2
    Process head -> info
STEP 3
    [move pointer to next node]
    head=head->next
STOP

Algorithm 6.2 : *To traverse reverse order*

START
    traverse_reverseorder(node *head)
STEP 1
    If head->next!=NULL
    Then goto step2.
STEP 2
    head=head->next
STEP 3
    Call traverse_reverseorder(head)
STEP 4
    Process head->info
STEP 5
    End If.
    STOP.

Algorithm 6.3 : *To insert a node at end*

START
    Void add_at_end(node ** head,int item)
STEP 1
    Declare *ptr and *loc of type node.
STEP 2
    Allocate free space
    Ptr=create new node.
STEP 3
    Ptr->info=item
STEP 4
    Ptr->next=NULL
STEP 5
    If list is empty then *head=ptr
    And EXIT else follow setep6.

STEP 6

loc=*head
Loop while loc!=NULL
loc=loc->next

STEP 7

loc->next=ptr

STEP 8

End Loop

STOP

We will cover operations 5 to 10 in the following listing of the same example.

LISTING 6.4

```
#include<stdio.h>
#include<conio.h>
#include<alloc.h>
typedef struct int_list
        {
            int info;
            struct int_list *next;
        }node;

void create_empty(node **head)
        {
            *head=(node *)NULL;
        }
        void traverse(node *head)
{
        while(head!=(node *)NULL)
        {
            printf("%d\n",head->info);
            head=head->next;
        }
}

void add_at_begning(node **head,int item)
        {
            node *ptr;
            ptr=(node *)malloc(sizeof(node));
            ptr->info=item;
            ptr->next=*head;
            *head=ptr;
        }
void * search(node *head,int item)
{
        while(head!=(node *)NULL && head->info!=item)
        head=head->next;
        return head;

}
```

```
void insert_after_node(node **head,int after,int item)
        {
            node *loc,*ptr;
            ptr=(node*)malloc(sizeof(node));
            ptr->info=item;
            loc=*head;
            loc=search(loc,after);
            if(loc!=(node *)NULL)
            {
                ptr->next=loc->next;
                loc->next=ptr;
            }
            else
            printf("Specefied node does not exist");
        }

void deletelist(node **head)
{
        node *ptr;
        while(*head!=(node *)NULL)
        {
            ptr=*head;
            *head=(*head)->next;
            free(ptr);
        }
}
void deletefromend(node **head)
{
        node *ptr,*loc;
        if(*head==(node *)NULL)
        return;
        else if((*head)->next==(node *)NULL)
        {
            ptr=*head;
            *head=(node *)NULL;
            free(ptr);
        }
        else
            {
                loc=*head;
                while((loc->next)->next!=(node *)NULL)
                loc=loc->next;
                ptr=loc->next;
                loc->next=(node *)NULL;
                free(ptr);
            }
}
void deletefrombegning(node **head)
{
            node *ptr;
            if(*head==(node *)NULL)
            return;
            else
```

```
            {
                ptr=*head;
                *head=(*head)->next;
                free(ptr);
            }
}
void main()
{
        node *head,*loc;
        int choice,item,after;
        create_empty(&head);
        while(1)
        {
            clrscr();
            printf("1. Insert node at begning the linked list\n");
            printf("2. Search an element\n");
            printf("3. Insert after given element\n");
            printf("4. delete entire list\n");
            printf("5. delete from end\n");
            printf("6. delete from begning\n");
            printf("7. Traverse\n");
            printf("8. exit");
            printf("\n enter your choice");
            scanf("%d",&choice);
            fflush(stdin);
            switch(choice)
            {
                case 1:
                            printf("\nEnter an element");
                            scanf("%d",&item);
                            add_at_begning(&head,item);
                            break;
                case 2:
                            printf("Enter element to search\n");
                            scanf("%d",&item);
                            fflush(stdin);
                            loc=search(head,item);
                            if(loc!=(node*)NULL)
                            printf("%d is found in list",loc->info);
                            else
                                printf("\n Element is not present in list");
                                getch();
                                break;
                case 3:
                            printf("Enter the element\n");
                            scanf("%d",&item);
                            printf("\nEnter the no after which you wants to insert
                            %d in list",item);
                            scanf("%d",&after);
                            insert_after_node(&head,after,item);
                            break;
```

```
                case 4:
                        deletelist(&head);
                        break;
                case 5:
                        deletefromend(&head);
                        break;
                case 6: deletefrombegning(&head);
                        break;
                case 7:
                        traverse(head);
                        getch();
                        break;
                case 8:
                exit();

            }
        }
}
```

You might be surprised to see that we have not written function prototype before function definition. This is because, if we define a function before main(), then there is no need to write function prototype but if you define function after main() function, then you should declare function prototype. Just see the deletelist() function. Prototype of this function is :

```
void deletelist(node ** head)
```

Last statement inside this function is free(ptr). free() function is used to free the memory referenced by a pointer. free(ptr) means free the memory referenced by ptr. You must remember that *malloc()* function is used to allocate the memory and free() is used to release the memory. Logic inside deletelist() function is to shift *head to next node and before shifting assign *head to ptr. Now program will free the ptr and repeat these steps till *head is not equal to NULL. Deletefrombegning() function is deleting a node from beginning of a list. Logic inside this function is that if the list is non empty then assign *head to ptr, shift *head to *head->next and free the ptr.

Assignment ptr=*head

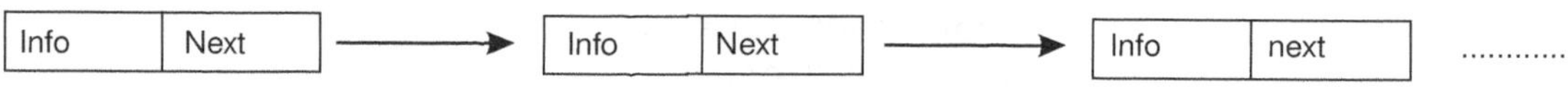

Fig. 6.5

*head=ptr

Shifting *haed to *head->next

ptr *head

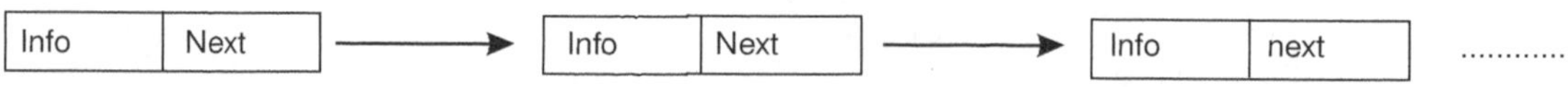

Fig 6.6

free ptr node

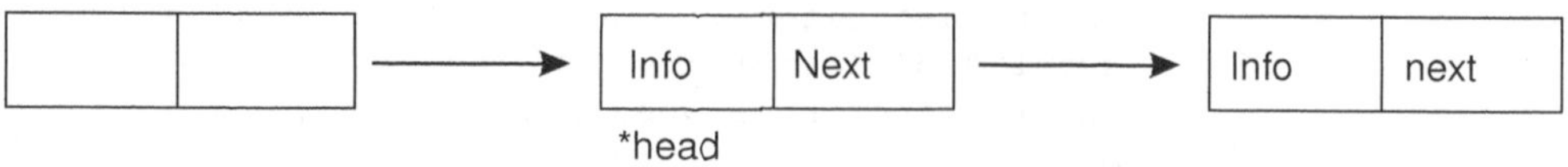

Fig. 6.7

Let's suppose our list contains only three nodes. We can delete entire list by following steps :

STEP 1

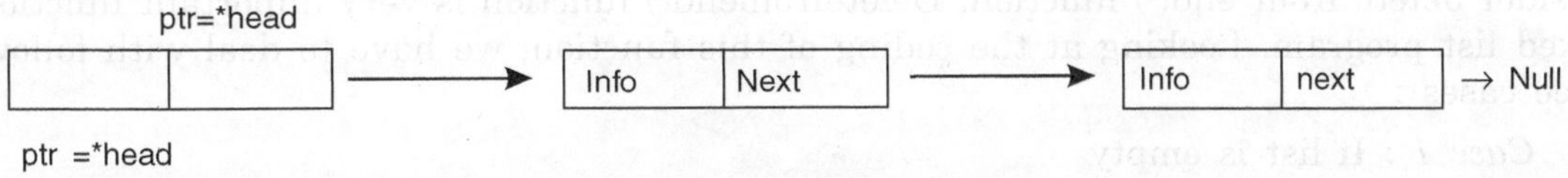

Fig. 6.8

STEP 2

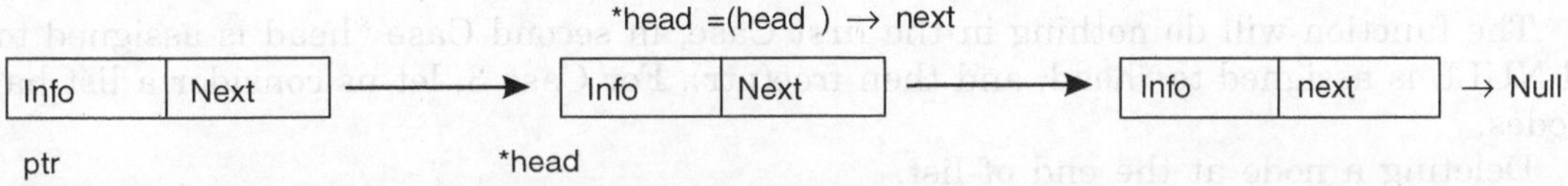

Fig. 6.9

STEP 3

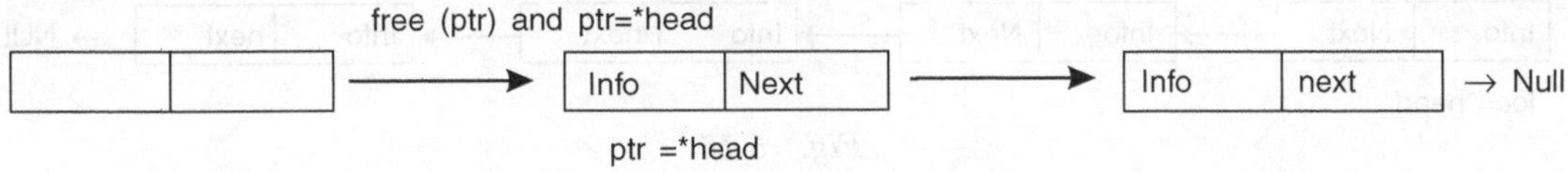

Fig 6.10

STEP 4

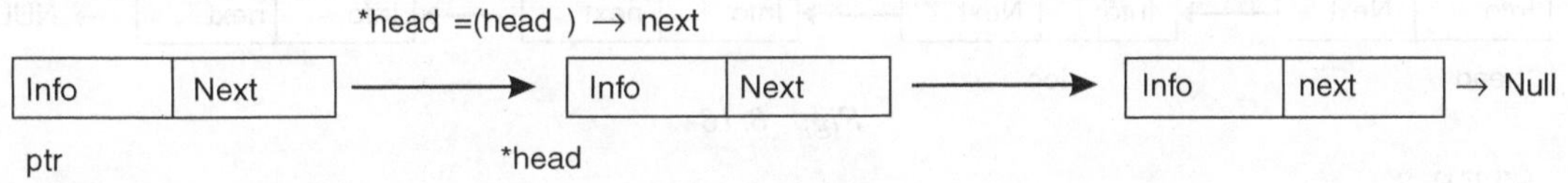

Fig 6.11

STEP 5

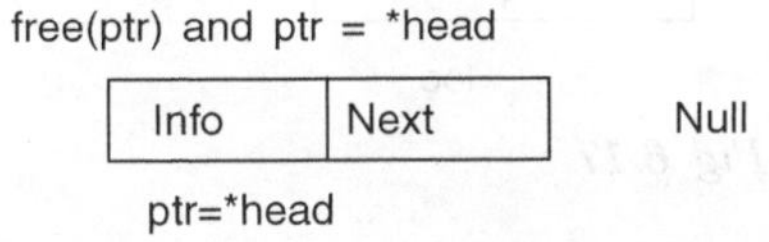

Fig. 6.12

STEP 6

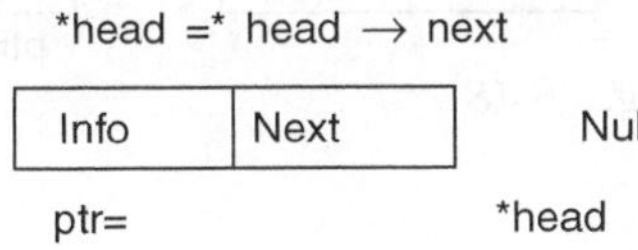

Fig. 6.13

STEP 7

Fig 6.14. Deleting entire list

You must notice from above figures that after STEP 3 there is repetition of previous steps. Dataflow in deleting list is very clear, so no extra explanation is required here. Now consider delete from_end( ) function. Deletefromend() function is very important function in linked list program. Looking at the coding of this function, we have to deal with following three cases :

Case 1 : If list is empty

Case 2 : If list have one node

Case 3 : If list have more than one node.

The function will do nothing in the first Case; in second Case *head is assigned to ptr and NULL is assigned to *head, and then free(ptr). For Case 3, let us consider a list having 4 nodes.

Deleting a node at the end of list.

STEP 1

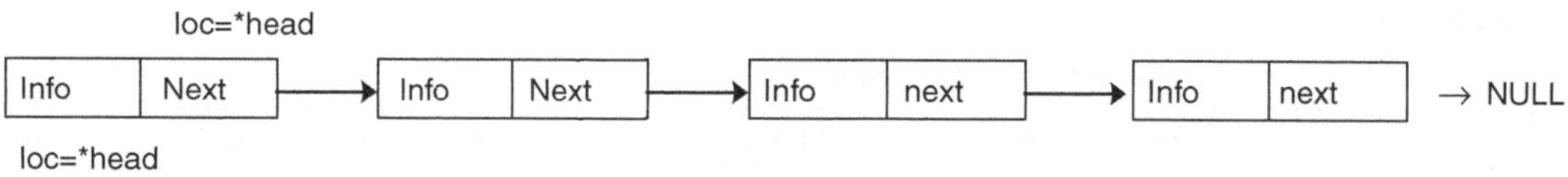

Fig. 6.15

STEP 2

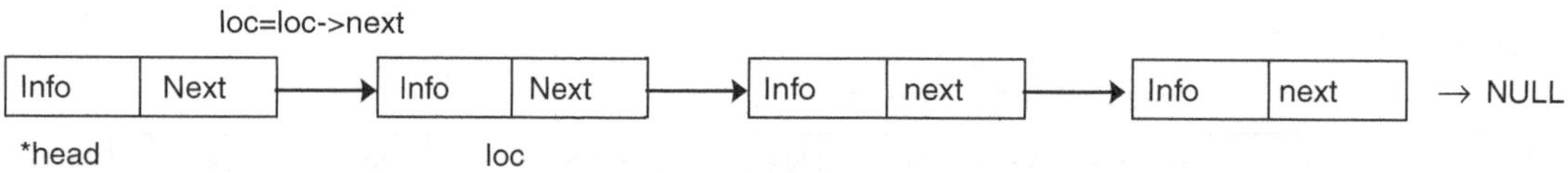

Fig. 6.16

STEP 3

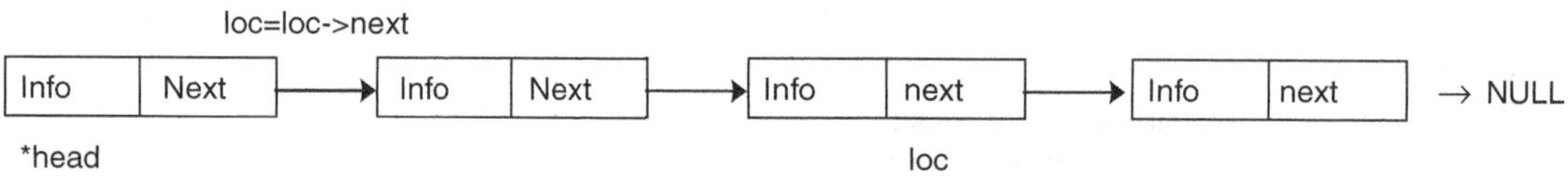

Fig 6.17

STEP 4

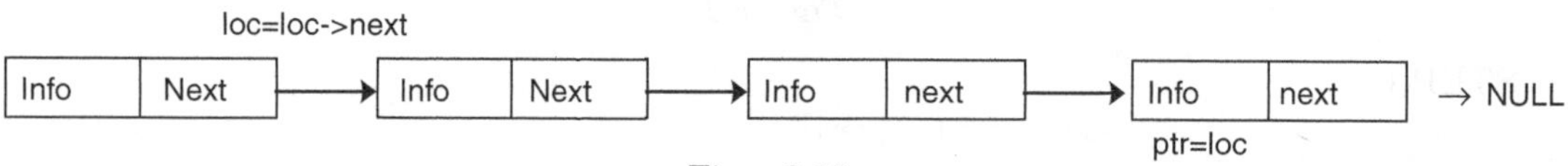

Fig. 6.18

STEP 5

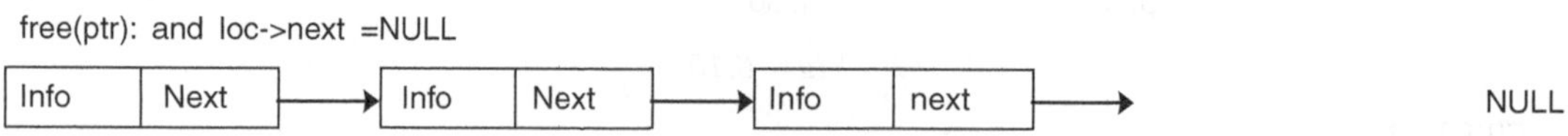

Fig. 6.19

Add_at_beginning() function adds a node at the beginning of linked list.

STEP 1

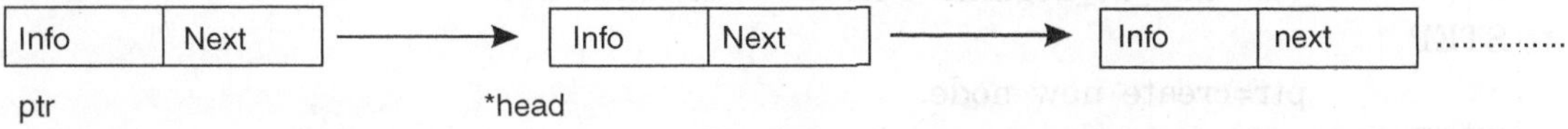

Fig 6.20

STEP 2

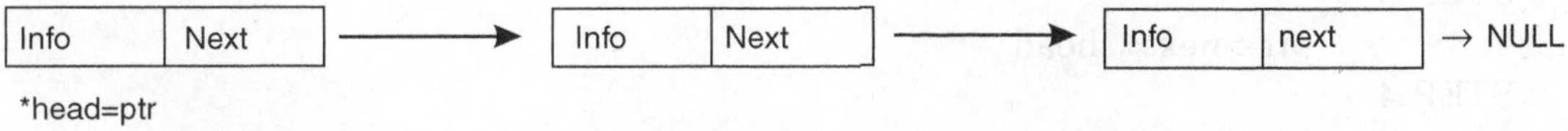

Fig. 6.21

Now we will discuss the most important operation in linked list that is search operation. Search can be made by different ways. In our program, we have made search for given info. We can also search a node at a specified position. Prototype of this function is node * search (node* hade,int item) ;

This function will return a pointer variable of node type (node*). Refer Case2 of main () function, third statement is

```
loc=search(head,item);
```

Now search()function will return a pointer variable and that will be assigned to loc. Look at search() function, there are two conditions inside while loop.

```
while(head!=(node *)NULL && head->info!=item)
head=head->next;
```

If either of the two conditions becomes false, then control comes out from *while* loop and head is returned to calling function, else head is shifted upward. In case when the item we are looking for is not present in the list, then head will reach to NULL, and NULL is returned to the calling function.

Our search() function can be modified to a search () function which returns a node at a specified position. Coding of modified function is given below :

```
node * search(node *head,int position)
{
        int x=1;
        while(head!=(node *)NULL)
        {
                if(x==position)
                     break;
                head=head->next;
                x++;
        }
        return head;
}
```

Function insert_after_node() is used to insert a node after a given node in a list, for that, search function is also used inside insert_after_node() function. You can understand the coding of this function very easily.

Algorithm 6.4 : *To insert a node at the beginning of a list*

START
    void add_at_beginning(node ** head,int item)
STEP 1
    ptr=create new node.
STEP 2
    ptr->info=item
STEP 3
    ptr->next=*head
STEP 4
    *head=ptr
STOP

Algorithm 6.5 : *To delete first node from linked list*

START
    void deletefrombeginning (node ** head)
STEP 1
    If *head=NULL
    Out put " list is empty"
    return.
    Else follow Step 2.
STEP 2
    ptr=*head
    *head=(*head)->next;
STEP 3
    Free the space associated with ptr.
STOP

Algorithm 6.6 : *To delete last node*

START
    void deletefromend(node **head)
STEP 1
    If(*head==NULL)
    Out put " List is EMPTY"
    EXIT.
    Else Follow step2:
STEP 2
    If ((*head)->next==NULL)
    Then ptr=*head
    *head=NULL
    free(ptr)
    Else follow STEP3:

STEP 3

loc=*head
Repeat while loc is not reach at second last node of list.
loc=loc->next.

STEP 4

ptr=loc->next
loc->next=NULL
free(ptr)

STOP

Algorithm 6.7 : *To delete entire linked list*

START

Void deletlist(node **head)

STEP 1

If *head=NULL
Out put "List is Empty"
EXIT
Else go to follow STEP 2:

STEP 2

Repeat while *head!=NULL
ptr=*head
***head=**(head)->next
free(ptr)
END LOOP.

STOP

Algorithm 6.8 : *To search a node*

START

node * search(node*head,int item)

STEP 1

Repeat while head!=NULL AND head->info!=item.
head=head->next
END LOOP.

STEP 2

Return head.

STOP

Algorithm 6.9 : *To insert after node*

START

void insert_after_node(node**head,int after,int item)

STEP 1

ptr=create new node.

STEP 2

ptr->info=item

STEP 3

loc=*head

STEP 4

loc=search(loc,after)

STEP 5

If loc= NULL
Output "node does not exist"
Else follow STEP6.

STEP 6

ptr->next=loc->next
loc->next=ptr

STOP

Algorithm 6.10 : ***To search a node in a linked list at a desired place, when the node number is known***

START

node*search(node*head,int position)

STEP 1

Initialise x=1

STEP 2

Repeat while head!=NULL
If x== position
Then
Return head
Else
head=next(head)
x=x+1
end loop.

STOP

Till now we have discussed our first example on linked list. In our first example we have considered a linked list of integers. Now in our second example we will discuss on the linked list of structure instances. Following listing explore our second example for storing students information in linked list.

LISTING 6.5

```
#include<stdio.h>
#include<malloc.h>
#include<conio.h>

typedef struct student
{
char name[20];
```

```
int age;
int rollno;
}stud;

typedef struct list
    {
        stud st;
        struct list *next;
    }   node;
        void create(node **head)
        {
        *head=(node *)NULL;
        }
        void addlist(node **head,stud st2)
        {
           node *ptr,*loc;
           ptr=(node *)malloc(sizeof(node));
           strcpy(ptr->st.name,st2.name);
           ptr->st.age=st2.age;
           ptr->st.rollno=st2.rollno;

           ptr->next=(node*)NULL;
           if(*head==(node*)NULL)
           *head=ptr;
           else
           {
                loc=*head;
                while(loc->next!=(node *)NULL)
                loc=loc->next;

                loc->next=ptr;
           }


        }
        void trav_inorder(node *head)

        {
           while(head!=NULL)
           {
                printf("%s\t",head->st.name);
                printf("%d\t",head->st.age);
                printf("%d\t\n",head->st.rollno);
                head=head->next;
           }

        }
        node * search(node *head,int position)
        { int x=1;

        while(head!=NULL)
        { if(x==position)
           {
           return head;
           }
```

```
    else
    {
    head=head->next;
    x++;
    }
}

    return head;

}


    void del_at_beg(node **head)
    {
    node *ptr=(node *)NULL;
    if(*head==NULL)
    {
    printf("list is empty");
    }
    else
         {
                ptr=*head;
                *head=(*head)->next;
                free(ptr);
         }
    }
    void trav_reverseorder(node *head)
    {
         if(head->next!=(node *)NULL)
         trav_reverseorder(head->next);
         printf("%s\t%d\t%d\n",(head->st).name,(head->st).age,
         (head->st) . rollno);
    }
    void insert_after_position(node **head,int position,stud s)
    {
         node *loc,*ptr;
         ptr=(node *)malloc(sizeof(node));
         ptr->st=s;
         loc=*head;
         loc=search(loc,position);
         if(loc!=(node *)NULL)
         {
         ptr->next=loc->next;
         loc->next=ptr;
         }
         else
         printf("position does not exist");
}

void del_at_pos(node **head,int position)
{
node *ptr,*loc;
```

```
        position=position-1;
                loc=search(*head,position);
                getch();
                if(loc==NULL)
                {
                printf("position does not exist");
                }
                if(loc!=NULL)
                {
                ptr=loc->next;
                loc->next=ptr->next;
                free(ptr);
                }
        }
void main()
{ int position,ch;
    stud st1;
    node *head,*loc;
    create(&head);
    while(1)
    { clrscr();
       printf("options are\n");
       printf("1. add at end\n");
       printf("2. Traverse in order\n");
       printf("3. Traverse in reverse order\n");
       printf("4. insert after a position\n");
       printf("5. Search\n");
       printf("6. delet at begning\n");
       printf("7. delet at any position\n");
       printf("8. exit\n");
       printf("enter your choice ");
       scanf("%d",&ch);
       switch(ch)
     {
     case 1:
                printf("enter a name");
                scanf("%s",st1. name);
                printf("enter age");
                scanf("%d",&st1. age);
                printf("enter rollno");
                scanf("%d",&st1. rollno);

                addlist(&head,st1);
                getch();
                break;
    case 2:
                trav_inorder(head);
                getch();
                break;
    case 3:
                trav_reverseorder(head);
                getch();
                break;
```

```
        case 4:
                printf("Enter position after which record to be added\n");
                scanf("%d",&position);
                fflush(stdin);
                printf("Enter name\n");
                gets(st1. name);
                fflush(stdin);
                printf("Enter age\n");
                scanf("%d",&st1. age);
                fflush(stdin);
                printf("enter Roll no\n");
                scanf("%d",st1. rollno);
                fflush(stdin);
                insert_after_position(&head,position,st1);
                break;

        case 5:
                printf("enter position to search\n");
                scanf("%d",&position);
                loc=search(head,position);
                getch();
                if(loc==NULL)
                {
                printf("position does not exist");
                }
                if(loc!=NULL)
                {
                printf("name is %s\n",loc->st. name);
                printf("age is %d\n",loc->st. age);
                printf("rollno is %d\n",loc->st. rollno);


                }

                getch();
                break;

        case 6:
                del_at_beg(&head);
                getch();
                break;

        case 7:
                printf("enter position");
                scanf("%d",&position);
                del_at_pos(&head,position);
                break;
        case 8:
                exit();

                }

        }

    }
```

6.2.2.2 Doubly Linked List

Doubly linked list or two-way list is a collection of homogeneous objects, in which each object is stored in a node with two additional variables which are the references of next and previous node in the list.

Hence from the definition of doubly linked list, each node is divided into three parts.

1. Previous pointer field.
2. Information of object.
3. Next pointer field.

By the term "object" we mean an entity, *e.g.* an integer value, string value or an struct value. Here you heed not to think object as an instance of a class because C does not support classes. Classes are supported by C++, Java and many other languages. Well, you can use linked lists in C++ or in Java also. Let's come back on our discussion on doubly linked lists. Following Fig. 6.22 shows a doubly linked list with 3 nodes.

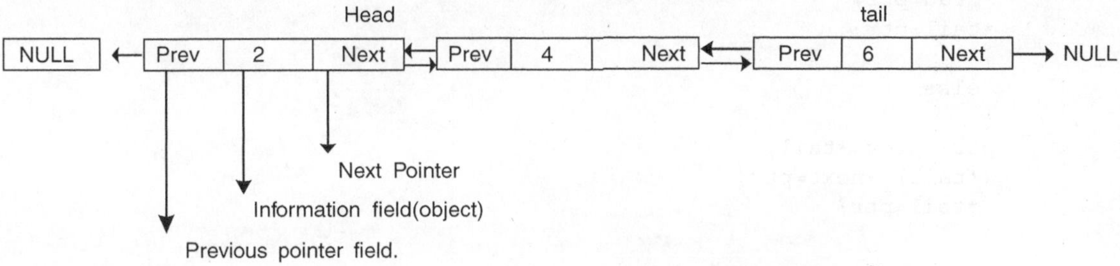

Fig. 6.22 Doubly linked list

Representation of doubly linked lists. For allocation of integers in a doubly liked list, we will represent the list as follows :

```
typedef struct doublylist
        {
           struct doublylist *prev;
           int info;
           struct doublylist *next;
        }node;
node *head,*tail;
```

Operations on Doubly Linked Lists. We will discuss all operations which we have discussed with respect to linked lists. We will also discuss an additional operation that is "to insert a node before a given node". Go through our first example of linked list, now we will do it using doubly linked list. All operations will be covered inside this listing.

LISTING 6.6

```
#include<stdio. h>
#include<conio. h>
#include<alloc. h>
    typedef struct doubly
    {
         int info;
          struct doubly *next;
          struct doubly *prev;
    } node;
```

```
// create_empty liked list

void create_empty(node **head, node **tail)
{
        *head= *tail=NULL;
}
   void add_at_end(node **head,node **tail,int element)
   {
        node *ptr;
        ptr=(node *)malloc(sizeof(node));
        ptr->info=element;
        ptr->next=NULL;

   if(*head==NULL)
   {
    ptr->prev=NULL;
   *head=ptr;
   *tail=ptr;
   }
    else
   {
   ptr->prev=*tail;
   (*tail)->next=ptr;
    *tail=ptr;
   }
}
void add_at_beg(node **head,node **tail,int item)
{
    node *ptr;
    ptr=(node *)malloc(sizeof(node));
    ptr->info=item;
    ptr->prev=(node *)NULL;
    ptr->next=*head;
    if(*head==(node *)NULL)
    *tail=ptr;
    *head=ptr;

}
void delete_at_beg(node **head,node **tail)
{
    node *ptr;
    if(*head==(node *)NULL)
    return;
    if((*head)->next==(node *)NULL)
    {
        ptr=*head;
        *head=*tail=(node*)NULL;
        free(ptr);
    }
    else
        {
        ptr=*head;
```

```
            *head=(*head)->next;
            (*head)->prev=(node *)NULL;
            free(ptr);
            }
    }

    void delete_at_end(node **head,node **tail)
    {
        node *ptr;
        if(*head==(node *)NULL)
            return;
        if((*head)->next==(node *)NULL)
        {
            ptr=*head;
            *head=*tail=(node*)NULL;
            free(ptr);
        }
        else
            {
            ptr=*tail;
            *tail=ptr->prev;
            (*tail)->next=(node *)NULL;
            free(ptr);
            }
    }

    void inordertrav(node *head)
    {
        while(head!=NULL)
        {
        printf("%d",head->info);
        head=head->next;
        }
    }
    void reverseordertrav(node *tail)
    {

        while(tail!=(node *)NULL)
        {
        printf("%d",tail->info);
        tail=tail->prev;
        }

    }
    node *search(node *head,int item)
    {
        while(head!=(node *)NULL && head->info!=item)
        head=head->next;
        return head;
    }
```

```
void insert_after_node(node **head,node **tail,int item,int after)
    {
        node *loc,*ptr;
        ptr=(node *)malloc(sizeof(node));
        ptr->info=item;
        loc=*head;
        loc=search(loc,after);
        if(loc==(node *)NULL)
        {
            printf("\nElement does not exist");
            return;
        }
        else if (loc->next==(node *)NULL)
        {
            ptr->next=(node *)NULL;
            ptr->prev=*tail;
            (*tail)->next=ptr;
            *tail=ptr;
        }
        else
        {
            ptr->next=loc->next;
            ptr->prev=loc;
            (loc->next)->prev=ptr;
            loc->next=ptr;
        }
    }

    void insert_before_node(node **head,int item,int before)
    {
        node *ptr,*loc;
        ptr=(node *)malloc(sizeof(node));
        ptr->info=item;
        loc=*head;
        loc=search(loc,before);
        if(loc==(node *)NULL)
        {
            printf("Element does not exist ");
            return;
        }
        else if (loc->prev==(node *)NULL)
        {
            ptr->prev=(node *)NULL;
            loc->prev=ptr;
            ptr->next=*head;
            *head=ptr;
        }
    else
    {
        ptr->prev=loc->prev;
        ptr->next=loc;
        (loc->prev)->next=ptr;
```

```
            loc->prev=ptr;
        }
    }

void delete_list(node **head,node **tail)
{

 node *ptr;

    while(*head!=(node *)NULL)
     {
            ptr=*head;
            *head=(*head)->next ;
            (*head)->prev=(node *)NULL;
            free(ptr);

     }

     *tail=(node *)NULL;
}


void main()
{
  node *head, *tail;
  int ch,element,after;
  create_empty(&head,&tail);
  while(1)
  {
    clrscr();
    printf("1. add at end\n");
    printf("2. add.  at begning\n");
    printf("3. Inorder traverse\n");
    printf("4. Reverse order traverse \n");
    printf("5. insert after a node\n");
    printf("6. insert before a node\n");
    printf("7. delete from begning\n");
    printf("8. delete from end\n");
    printf("9. delete entire list\n");
    printf("10. Exit\n");
    printf("enter your choice\n");
    scanf("%d",&ch);
    switch(ch)
       {

    case 1:
              printf("Enter element");
              scanf("%d",&element);
              add_at_end(&head,&tail,element);
              getch();
              break;
```

```
        case 2:
                printf("Enter element");
                scanf("%d",&element);
                add_at_beg(&head,&tail,element);
                break;
        case 3:
                inordertrav(head);
                getch();
                break;
        case 4:
                reverseordertrav(tail);
                getch();
                break;
        case 5:
                printf("Enter element after which new element have to
                insert\n");
                scanf("%d",&after);
                printf("Enter element");
                scanf("%d",&element);
                insert_after_node(&head,&tail,element,after);
                break;
        case 6:
                printf("Enter element before which new element have to
                insert\n");
                scanf("%d",&after);
                printf("Enter element");
                scanf("%d",&element);
                insert_before_node(&head,element,after);
                break;
        case 7:
                delete_at_beg(&head,&tail);
                break;
        case 8:
                    delete_at_end(&head,&tail);
                         break;
        case 9:
                delete_list(&head,&tail);
                    break;
        case 10:
                exit();
        }
      }

    }
```

Algorithm 6.11 : *To add a node at end*

```
void add_at_end (node **head,node **tail,int item)
```

STEP 1 Declare *ptr of node type.

STEP 2 ptr=create new node.

STEP 3

ptr->info=item
ptr->next=NULL

STEP 4

If list is EMPTY then
*head=tail=ptr
ptr->prev=NULL
exit()

STEP 5

ELSE
(*tail)->next=ptr
ptr->prev=*tail
*tail=ptr

STOP

Algorithm 6.12 : *To traverse in reverse order*

START

void traverseinreverseorder(node *tail)

STEP 1

Repeat while tail!=NULL
OUT PUT tail->info

STEP 2

tail=tail->prev
END LOOP.

STEP 3

Return.

STOP

Algorithm 6.13 : *To insert after a given node*

START

void insert_after_node(node **head,node**tail,int item,int after)

STEP 1

Declare *ptr, *loc of node type.

STEP 2

ptr=create new node.

STEP 3

ptr->info=item

STEP 4

loc=*head

STEP 5

loc=search(loc,after)

STEP 6

If loc==NULL
Then

OUT PUT "Element does not exist"
Return

STEP 7

If loc->next==NULL
ptr->next=NULL
ptr->prev=*tail
(*tail)->next=ptr
*tail=ptr
return

STEP 8

Else
    ptr->next=loc->next
    ptr->prev=loc
    (loc->next)->prev=ptr
    loc->next=ptr

STEP 9

Return

STOP

Algorithm 6.14 : *To insert before a node*

START

void insert_before_node(node **head,int item,int before)

STEP 1

Declare* ptr,* loc of node type.

STEP 2

ptr=create new node.

STEP 3

ptr->info=item

STEP 4

loc=*head
(point loc to beginning)

STEP 5

loc=search(loc,before)

STEP 6

If loc==NULL
Then
OUT PUT "node does not exist"
Return

STEP 7

If loc->prev==NULL
Then
ptr->prev=NULL

```
        loc->prev=ptr
        ptr->next=* head
          * head=ptr
        return
STEP 8
        Else
          ptr->prev=loc->prev
          ptr->next=loc
          (loc->prev)->next=ptr
          loc->prev=ptr
STEP 9
        Return
STOP
```

6.2.2.3 Circular Linked List

It is a linear linked list except that the last node points to the first node. All operations applied on linear linked lists are also valid for circular linked list with following exceptions.

1. When we add a node at the end of linked list, its next pointer field is made to point to the first node.
2. While testing for end of the lists, we compare the next pointer field with the address of the first node.

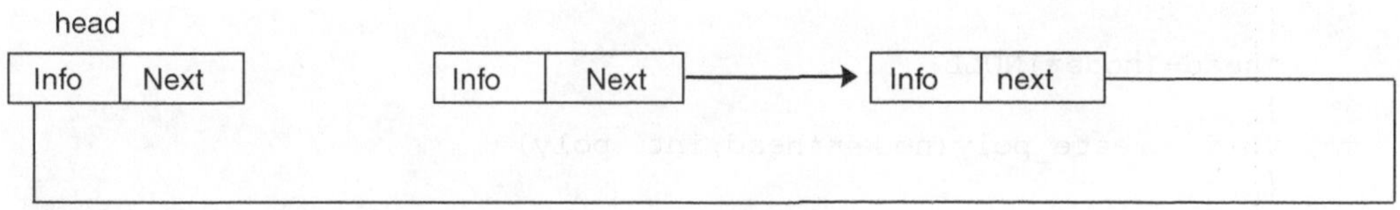

Fig 6.23 Circular linked list

Listing and algorithm for circular linked list are left as an exercise for you.

6.3 STORAGE OF SPARSE MATRICES USING LINKED LISTS

In first chapter, we have discussed a method (3-tuple) to store sparse matrices in main memory. Now, we will discuss second method to store sparse matrices in main memory. In a sparse matrix only non-zero elements are needed to store in memory. Let's consider the following sparse matrix :

0	0	0	0	0	1	0
0	0	0	0	1	0	0
0	0	0	0	0	0	0
0	0	0	0	3	0	0

Fig. 6.24 Sparse matrix

Fig 6.25 Illustrates the linked list for the sparse matrix given in Fig. 6.25.

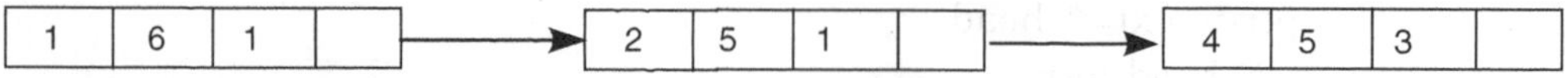

Fig. 6.25

CONCEPTUAL PROBLEMS

Problem 6.1 : *Write a C program to perform following operations on the polynomials (using Arrays/Linked list) :*

(*i*) *Read and Display the polynomials.*

(*ii*) *Add two polynomials.*

(*iii*) *Multiply two polynomials.*

Solution :

```
#include<stdio.h>
#include<conio.h>
typedef struct link_list
{
   float coef;
   int exp;
   struct link_list *next;
}node;
void empty_list(node **head}
{
*head=(node*)NULL;
}
void create_poly(node **head,int poly)
{
   node *ptr,*loc;
        char ch='y';
        float coef;
        int exp;
        clrscr();
        while(ch=='y'||ch=='Y')
        {
              ptr=(node*)malloc(sizeof(node));
              printf("\nenter coeff of Polynomial %d",poly);
              scanf("%f", &coef);
              printf("\nenter exp");
              scanf("%d",&exp);
              ptr->coef=coef;
              ptr->exp=exp;
              ptr->next=(node*)NULL;
              if(*head==(node*)NULL)
              *head=ptr;
              else
              {
              loc=*head;
              while(loc->next!=(node*)NULL)
```

```
                loc=loc->next;
                loc->next=ptr;
                }
                printf("\ncontinue y/n");
                ch=getch();
            }
            clrscr();
        getch();
        }

        void  display_poly(node*head)
        {
            if(head==(node*)NULL)
            {
            printf("Polynomial  is  empty");
            return;
            }
            while(head!=(node*)NULL)
            {
                if(head->coef>0)
                printf("+");
                printf("%.2fX^%d  ",head->coef,head->exp);
                head=head->next;
            }
            getch();
            return;
        }

        void  sum_poly(node *head1,node *head2,node **sumofpoly)
        {
            node *loc_poly,*loc_head2,*ptr;
            int  x;
            if((!head1)&&(head2))
            {
                *sumofpoly=head2;
                display_poly(*sumofpoly);
                return;
            }
            if(!head2)&&head1)
            {
                *sumofpoly=head1;
                display_poly(*sumofpoly);
            return;
            }
            if((!head1)&&(!head2))
            {
                printf("Polynomials  are  empty");
                return;
            }
```

```
        while(head1)
        {
                loc_head2=head2;
                ptr=(node*)malloc(sizeof(node));
                x=head1->exp;
                while(loc_head2->exp!=x&&loc_head2->next!=(node*)NULL)
                loc_head2=loc_head2->next;
                if(loc_head2->exp==x)
                {
                        ptr->coef=head1->coef+loc_head2->coef;
                        ptr->exp=x;
                        ptr->next=(node*)NULL;
                }
                if(loc_head2->exp!=x)
                {
                        ptr->coef=head1->coef;
                        ptr->exp=x;
                        ptr->next=(node*)NULL;
                }
                if(*sumofpoly==(node*)NULL)
                {
                *sumofpoly=ptr;
                }
                else
                {
                        loc_poly=*sumofpoly;
                        while(loc_poly->next!=(node*)NULL)
                        loc_poly=loc_poly->next;
                        loc_poly->next=ptr;
                }
    head1=head1->next;
    }
    while(head2)
    {
                ptr=(node*)malloc(sizeof(node));
                x=head2->exp;
                loc_poly=*sumofpoly;
                while(loc_poly->exp!=x&&loc_poly->next!=(node*)NULL)
                loc_poly=loc_poly->next;
                if(loc_poly->exp!=x)
                {
                        ptr->coef=head2->coef;
                        ptr->exp=x;
                        ptr->next=(node*)NULL;

                        if(*sumofpoly==(node*)NULL)
                        {
                        *sumofpoly=ptr;
                        }
                        else
                        {
                                loc_poly=*sumofpoly;
```

```
                        while(loc_poly->next!=(node*)NULL)
                        loc_poly=loc_poly->next;
                        loc_poly->next=ptr;
                    }
            }
            head2=head2->next;
            }

    clrscr();
    display_poly(*sumofpoly);
    getch();
    }
    void  mul_poly(node *head1,node *head2,node **mulofpoly)
    {
        node *loc_poly,*loc_head2,*ptr;
        if((!head1)&&(head2))
        {
        *mulofpoly=head2;
        printf("Result  is  zero  polynomial");
        return;
        }
        if((!head2)&&head1)
        {
        *mulofpoly=head1;
        printf("Result  is  zero  polynomial");
        return;
        }
        if((!head1)&&(!head2))
        {
            printf("Result  is  zero  polynomial");
            return;
        }
        while(head1)
        {
            loc_head2=head2;

            while(loc_head2!=(node*)NULL)
            {     ptr=(node*)malloc(sizeof(node));
                  ptr->coef=(head1->coef)*(loc_head2->coef);
                  ptr->exp=head1->exp+loc_head2->exp;
                  ptr->next=(node*)NULL;

                  if(*mulofpoly==(node*)NULL)
                  {
                  *mulofpoly=ptr;
                  }
                  else
                  {
                        loc_poly=*mulofpoly;
                        while(loc_poly->next!=(node*)NULL)
                        loc_poly=loc_poly->next;
```

```
                        loc_poly->next=ptr;
                    }
                loc_head2=loc_head2->next;
                }
        head1=head1->next;
        }
        clrscr();
        display_poly(*mulofpoly);
        getch();

}

void main()
{
        char ch;
        node *head1,*head1,*sumofpoly,*mulofpoly;
        empty_list(&head1);
        empty_list(&head2);
        empty_list(&sumofpoly);
        clrscr();
        while(1)
        {
        printf("\n1.Enter polynomial 1.");
        printf("\n2.Enter polynomial 2");
        printf("\n3.View polynomials");
        printf("\n4.Add two Polynomials");
        printf("\n5.Multiply two Polynomials");
        printf("\n6.Exit");
        printf("\nEnter your choice");
        ch=getch();
        switch(ch)
        {
        case '1':
                    empty_list(&head1);
                    create_poly(&head1,1);
                break;
        case '2':
                    empty_list(&head2);
                    create_poly(&head2,2);
                    break;
        case '3':
                    clrscr();
                    printf("Polynomial 1/t");
                    display_poly(head1);
                    printf("\n\nPolynomial 2/t");
                    display_poly(head2);
                break;
        case '4':
                    empty_list(&sumofpoly);
                    sum_poly(head1,head2,&sumofpoly);
                    break;
```

```
        case  '5';
                  empty_list(&mulofpoly);
                  mul_poly(head1,head2,&mulofpoly);
                  break;
        case  '6';
              exit();
        }
    }
}
```

Problem 6.2 : *Write a C program to perform the following operations on the following sparse matrices (using/Arrays/Linked lists).*

(*i*) *Read and display the sparse matrix*

(*ii*) *Add two sparse matrix.*

Solution :

```
#include>stdio.h>
#include<conio.h>
#include<alloc.h>
typedef  struct  sparse
{
   int  column,row;
   int  value;
   struct  sparse *next,*prev;
}node;
void  create_empty(node **head,node **tail)
{
   *head=*tail=NULL;
}
void store_element(node **head,node **tail,int row,int col,int element)
{
   node *ptr;
   if(element)
   {
       ptr=(node*)malloc(sizeof(node));
       ptr->column=col;
       ptr->row=row;
       ptr->value=element;
       ptr->next=NULL;
       if(*head==NULL)
       {
           ptr->prev=NULL;
           *head=ptr;
           *tail=ptr;
       }

       else
       {
           ptr->prev=*tail;
           (*tail)->next=ptr;
           *tail=ptr;
       }
   }
}
```

```
void  display(node *head,int row,int col)
{
   node *loc;
   int  i,j;

   for(i=0;i<row;i++)
   {
        printf("\n");
        for(j=0;j<col;j++)
        {
              loc=head;
              while(loc!=NULL)
              {
                     if(loc->row==i&&loc->clumn==j)
                     {
                         printf("\t%d",loc->value);
                         break;
                     }
                     loc=loc->next;
              }
                     if(loc==NULL)
                     printf("\t0");
        }
   }
   getch();
}

void  sum(node *head_a,node *head_b,int  row,int  col)
{
   node *loc1,*loc2;
   int  i,j,s;
   s=0

   for(i=0;i<row;i++)
   {
        printf("\n");
        for(j=0;j<col;j++)
        {
              loc1=head_a;
              loc2=head_b;
              while(loc1!=NULL)
              {
                     if(loc1->row==i&&loc1->column==j)
                     {
                            s=loc1->value;
                        break
                     }
                     loc1=loc1->next;
              }
              if(loc1==NULL)
              s=0;
                     while(loc2!=NULL)
              {
```

```
                    if(loc2>row==i&&loc2->column==j)
                    {
                          s+=loc2->value;
                       break;
                    }
                    loc2=loc2->next;
               }
               if(loc2==NULL)
               s+=0;
               printf("\t%d",s);
          }
     }
getch();
}

void main()
{
   node *head_a,*tail_a,*head_b,*tail_b;
   int col,row,col1,row1,item,choice;
   int i,j;
   char ch;
   while(1)
   {
        clrscr();
        printf("\n1.Store the values of sparse matrix A");
        printf("\n2.Store the values of sparse matrix B");
        printf("\n3.Read A/B and SUM");
        printf("\n4.EXIT");
        printf("\nenter your choice");
        ch=getch();
        switch(ch)
        {
             case '1';
             create_empty(&head_a,&tail_a);
             printf("\nenter number of rows");
             scanf("%d",&row);
             printf("\nenter number of columns");
             scanf("%d",&col);
             for(i=0;i<row;i++)
             for(j=0;j<col;j++)
             {
                    printf("\nenter value at [%d}{%d]",i,j);
                    scanf("%d",&item);
                    store_element(&head_a,&tail_a,i,j,item);
             }
             break;
             case '2';

             create_empty(&head_b,&tail_b);
             printf("\nenter number of rows");
             scanf("%d",&row1);
             printf("\nenter number of columns");
             scanf("%d",&col1);
```

```
                        if(row!=row1||col!=col1)
                        {
                              printf("Two matrices should be of same order to
                              find the sum");
                              break;
                        }
                        for(i=0;i<row;i++)
                        for(j=0;j<col;j++)
                        {
                              printf("\nenter value at [%d}{%d]",i,j);
                              scanf("%d",&iem);
                              sore_element(&head_b,&tail_b,i,j,item);

                        }
                        break;
                        case '3':
                              printf("\nEnter 1 to display Matrix A,2 for
                              Matrix B, 3 for sum of A and B");
                              scanf("%d",&choie);
                              if(choice==1)
                              display(head_a,row,col);
                              if(choice==2)
                              display(head_b,row,col);
                              if(choice==3)
                              sum(head_a,head_b,row,col);
                        break;
                        case '4';
                        exit();
                  }
            }
      }
```

Problem 6.3 : *Write a C program to find multiplication of two sparse matrices.*

Solution :

```
#include<stdio.h>
#include<conio.h>
#include<alloc.h>
typedef struct sparse
{
   int column;row;
   int value;
   struct sparse *next,*prev;
}node;

void create_empty(node **head,node **tail)
{
   *head=*tail=NULL;
}
void store_element(node **head,node **tail,int row,int col,int element)
{
   node *ptr;

   if(element)
   {
```

```
    ptr=(node*)malloc(sizeof(node));
    ptr->column=col;
    ptr->row=row;
    ptr->value=element;
    ptr->next=NULL;
    if(*head==NULL)
    {
        ptr->prev=NULL;
        *head=ptr;
        *tail=ptr;
    }

    else
    {
        ptr->prev=*tail;
        (*tail)->next=ptr;
        *tail=ptr;
    }
    }
}

void  display(node *head,int row,int col)
{
        node *loc;
        int  i,j;
        for(i=0;i<row,i++)
        {
             printf("\n");
             for(j=0;j<col;j++)
             {
                   loc=head;
                   while(loc!=NULL)
                   {
                          if(loc->row==i&&loc->column==j)
                          {
                                printf("\t%d",loc->value);
                                break;
                          }
                          loc=loc->next;
                   }
                   if(loc==NULL)
                   printf("\t0");
             }
        }
getch();
}

void  mul(node *head_a,node *head_b,int col2,int row1,int col1)
{
   node  *loc_head_a,*loc_head_b;
        int  c1,c2,r1;
        int  a,b,c;
```

```
        int cp,rp,p; /*cp,rp,p used for positioning for gotoxy()"/
        p=0;
        gotoxy(5,20);
        printf("MULTIPLICATION=")
        for(c2=0;c2<col2;c2++)
        {
        cp=rp=20;
        cp=cp+p;

        for(r1=0;r1<row1;r1++)
        {
        c=0;
              for(c1=0;c1<=col1;c1++)
              {
              loc_head_a=head_a;
              while(loc_head_a!=NULL)
              {
              if(loc_head_a->row==r1&&loc_head_a->column==c1)
                     {
                            a=loc_head_a->value;
                                   break;
                     }
                     loc_head_a=loc_head_a->next;
              }
              if(loc_head_a==NULL)
              a=0;
              loc_head_b=head_b;
              while(loc_head_b!=NULL)
              {
              if(loc_head_b->row==c1&&loc_head_b->column==c2)
                     {
                            b=loc_head_b->value;
                                   break;
                     }
                     loc_head_b=loc_head_b->next;
              }
              if(loc_head_b==NULL)
                     b=0;
                     c+=a*b;
              }
              gotoxy(cp,rp=rp+4);
              printf("%d:,c);

              }
              p=p+4; /*p is used for Positioning for gotoxy()*/
        }
        getch();
}

void main()
{
   node *head_a,*tail_a,*head_b,*tail_b,*mul_head,*mul_tail;
   int  col1,row1,col2,row2,item,choice;
```

```
int i,j;
char ch;
while(1)
{
    clrscr();
    printf("\n1.Store the values of sparse matrix A");
    printf("\n2.Store the values of sparse matrix B");
    printf("\n3.Read A/B and Multiplication A*B");
    printf("\n4.EXIT");
    printf("\nenter your choice");
    ch=getch();
    switch(ch)
    {
        case '1';
        create_empty(&head_a,&tail_a);
        printf("\nenter number of rows");
        scanf("%d",&row1);
        printf("\nenter number of columns");
        scanf("%d",&col1);
        for(i=0;i<row1;i++)
        for(j=0;j<col1;j++)
        {
        printf("\nenter value at [%d}{%d]",i,j);
        scanf("%d",&item);
        store_element(&head_a,&tail_a,i,j,item);
        }
        break;
        case '2';

        create_empty(&head_b,&tail_b);
        create_empty(&mul_head,&mul_tail);
        printf("\nenter number of rows");
        scanf("%d",&row2);
        printf("\nenter number of columns");
        scanf("%d",&col2);
        if(col1!=row2)
        {
            printf("Multiplication not possible, order of
            matrices is not valid");
            getch();
            break;
        }
        for(i=0;i<row2;i++)
        for(j=0;j<col2;j++)
        {
        printf("\nenter value at[%d}{%d]",i,j);
        scanf("%d",&item);
        store_element(&head_b,&tail_b,i,j,item);
        }
        break;
        case '3':
            printf("\nEnter 1 to display Matrix A,2 for
            Matrix B, 3 for sum of A and B");
```

```
                scanf("%d",&choice);
                if(choice==1)
                display(head_a,row1,col1);
                if(choice==2)
                display(head_b,row2,col2);
                if(choice==3)
                mul(head_a,head_b,col2,row1,col1);
            break;

            case '4':
            exit();
        }
    }
}
```

Problem 6.4 : *Write a C function to count the number of nodes in a linked list.*

(MCA June, 1996)

Solution :

```
int  countnodes(node  *head)
{
        int  n=0;
        while(head!=(node  *)NULL)
        {
              n++;
                head = head → next
        }
        return  n;
}
```

Problem 6.5 : *Write short note on "Garbage Collection and Compaction."*

(MCA June, 2001)

Solution : ***Garbage Collection :*** It is a method by which Operating System deallocates the nodes. This requires the presence of a Marking bit on each node.

Deallocation of a node is done in two levels :

1. The application which claimed the node releases it back to the operating system.
2. The operating system calls storage management routines to return free nodes to the free space.

Application level deallocation

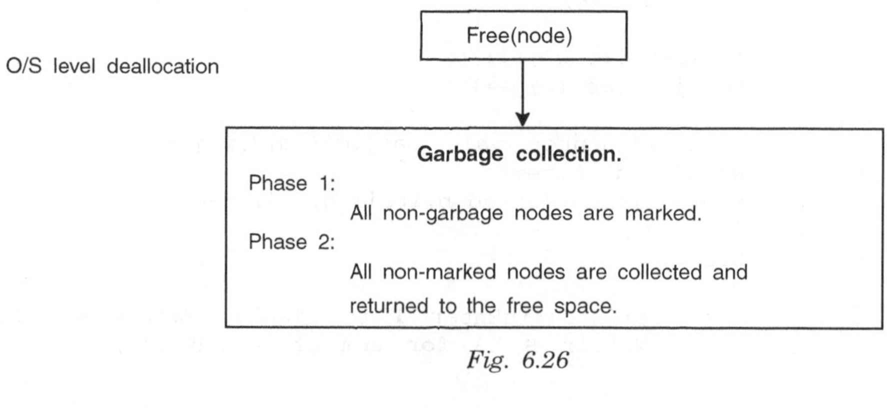

Fig. 6.26

Where variable size nodes are used it is desirable to keep the space as one contiguous block. In this case, the second phase of garbage collection is called **memory compaction.**

Problem 6.6 : *Write a 'C' function to delete a node at a specified position in linked list.*

(BCA June, 1999)

Solution : *Refer. Listing 6.5.*

KEY POINTS

- A collection object which is used to store homogeneous elements in computer memory is called a LIST.
- Linked list is a dynamic implementation of list.
- A linked list can be singly, doubly or circular.
- Node of a singly linked list contains a value and a pointer to next node.
- Use malloc function to allocate the memory to a pointer of node type.
- When a function accepts address of a pointer like &head in **head, then we use *head inside the body of that function and if a function accepts a pointer like head in *head, then we should write head instead of *head in function body whenever needed.
- Doubly linked list is the collection of homogeneous objects, in which each object is stored in a node with two additional variables which are references of next and previous node in the list.

EXERCISE

1. Write an algorithm and a program to count the number of elements in a circular singly linked list.
2. Write a C routine to insert a value N after the node in the linked list.
3. Write a segment of code to delete the first element of the linked list.
4. Give advantages and disadvantages of using linked lists.
5. Define a self referential structure for representing a simple linked list of integers. Write a 'C' function to split the list into two lists so that the first contains all even numbered elements and the second list contains only odd numbered elements.

7

STACK AND QUEUES

STACK

7.1 INTRODUCTION

A stack is a homogeneous collection of items, arranged linearly with access at one end only, called *the top*. This means that data can be added or removed from only the top. Formally, this type of stack is called a *Last In First Out (LIFO) stack*. Data is added to the stack using the *Push* operation, and removed using the *Pop* operation. These will be covered in coming sections.

In order to clarify the idea of a stack, let us look at a "real life" example of a stack. Think of a stack of plates in a high school cafeteria. When the plates are being stacked, they are added one on top of each other. It does not make much sense to put each plate on the bottom of the pile, as that would be far more tedious a job, and would accomplish nothing over stacking them on top of each other. Similarly, when a plate is taken out, it is usually taken from the top of the *stack*.

A *stack* can be implemented in two ways :

1. *Array implementation*
2. *Linked list implementation.*

7.2 ARRAY IMPLEMENTATION

One of two ways to implement a *stack* is by using a one dimensional array. When implemented this way, the data is simply stored in the array. Top is an integer value, which contains the array index for the top of the stack. Each time data is added or removed, top is incremented or decremented accordingly, to keep track of the current top of the *stack*. By convention, an empty stack is indicated by setting top to be equal to –1.

Operations on *stacks*

1. Create empty *stack*.
2. Push operation (to push element in *stack*).
3. Pop-to access and remove the top element of the *stack*.
4. Is full-to check whether the *stack* is full or not.
5. Is empty-to check whether the *stack* is empty or not.
6. Traversing.

Is it possible to pop the *stack* if *stack* is empty ? Certainly, not. Similarly if the stack is full, then push operation is invalid.

7.2.1 Representation of a Stack in Memory

Representing a *stack* using an Array. Consider an example to store integers inside a *stack*. Listing of such an example is as follows :

LISTING 7.1

```
#include<stdio.h>
#include<conio.h>
#include<alloc.h>
#define MAX 5
typedef struct stack
{
int ele[MAX];
 int top;
}stack;

void create_empty_stack(stack *s)
      {
            s->top=-1;
      }
int isfull(stack *s)
      {

            if(s->top==MAX-1)
            return 1;
            else
            return 0;
      }
int isempty(stack *s)
 {
       if(s->top==-1)
       return 1;
       else return 0;
 }

void push(stack *s,int item)
 {
       if(isfull(s))
       {
            printf(" Overflow");
            return;
       }
       else
       s->top++;
       s->ele[s->top]=item;
}
void pop(stack *s)
 {
 if(isempty(s))
 {
 printf("Underflow");
 return;
 }
 else
 return(--s->top)

 }
```

```
void trav(stack *s)
 {
        int i=0;
        while(i<=s->top)
        {
        printf("%d\n",s->ele[i]);
        i++;
        }
 }
int peek(stack *s)
        {
             if(isempty(s))
             printf("underflow");
             return s->top;
        }

void main(void)
 {

        stack *s;
        int p;
        int item,choice;
        create_empty_stack(s);
        while(1)
        {
             clrscr();
             printf("1.Push\n");
             printf("2.Pop\n");
             printf("3.Trav");
             printf("4.Peek \(uper most element\)\n");
             printf("5.exit\n");
             printf("entaer your choice");
             scanf("%d",&choice);
             switch(choice)
             {
             case 1:
             printf("\nEnter a number");
             scanf("%d",&item);
             push(s,item);
             break;
             case 2:
             printf("%d", pop(s));
             break;
             case 3:
             trav(s);
             getch();
             break;
             case 4:
         p=peek(s);
                 if(p!=-1)
                 {
         printf("%d",s->ele[p]);
         getch();
```

```
            }
        break;
            case 5:
            exit();
            }
        }
}
```

Algorithm 7.1 : *To push item in the stack*

START

Void push(stack * s,int item)

STEP 1

Check for stack overflow
If s–>top=size
OUT PUT "stack overflow"
Exit().

STEP 2

s–>top++

STEP 3

s–>element[s–>top]=item

STEP 4

Exit

STOP

Algorithm 7.2 : *To pop operation*

START

int pop(stack *s)

STEP 1

Check whether the stack is empty.
If s–>top=0
Out put "stack under flow"
Exit

STEP 2

p=s–>top
s–>top
(decrement top by 1)

STEP 3

Return (s–>element[s–>p])

STOP

Algorithm 7.3 : *To traverse*

START

void traverse (stack * s)

STEP 1

Set i=0

STEP 2

Repeat while

i<=s–>top

STEP 3

Increment i by 1

STEP 4

End While

STEP 5

Exit

STOP

7.3 LINKED LIST IMPLEMENTATION OF STACKS

Like lists, stacks can also be implemented as linked data structure. As you have seen the consequences of array implementation of stacks, the main problem was overflow condition which is faced when stacks try to cross size of array. This problem can be solved by linked implementation. Here we will follow the principle of dynamic memory allocation. Every time memory will be allocated at runtime, whenever new element is pushed into the stack. Similarly, memory will be freed when we pop an element from the stack.

If you have read previous chapters then there is nothing new. We will use singly linked list program for linked implementation of stacks. You have to follow following points :

1. Head will be referred by top.
2. We will use a C routine, "insert a node at beginning" to push an element.
3. Reverse order traversal can be used to read from bottom of stack.

We are giving listing for following operations :

1. create empty stack
2. push
3. pop
4. traverse
5. peek (to read topmost element).

LISTING 7.2

```
#include<stdio.h>
#include<conio.h>
#include<alloc.h>
typedef struct stack
       {
            int info;
            struct stack *next;
       }node;

void create_empty(node **top)
       {
            *top=(node *)NULL;
       }
```

```
        void push(node **top,int item)
        {
             node *ptr;
             ptr=(node *)malloc(sizeof(node));
             ptr->info=item;
             ptr->next=*top;
             *top=ptr;
        }
             void traverse(node *top)
        {
             if(top->next!=(node *)NULL)

             traverse(top->next);
             printf("%d",top->info);
        }

   void pop(node **top)
   {
             node *ptr;
             if(*top==(node *)NULL)
             {
             printf("Underflow");
             return;
             else
             {
                  ptr=*top;
                  *top=(*top)->next;
                  free(ptr);
             }
   }

   int peek(node *top)
   {
   return top->info;
   }
   void main()
   {
        node *top;
        int item,choice,p;
        create_empty(&top);
        while(1)
        {

             clrscr();
             printf("1.Push new element in list\n");
             printf("2.Pop an element from stack \n");
             printf("3.Trverse:");
             printf("4.Peek element");
             printf("5.EXIT\n");
```

```
            printf("\nEnter your choice");
            scanf("%d",&choice);
            switch(choice)
            {
            case 1:
                    printf("\nEnter a no");
                    scanf("%d",&item);
                    push(&top,item);
                    break;
            case 2:
                    pop(&top);
                    break;


            case 3:
                    traverse(top);
                    getch();
                    break;
            case 4:
                    if(top!=(node *)NULL)
                    {
                    p=peek(top);
                    printf("top most element is %d",p);
                    getch();
                    }
                    else
                    printf("stack is empty");
                    break;

            case 5:
                    exit();
            }
        }
}
```

7.4 APPLICATIONS OF STACKS

1. Stacks are used to pass parameters between functions.
2. Stacks are used in recursion.

In addition, stacks are used when a program uses subprograms. Let a program A call a subprogram B and B call C. Now, first of all C will be completed and then B and in the last A will be completed. Thus the sequence by which subprograms activity proceeds are summed up as the property Last In First Out (LIFO).

7.4.1 Polish Notations

The process of writing the operators of an expression in a particular position is called *polish notation*. The basic rule of polish notation states that the order in which the operations are to be performed is completely determined by the positions of the operations and operand in the expression. Accordingly, one never needs parenthesizing these when writing expressions in polish notation. The polish notations are classified into three categories.

1. *Infix*
2. *Prefix*
3. *Postfix.*

7.4.1.1 Infix Polish Notation

When the operators exist between two operands, then the expression is called *infix*. For example : A+B–C. In this expression operator + is placed between A and B and – is placed between B and C.

7.4.1.2 Prefix Polish Notation

Operator symbol is placed before its two operands. For example,

* To add A to B, we can write as +AB or +BA.
* To subtract A from B, we have to write as –AB not as –BA.

In order to translate an arithmetic expression from infix notation to polish notation, we do step by step using brackets [ ] to indicate the partial translation. Consider the following expression in infix notation.

```
(A+B/C)*(X*Y+Z)
(A-[/BC])*([*XY]+Z)
[-A/BC]*[+*XYZ]
* -A/BC+*XYZ
```

7.4.1.3 Postfix Polish Notation

In this notation the operator symbol is placed after its two operands. For example,

* To add A to B we can write as AB+ or BA+.
* To subtract A from B we have to write AB–

In order to translate an arithmetic expression from infix notation to reverse polish notation we will discuss two method.

1. *Partial translation ([ ]) method :* As we have done in converting infix to prefix, similarly this method can be used to convert an infix to postfix. Consider the following expression.

```
(A+B/C)*(X*Y+Z)
(A+[BC/])*([XY*]+Z)
[ABC/+]*[XY*Z+]
ABC/+XY*Z+*
```

2. *Stack of operators method :* When we have to write an algorithm to convert infix expression to postfix, then we use a stack of operators. Let us see an expression :

```
A+B/C
```

To convert the above expression into postfix notation, follow the following steps :

STEP 1

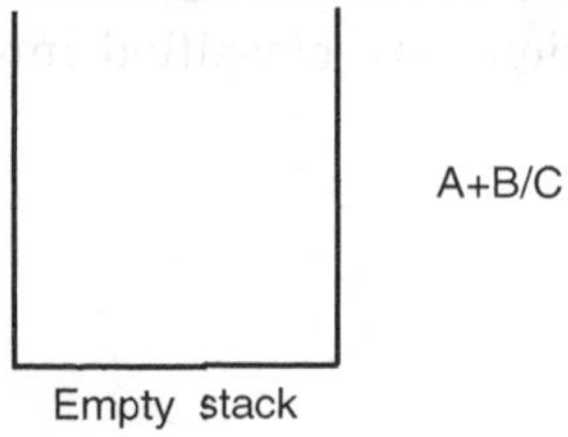

Fig. 7.1

STEP 2

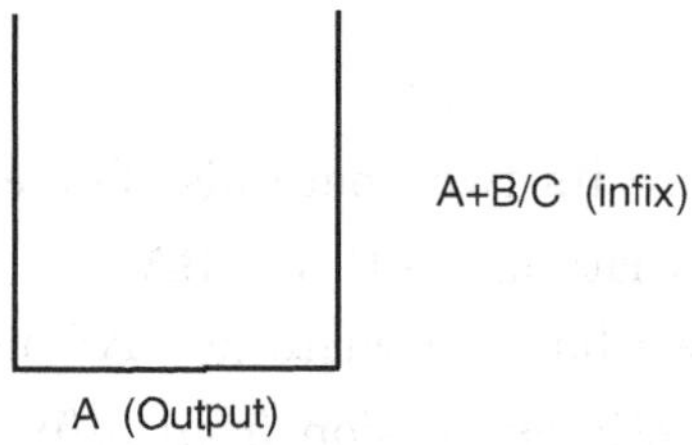

Fig. 7.2

STEP 3

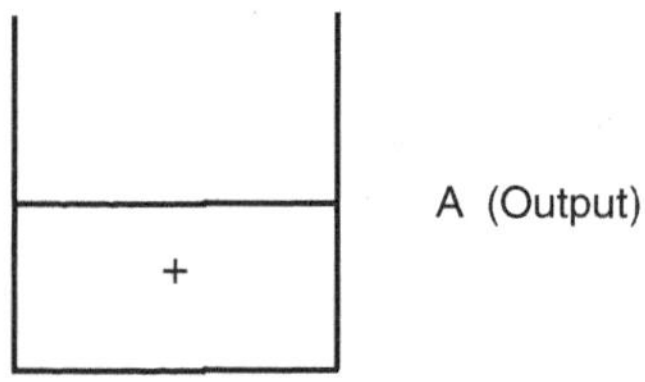

Fig. 7.3

STEP 4

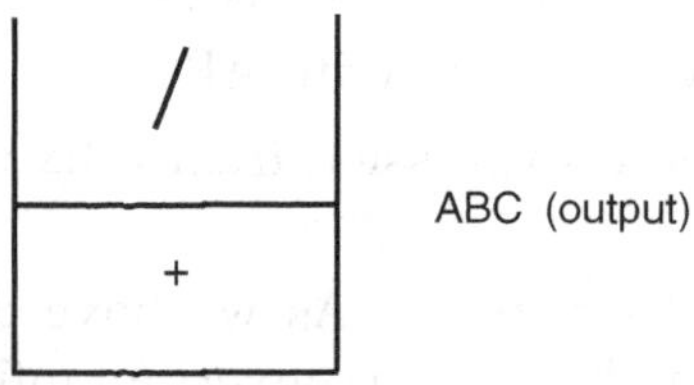

Fig. 7.4

STEP 5

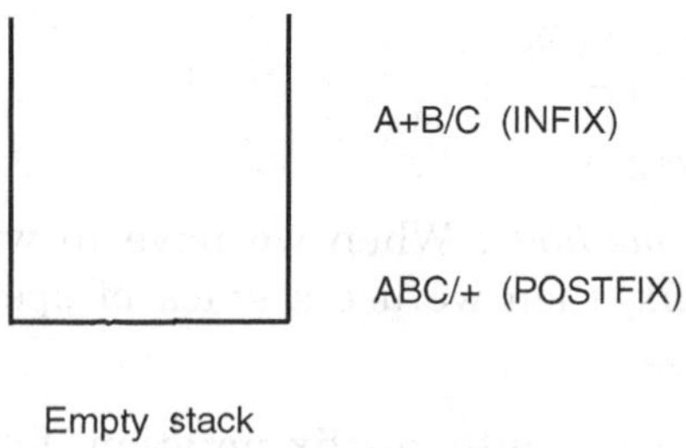

Fig. 7.5

Algorithm 7.4 : *To convert infix notation to postfix notation*

START

STEP 1

Declare a stack.

STEP 2

Scan the leftmost symbol from the given infix expression, and denote it as current symbol.

STEP 3

If current symbol is an operand, then append this to output string.
Else
Follow step 4.

STEP 4

If current input symbol is an operator, then all stack symbols whose precedence values are greater than or equal to the precedence of the current symbol are removed and appended to the output string.

STEP 5

Push the current symbol on to the stack.

STEP 6

Scan the leftmost symbol from the infix and let it be the current input symbol.

STEP 7

Repeat STEP 3 to STEP 6 while current symbol is not the last symbol of infix expression.

STEP 8

Append current symbol to the output string.

STEP 9

Pop up all symbols from the stack and append at output string.

STEP 10

Display output string.

STEP 11

EXIT

STOP

According to above algorithm, we have to read the characters of an infix expression from the left side. And if the character is an operator, then it is pushed into a stack and if it is an operand, then it is appended to the output string. Again if we have read an operator and if there is already an operator inside the stack, then we check if the precedence of incoming operator is higher than that of the existing operator, then we push incoming operator. And if precedence of incoming operator is less than or equal to the existing operator, then existing operator is popped up and appended to the output string and incoming operator is pushed into the stack.

For example,

A+B–C/D

STEP 1

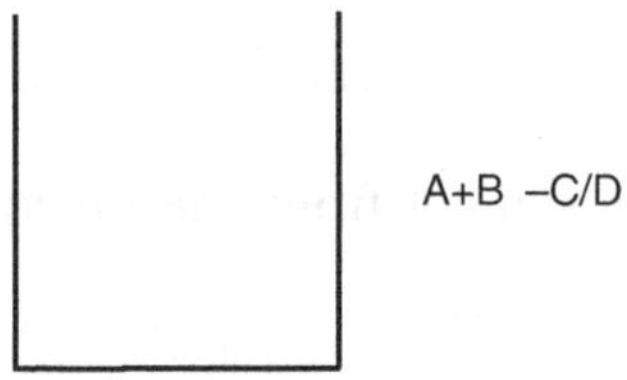

Fig. 7.6

STEP 2

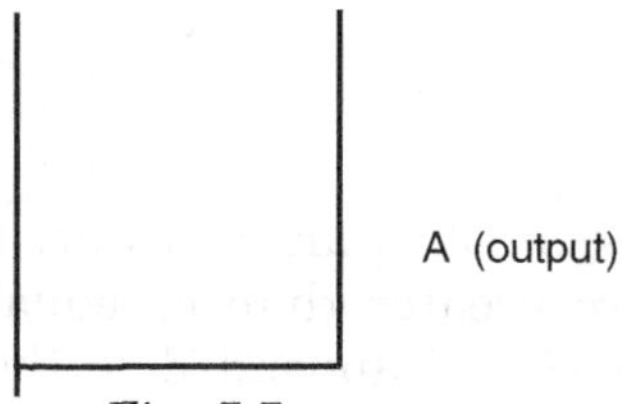

Fig. 7.7

STEP 3

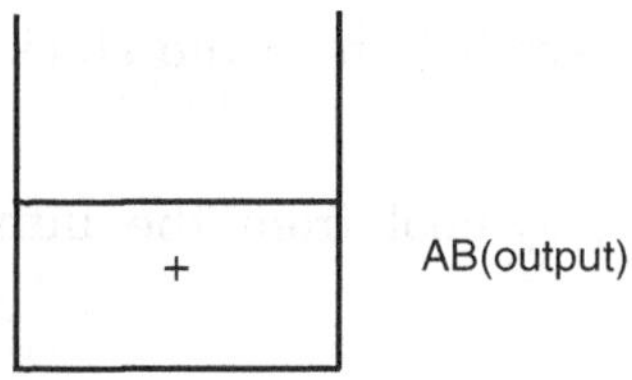

Fig. 7.8

STEP 4

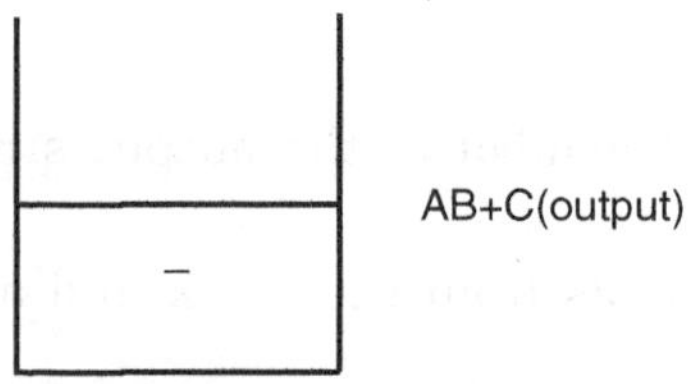

Fig. 7.9

STEP 5

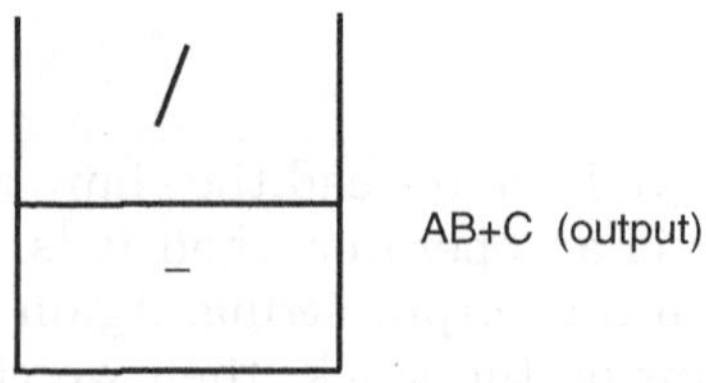

Fig. 7.10

STEP 6

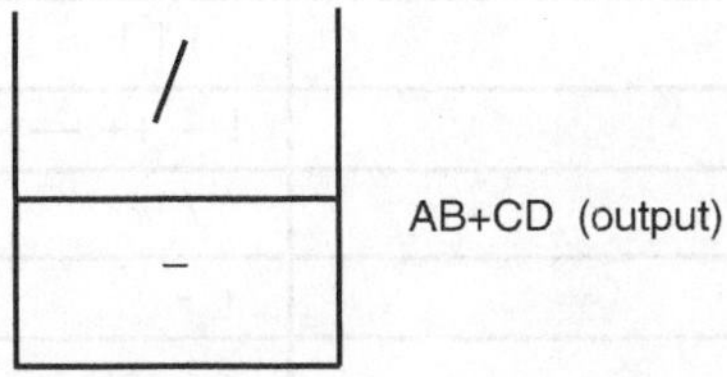

Fig. 7.11

STEP 7

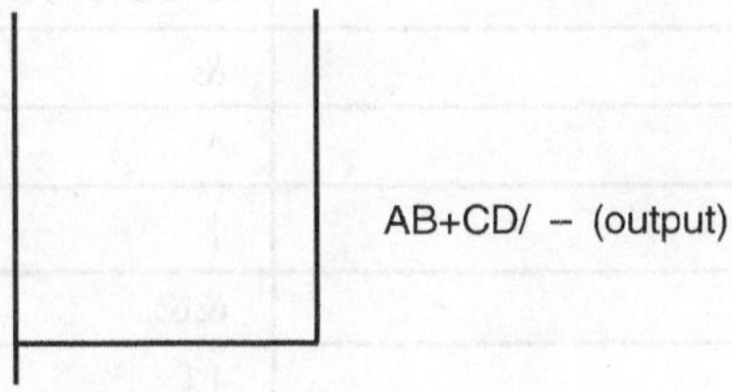

Fig. 7.12

Hence postfix notation is AB+CD/-

7.4.2 Operator Precedence

Operator precedence is the most important topic for polish conversions. So you must be very clear about the precedence of operators. An expression can have different types of operators. There are four types of operators :

1. Arithmetic operators : We are giving operators with their precedence. Level 1 operators are of higher precedence than level 2 operators. In any level precedence of operators is from left to right.

Level 1	*	/	%
Level 2	+	–	

2. Relational operators:

Level 1	<	<=	>	>=
Level 2	==	!=		

3. Logical operators:

Level 1	!	(NOT)
Level 2	&&	(AND)
Level 3	||	(OR)

4. Bit wise operators:

Level 1	>>	<<
Level 2	~	(1's complements)
Level 3	&	(bit-wise AND)
Level 4	^	bit-wise exclusive OR
Level 5	|	inclusive OR

<table>
<tr><th>Level</th><th>Operators</th></tr>
<tr><td>1</td><td>( ) [ ] -></td></tr>
<tr><td>2</td><td>! ~ ++ — + - * & (type) sizeof</td></tr>
<tr><td>3</td><td>* / %</td></tr>
<tr><td>4</td><td>+ -</td></tr>
<tr><td>5</td><td><< >></td></tr>
<tr><td>6</td><td>== !=</td></tr>
<tr><td>7</td><td>< <= > >=</td></tr>
<tr><td>8</td><td>&</td></tr>
<tr><td>9</td><td>^</td></tr>
<tr><td>10</td><td>|</td></tr>
<tr><td>11</td><td>&&</td></tr>
<tr><td>12</td><td>||</td></tr>
<tr><td>13</td><td>?</td></tr>
<tr><td>14</td><td>= += -= *= /= %= &= ^= != <<= >>=</td></tr>
</table>

Table 7.1

Table of Precedence of Operator

Associativity of the operators in level 2, 13 and 14 are from right to left and rest of operators have associativity from left to right. For example, see the association of operators in the following example :

```
2+3++
```

Associativity between operators of this example is from right to left *means* first ++ operator is operated on 3 which becomes 4 after operation and then this is added to 2 which finally becomes 6.

Algorithm 7.5 : *To evaluate expression in postfix notation*

START

STEP 1

Create empty stack.

STEP 2

Repeat while not end of expression.

STEP 3

If (element is operand) then push element on to stack.

Else

Pop two elements and let first be a and second be b. Evaluate b ⊗ a. Let its value be c, where ⊗ is an operator.

STEP 4

push c onto stack.

STEP 5

End While.

STEP 6

Pop the result.

STEP 7

Exit

STOP

Consider the following expression :

`35-83/*`

Character scanned	Stack
3	3
5	3,5
–	–2
8	–2,8
3	–2,8,3
/	–2,2.6
*	–5.2

Table 7.2

Hence the result is –5.2

QUEUES

7.5 INTRODUCTION

This is a linear data structure used to represent a linear list and permits deletion to be performed at one end of the list and the insertion at the other end.

7.5.1 Implementation of Queues

Two ways in which queues may be implemented are as follows :

1. Arrays.
2. Pointers (linked list)

Operation on Queues :

The following operations are performed on queues.

1. Create queue (q) : to create q as an empty queue.
2. Enqueue (q,I) to insert element I in a queue q.
3. Dequeue (q) to access and remove an element of queue q.
4. Peek (q) to access the first element of the queue q without removing it from the queue q.
5. Isfull (q) to check whether the queue q is full.
6. Is empty(q) to check whether the queue q is empty.
7. trav(q)_ to read entire queue.
   all these operations run in O(1) time.

7.5.1.1 Representing a Queue Using an Array

Two variables *front* and *rear* are used to implement a queue. These two variables hold index of the first and last element of the queue and an array is used to hold the elements of the queue. Let us declare a queue of 5 integers.

```
# define MAX 5
typedef struct
        {
           int front,rear;
           int element [MAX];
        }queue;
```

You can think linear queue as a one dimensional array in which insertion of new elements is done at front end and deletions are done from other end. Empty queue for above declared queue will be represented in computer memory as shown in following figures :

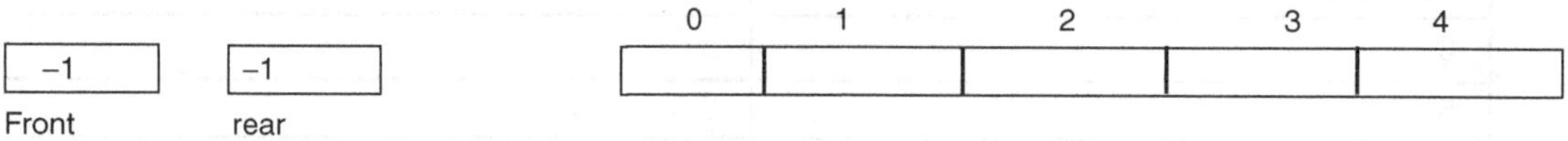

Fig. 7.13

Let us insert two numbers 2, 4 in our queue.

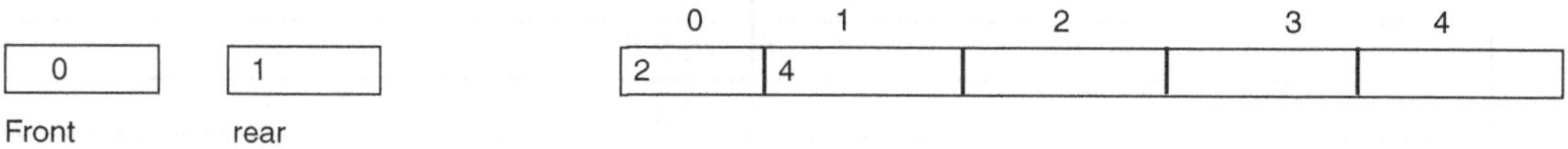

Fig. 7.14

Operation enqueue(q, 6)

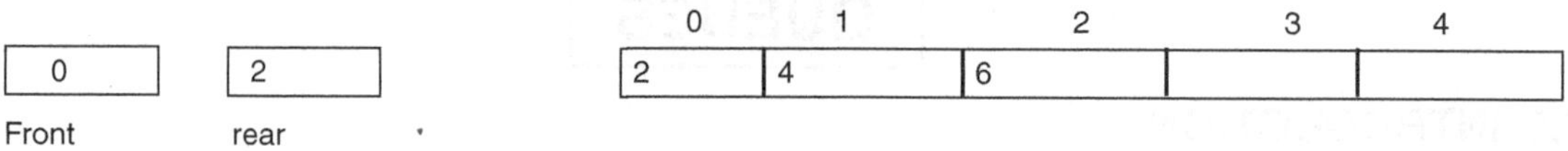

Fig. 7.15

Operation dequeue(q):

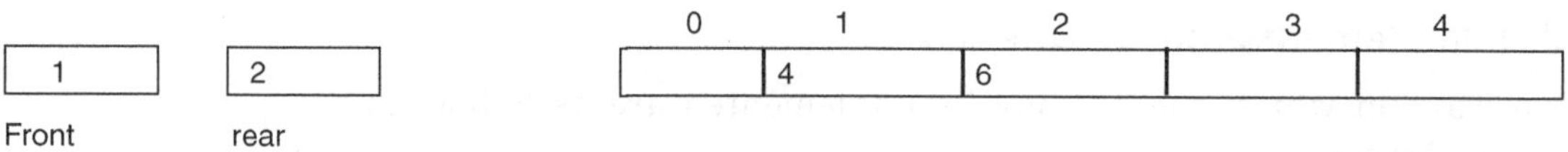

Fig. 7.16

Operation enqueue(q,8):

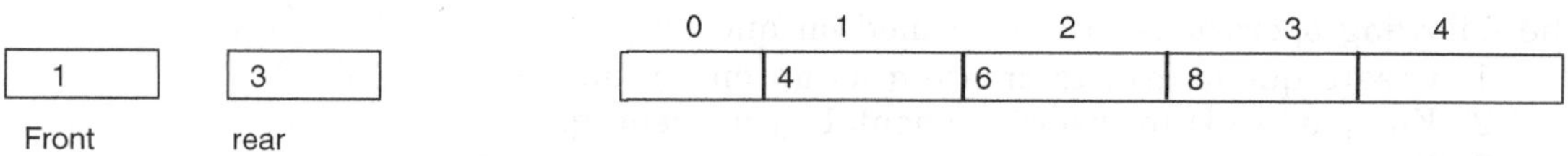

Fig 7.17

Operation enqueue(q,10):

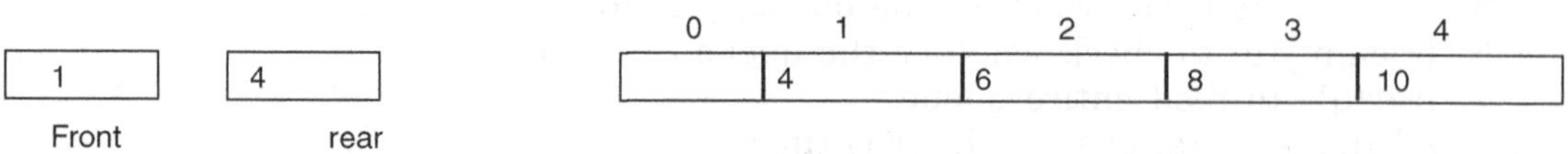

Fig. 7.18

Opearation dequeue(q):

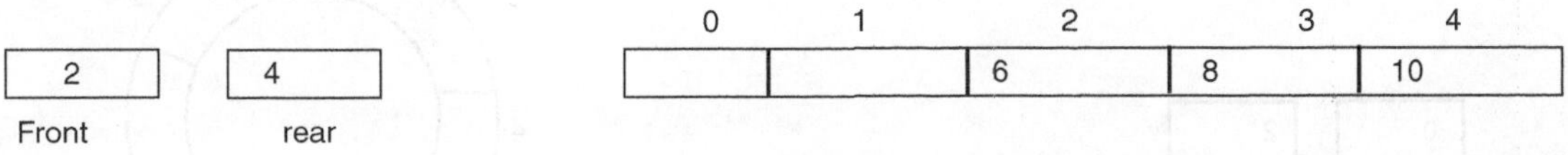

Fig 7.19

You must have observed as shown in Fig. 7.19 that it is not possible to enqueue more elements as such though two positions in the linear queue are vacant. To overcome this problem, the elements of the queue are moved forward so that vacant positions are shifted towards rear end. After shifting, front and rear are adjusted properly and then the elements are inserted. For example, we want to insert one more element (12). After enqueuing the element, now our queue will be as shown next :

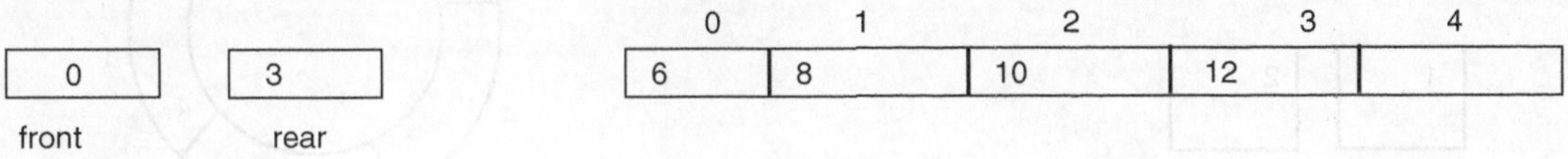

Fig 7.20

However, this difficulty can be overcome if we treat queue position with index 0 as a position that comes after position with index 4, *i.e,* we treat the queue as circular as shown in Fig. 7.21

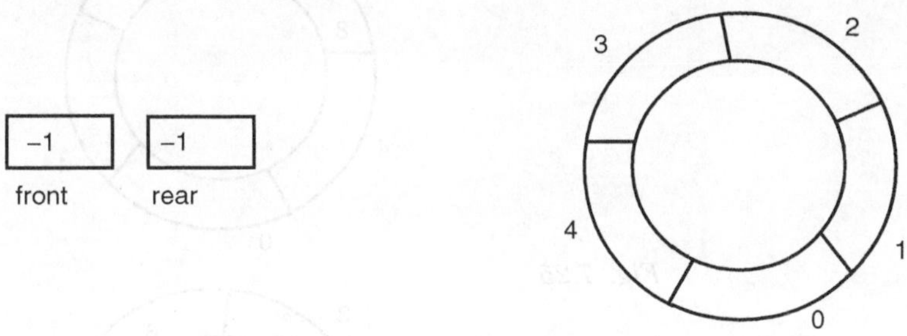

Circular queue.

Fig. 7.21

Enqueue(q,2) and enque(q,4):

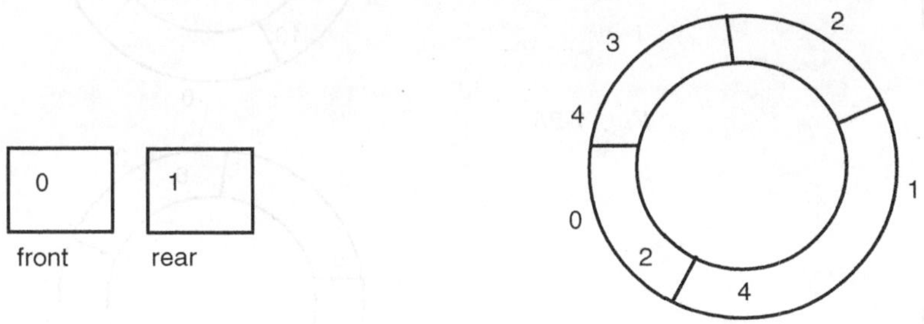

Fig. 7.22

Enqueue(q,6)

Fig. 7.23

Dequeue(q):

Fig. 7.24

Enqueue(q,8)

Fig. 7.25

Enqueue(q,10)

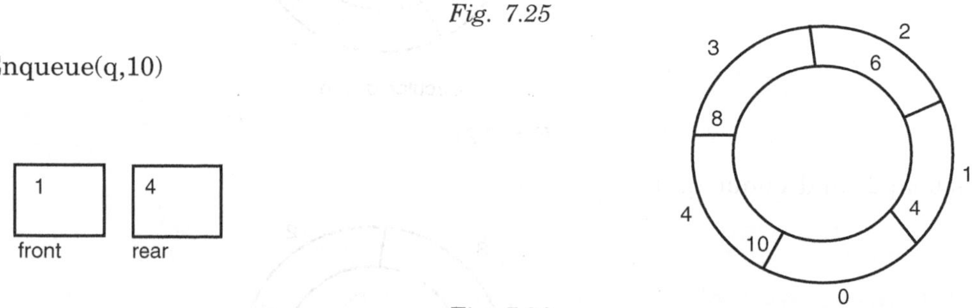

Fig. 7.26

Dequeue(q):

Fig. 7.27

Enqueue(q,12):

Fig. 7.28

We can enqueue one more number in our queue.

Enqueue(q,14) :

Fig. 7.29

Following points must be noticed while enqueuing or dequeuing in a linear queue or in circular queue.

1. Before *dequeue* operation, you must check whether the queue is already empty or not. This can be done by following function :

```
int isempty(queue * q)
{
   if (q->front ==-1 && q->rear ==-1)
   return 1;
   else
   return 0;
}
```

The above function returns 1 if queue is empty and returns 0 if queue is not empty. This function will be used in both linear and circular queues.

2. Before *enqueue* operation, you must check whether queue is full or not. If queue is full, then enqueue operation is not possible. Checking the linear queue,

```
int isfull (queue*q)
{
   if ((q->front==0)&&(q->rear==(MAX-1))
   return 1;
   else
   return 0;
}
```

Checking the circular queue,

```
int isfull ( queue *q)

        {
            if(((q->front==0)&&(q->rear==MAX-1))||(q->front==q->rear+1))
             return 1;
            else
            return 0;
        }
```

The above function returns value 1 if the test condition is satisfied; otherwise it returns 0.

Note. *If a queue is empty, then this condition is called underflow and if a given queue is full, then this condition is called overflow. Now we will consider all the operations on a linear and circular queue by an example. Let us create a queue for integers. First we will consider linear queue and then circular queue.*

LISTING 7.3

```
#include<stdio.h>
#include<conio.h>
#include<alloc.h>
# define MAX 5
typedef struct quetype
{
int front;
int rear;
int element[MAX];
} que;

void create_empty(que *q)
 {
 q->front=q->rear=-1;
 }
        int isfull(que *q)
        {
            if(q->front==0 && q->rear==MAX-1)
            return 1;
            else
            return 0;
        }
        void enqueue(que *q,int item)
        {

            int i;
            if(q->front==-1)
            {
                q->front=q->rear=0;
                q->element[0]=item;
                return;
            }
            if(q->rear!=MAX-1)
                q->rear++;
            else
            {
```

```
                for(i=q->front;i<=q->rear;i++)
                {
                    q->element[i-(q->front)]=q->element[i];

                }

                q->rear=q->rear-q->front;
                q->rear++;
             q->front=0;
            }
                q->element[q->rear]=item;

        }

        void trav(que *q)
        {

         int i;
         for(i=q->front;i<=q->rear;i++)
             printf("%d\n",q->element[i]);

        }
        void dequeue(que *q)
        {
            if(q->front==q->rear)
            q->front=q->rear=-1;
            else
            q->front++;
        }

        int isempty(que *q)
{
         if(q->front==-1)
                return 1;
            else
                return 0;
}

void main()
{
                int item,ch;
                que v;
                create_empty(&v);
                while(1)
                {
                    clrscr();
                    printf("1.enqueue\n");
                    printf("2.dequeue\n");
                    printf("3.traverse\n");
                    printf("4.exit\n");
                    printf("enter your choice\n");
                    scanf("%d",&ch);
                    getch();
```

```
                switch(ch)
                {
                case 1:
                     if(isfull(&v))
                 {
                 printf("list is full\n");
                 getch();
                 }
                 else
                 {
                        printf("\n enter a no");
                        scanf("%d",&item);
                        enqueue(&v,item);

                        }
                        break;
                case 2:

                          if(isempty(&v))
                          printf("que is empty");
                          else
                          {
                          dequeue(&v);
                          }
                         break;
                case 3:
                         trav(&v);
                          getch();
                         break;
                case 4:
                          exit();
                 }

            }

}
```

LISTING 7.4

(Listing for circular queue).

```
#include<stdio.h>
#include<conio.h>
#include<alloc.h>
# define MAX 5
typedef struct quetype
{
int front;
int rear;
int element[MAX];
} que;

void create_empty(que *q)
 {
```

```
q->front=q->rear=-1;
}
        int isfull(que *q)
        {
              if((q->front==0 && q->rear==MAX-1)||(q->front==q->rear+1))
              return 1;
              else
              return 0;
        }
        void enqueue(que *q,int item)
        {

              if(isempty(q))
              {
                    q->front=q->rear=0;
                    q->element[0]=item;
                    return;
              }
              if(q->rear==MAX-1)
                    q->rear=0;
              else
                    q->rear++;
                    q->element[q->rear]=item;

        }

        void trav(que *q)
        {
         int i=q->front;
         while(i<=MAX-1||i<=q->rear)
         {
              if(i==-1)
              return;
              printf("%d\n",q->element[i]);
              if(i==q->rear)
              return;
              if(i==MAX-1)
              i=-1;
              i++;
         }

        }
        int dequeue(que *q)
        {
              int d;
              d=q->element[q->front];
              if(q->front==q->rear)
              {
              q->front=q->rear=-1;
              return d;
              }
              else
              q->front++;
```

```
            return d;
        }

        int isempty(que *q)
    {
         if(q->front==-1)
                return 1;
            else
                return 0;
    }
    void main()
    {
                int item,ch,d;
                que v;
                create_empty(&v);
                while(1)
                {
                    clrscr();
                    printf("1.enqueue\n");
                    printf("2.dequeue\n");
                    printf("3.traverse\n");
                    printf("4.exit\n");
                    printf("enter your choice\n");
                    scanf("%d",&ch);
                    getch();
                switch(ch)
                {
                case 1:
                            if(isfull(&v))
                 {
                 printf("list is full\n");
                 getch();
                 }
                 else
                 {
                        printf("\n enter a no");
                        scanf("%d",&item);
                        enqueue(&v,item);

                  }
                  break;
                case 2:

                     if(isempty(&v))
                     printf("que is empty");
                     else
                     {
                 d=dequeue(&v);
                    printf("Dequeued element is %d",d);
                     }
                    break;
                case 3:
                    trav(&v);
```

```
                        getch();
                       break;
                case 4:
                        exit();
                }
            }
    }
```

Look at enqueue( ) function of linear queue listing. First three statements of this function are :

```
    if (isfull(q))
    {
          printf("list is full");
          return;
    }
```

use of *isfull ()* function inside *if* must be clear to you, isfull( ) function will return either 1 or 0. If this function returns 1, it means list is already full. Then two statements inside block will be executed and if it returns 0, it means list is not full, so enqueue operation is possible.

Both the listings are very simple to understand.

7.5.1.2 Pointer Implementation of Queue

To overcome the problem of overflow, pointer (linked list implementation) is used.

This is very much similar to doubly linked list. Only following points should be kept in mind to implement a queue as a linked list.

1. To refer head, use front and to refer tail, use rear.
2. To enqueue an element *"insert at end"* C routine is used.
3. To dequeue an element *"delete from beginning"* routine is used.

LISTING 7.5

```
#include<stdio.h>
#include<conio.h>
#include<alloc.h>
 typedef struct queue_list
 {
       int info;
       struct queue_list *next;
       struct queue_list *prev;
 } node;

      void create_empty(node **front, node **rear)
       {
          *front= *rear=NULL;
       }
       void enqueue(node **front,node **rear,int element)
       {
          node *ptr;
          ptr=(node *)malloc(sizeof(node));
          ptr->info=element;
          ptr->next=NULL;
      if(*front==NULL)
```

```
        {
         ptr->prev=NULL;
        *front=ptr;
        *rear=ptr;
        }
         else
        {
         ptr->prev=*rear;
         (*rear)->next=ptr;
         *rear=ptr;
        }
  }
  void dequeue(node **front,node **rear)
  {
  node *ptr;
  if(*front==(node *)NULL)
        {
              printf("Underflow");

              return;
        }
  if((*front)->next==(node *)NULL)
  {
        ptr=*front;
        *front=*rear=(node*)NULL;
        free(ptr);
  }
  else
        {
        ptr=*front;
        *front=(*front)->next;
        (*front)->prev=(node *)NULL;
        free(ptr);
        }
  }

  void traverse(node *rear)
  {

        while(rear!=(node *)NULL)
        {
        printf("%d",rear->info);
        rear=rear->prev;
        }

  }


 void main()
 {
  node *front, *rear;
  int ch,element,after;
  create_empty(&front,&rear);
  while(1)
```

```
    {
        clrscr();
        printf("1Enqueue\n");
        printf("2.Dequeue\n");
        printf("3.traverse\n");
        printf("4.Exit\n");
        printf("enter your choice\n");
        scanf("%d",&ch);
        switch(ch)
        {
        case 1:
                printf("Enter element");
                scanf("%d",&element);
                enqueue(&front,&rear,element);
                getch();
                break;
        case 2:
                dequeue(&front,&rear);
                break;
        case 3:
                traverse(rear);
                getch();
                break;
        case 4:
                exit();
        }
    }
  }
```

7.6 DEQUE

A deque is a kind of queue in which elements can be added or removed from the either end but not from the middle. The term deque is taken from double ended queue.

There are two types of deque :

1. **Input-restricted deque—**This queue allows insertions only at one end but allows deletions at both ends.
2. **Output-restricted deque—**This queue allows insertions at both ends but deletions only at one end.

7.7 PRIORITY QUEUE

A priority queue is that in which each element is assigned a priority and the order in which elements are deleted and processed. Best application of priority queue is observed in CPU scheduling. Jobs which have higher priority are processed first. If the priority of two jobs is same then these jobs are processed according to their position in queue. A short job is given higher priority over the longer one.

Representations of a priority Queue in Memory :

- Using a linear linked list
- Using multiple queues
- Using heap

7.7.1 Linked List Representation

Each node of linked list will have three fields:

1. Info(information field)
2. A priority field p which holds the priority number of the element
3. A next pointer.

7.7.2 Multiple Queue Representation

In this representation, one queue is maintained for each priority number. And second queue is used to hold actual values of elements but order of elements in both the queues must be same.

7.7.3 Heap Representation

A heap is a complete binary tree. But heaps have an additional property: The root element is either smallest or largest from its children.If root element of the heap is largest from its children,it is known as **max heap.** If root element of heap is smallest from its children, it is known as **min heap.** A priority queue having highest priority for lower numbers can be represented using min heap and a priority queue having highest priority for highest number can be represented using max heap.

CONCEPTUAL PROBLEMS

Problem 7.1 : *Sometimes, a stack data structure uses an operation top, where top(S) returns the top element of stack S, which must be checked non-empty before doing the operation. Write C-program/function that can be used with* (MCA January, 2001)

(*a*) *The array data structure.*
(*b*) *The linked list data structure.*

Solution (*a*) :

```
int isempty(stack *s)
   {
   if(s->top==-1)
   return 1;
   else return 0;
   }
   int top(stack *s)
   {
   if(isempty(s))
   {
   printf("underflow");
   return 0;
   }
   else
   return s->top;
   }
```

Solution (*b*) :

```
int top(node *top)
{
   if(top==(node *)NULL)
```

```
    {
    printf("Underflow");
    return 0;
    else
    return top->info;
}
```

Problem 7.2 : *Assuming a queue representation through circular array, write algorithm for addition and deletion of an element into queue.*

(PGDCA December, 1995; MCA December, 2001)

Solution :

Algorithm for addition of an element in circular queue :

START
    Void enque(queue *q,item)
STEP 1
    If(isfull(q)) is true then Output "Overflow"
    Exit.
    End if.
STEP 2 If(isempty(q)) is "true"
    Then
    q->front=q->rear=0
    q->element[0]=item
    return
    end if.
STEP 3
    If q->rear==MAX-1
    Then
    q->rear=0
    else
    q->rear=q->rear+1
    q->element[q->rear]=item
STOP

Algorithm for deletion of element :

START
    Int deque(queue q)
STEP 1
    If(isempty(q)) is "true" then output"Overflow"
    exit.
STEP 2 d=q->element[q->front]
STEP 3
    If(q->front==q->rear)
    q->front=q->rear=-1
    return d
    end if.

```
STEP 4
        q->front++
        return d
STOP
```

Problem 7.3 : *A recursive function f is shown below, what is the value of f(5)?*

(PGDCA Dec., 1996)

```
int f(int x)
{
if(x<2)
return(1);
else
return f(x-1)+f(x-2);
}
```

Solution :

```
STEP 1    f(4)+f(3)
STEP 2    [f(3)+f(2)]+[f(2)+f(1)]
STEP 3    [f(2)+f(1)+f(1)+f(0)]+[f(1)+f(0)+1]
STEP 4    [f(1)+f(0)+1+1+1]+[1+1+1]
STEP 5    [1+1+1+1+1]+[1+1+1]
STEP 6    return 5+3
```

Return value =8.

KEY POINTS

- A stack is a homogeneous collection of items, arranged linearly with access at one end only.
- Stack is also known a Last in First Out (LIFO) data structure.
- Data is added to stack using a push operation.
- Data is removed from a stack using POP operation.
- A stack can be implemented either using array or linked list.
- A run time stack is used to pass parameters between two functions.
- Stack is used in recursion.
- The process of writing the operators of an expression in a particular position is called **polish notation.**
- Infix, Prefix and Postfix are three types of polish notations.
- A **Queue** is a linear data structure used to represent a linear list and permits deletion to be performed at one end of the list and the insertion at the other end.
- A queue can be implemented either using array or linked list implementation.
- A Deque (Double ended queue) is a kind of queue in which elements can be added or removed from the either end but not from the middle.
- A Priority queue is a queue in which each element is assigned a priority and the order in which elements are deleted and processed.

EXERCISE

1. It is possible to keep two stacks in a single array. If one grows from position 1 of the array, and the other grows from the last position, write a procedure PUSH(x,S) that pushes element x onto stack S, where S is one or the other of these two stacks. Include all necessary error checks in your procedure. The procedure should be written in "C" language.
2. What are the differences between queue and deque?
3. Write an algorithm to evalute a prefix expression.
4. Write the prefix form of the following expressions :
   * !|a&&!(b<c)||(c<e)
   * a&&b||c!(e>f)
5. What are the differences between stacks and queues ?
6. Assuming a queue representation through circular array, write algorithm for addition and deletion of an element in a queue.

8

GRAPHS

8.1 INTRODUCTION

Geometrical arrangements are very important while working with real life projects. For example, let us suppose there are five villages separated by a river. Now we want to construct bridges to connect these villages.

Fig. 8.1

We can reduce the landmass of villages to a dot and we can change the shape of bridges. This will not change geometric arrangement of paths to connect different villages. We can draw a similar geometry of our project as follows:

Fig. 8.2

We have represented villages by dots (which we call vertex or node) and bridges by lines which are called edges. This type of drawing is called *graph*. Hence a graph can be defined as a ordered set (V, E), where *V(G) represents the set of all elements called vertices and E(G) represents the edges between these vertices*.

Fig. 8.2 shows a graph, for which V(G)={v1, v2, v3, v4, v5} and E(G)={b1, b2, b3, b4}.

8.1 INTRODUCTION

Geometrical arrangements are very important while working with real life projects. For example, let us suppose there are five villages separated by a river. Now we want to construct bridges to connect these villages.

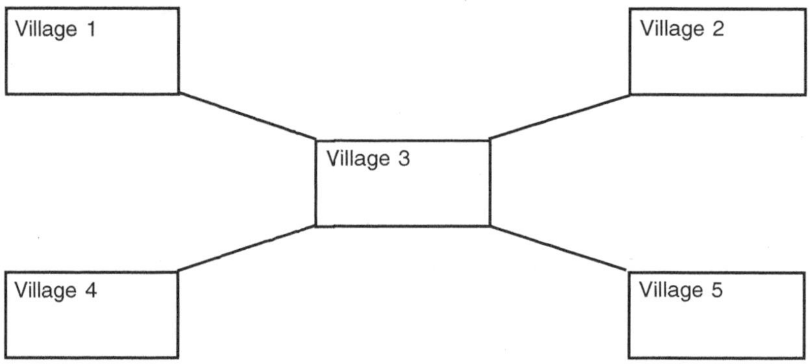

Fig. 8.1

We can reduce the landmass of villages to a dot and we can change the shape of bridges. This will not change geometric arrangement of paths to connect different villages. We can draw a similar geometry of our project as follows.

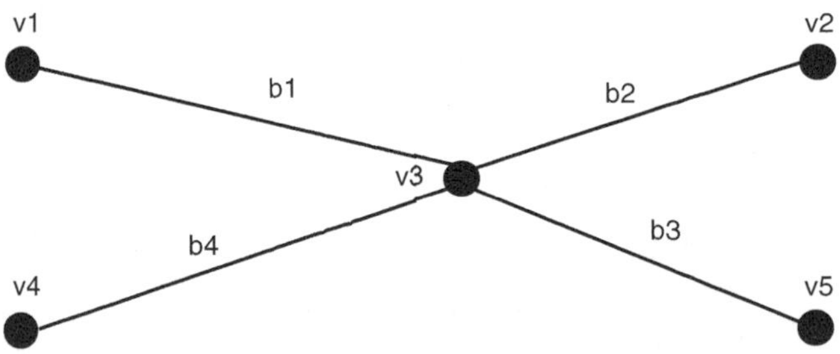

Fig 8.2

We have represented villages by dots (which we call vertex or node) and bridges by lines which are called edges. This type of drawing is called *graph*. Hence a graph can be defined *as a ordered set (V, E), where V(G) represents the set of all elements called vertices and E(G) represents the edges between these vertices.*

Fig. 8.2 shows a graph, for which V(G)={v1, v2, v3, v4, v5} and E(G)={b1, b2, b3, b4}.

8.2 BASIC TERMINOLOGY

Adjacent vertices

Vertex v1 is said to be adjacent to vertex v2, if there is an edge (v1, v2) or (v2, v1). From Fig. 8.2 vertices adjacent to node v3 are v1, v2, v4, v5 and verices adjacent to v1 is v3. Similarly vertex adjacent to v4 and v5 is v3.

Path

A path between any two vertices is a sequence of vertices between these two vertices. There may be more than one path to traverse from one vertex to another. In Fig. 8.2, v1, v3, v2 is a path to traverse from v1 to v2. Path can also be defined as number of edges between two verticles.

Cycle

A cycle is a path in which first and last vertices are the same.

Connected graph

A graph G is said to be connected if there is a path between any vertex to any other vertex. Fig. 8.2 is a connected graph. There is no isolated vertex.

Complete graph

A graph G is said to be complete or fully connected if there is a path from every vertex to every other vertex. A complete graph with *n* vertices will have n(n–1)/2 edges.

Unconnected graph

The graph which is not a connected graph, is called an *unconnected graph*. Consider the following example:

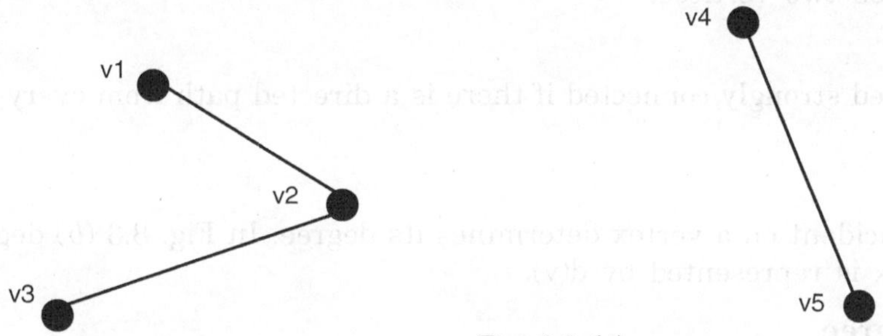

Fig. 8.3 (a)

Fig. 8.3(*a*) is an unconnected graph. You may think that these are two graphs, but by the definition of graph it is a single graph. It is one graph having two unconnected components.

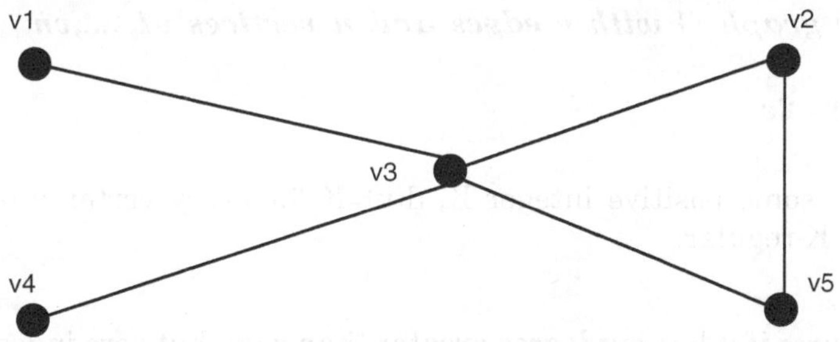

Fig 8.3 (b)

There is one cycle in this graph, path of cycle is v3, v2, v5, v3.

Undirected graph

There is no specific direction associated with edge. In an undirected graph, an edge is represented by an unordered pair $[v_x, v_y]$. Figs. 8.1, 8.2 and 8.3 represent undirected graph.

Directed graph

A graph is called directed in which an edge is represented by an ordered pair$[v_x, v_y]$.

Example:

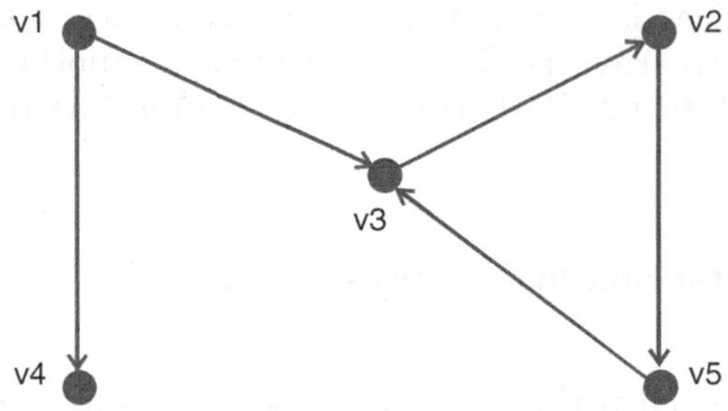

Fig. 8.4

In a directed graph the path is called *directed graph* and a cycle is known as a *directed cycle*. In the above Fig. 8.4, v1, v3, v2 is a directed path but v1, v3, v5 is not a directed path.

Weighted graph

A graph is said to be a weighted graph if every edge in the graph is assigned some data. The value of an edge is a non-negative value that may represent the cost of moving along that edge or distance between two vertices.

Strongly connected

A directed graph is called strongly connected if there is a directed path from every vertex to every other vertex.

Degree

The number of edges incident on a vertex determines its degree. In Fig. 8.3 (*b*) degree of v3 is 4. Degree of a vertex is represented by d(v).

Outdegree and Indegree

Outdegree of vertex v is the number of edges originating from v and Indegree of vertex v is the number of edges coming towards v. In Fig. 8.4 outdegree of v3 is 1 and indegree of v3 is 2.

Theorem 1 : ***For any graph G with e edges and n vertices v1,.....,vn***

$$\sum_{i=1}^{n} d(vi) = 2e$$

Regular graph : If for some positive integer K, d(v)=K for every vertex v of the graph G. The Graph G is called K-regular.

Source and Sink

A vertex v is called a *source* if it has outdegree greater than zero, but zero indegree. Similarly, a vertex v is called *sink* if it has indegree greater than zero, but zero outdegree.

Tree

A connected graph without any cycle is called a *tree*.

Planar graphs

A graph is planar if it can be drawn (on a plane) so that the edges intersect only at the vertices. Note that it does not matter how it is drawn, it is planar if it is possible to draw it on a plane without edges crossing. For example, consider the five complete graphs :

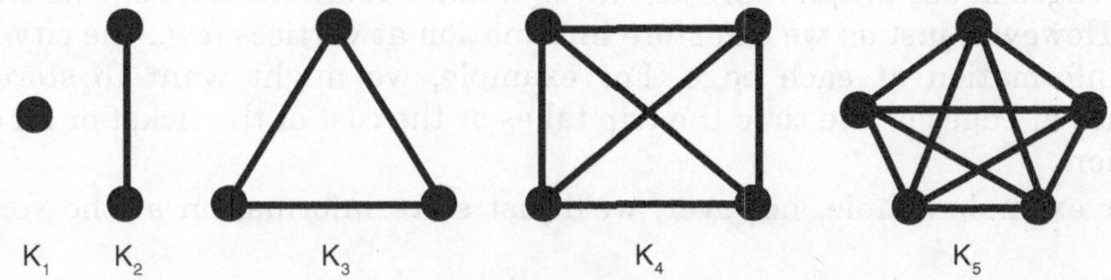

Fig. 8.5

The first three are obviously planar, as is the fourth since it can be drawn without the diagonals' intersecting.

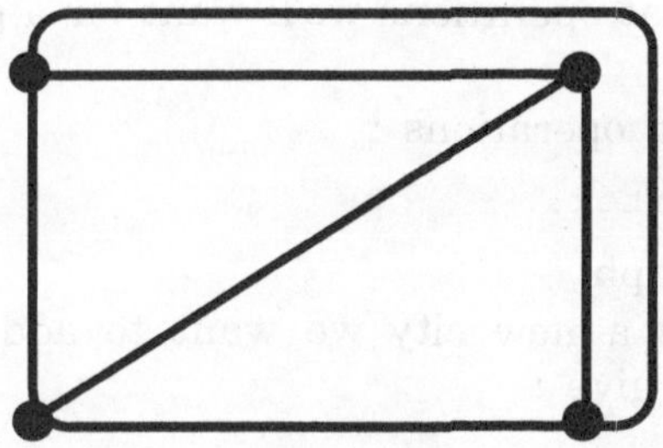

Fig. 8.6

But what about the fifth ? This is left as an exercise of reader.

8.3 USES OF GRAPHS

Why would we want to store information in a graph? Well, some types of information are naturally represented in a graph.

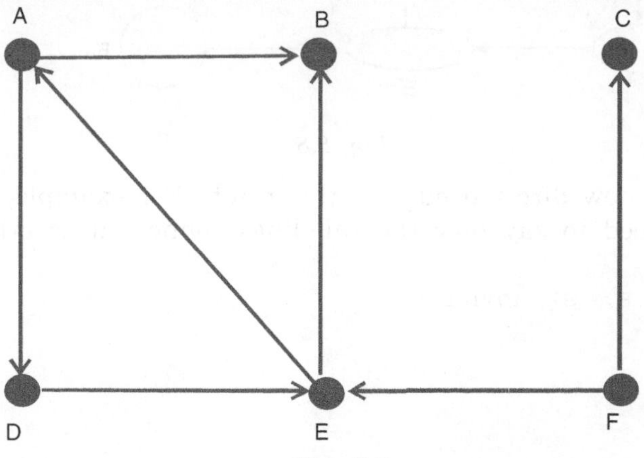

Fig. 8.7

For example, the above graph could be viewed as a map of what cities are connected by train routes. Viewing it this way, each vertex represents a particular city and each edge represents whether there is a train route from one city to another. We can imagine that the edges are unidirectional since trains are only allowed to go in one direction on the tracks (a new government rule so trains don't crash into each other any more).

Since the graph has different components, there are some cities that are not connected by train routes. For example, there is no way to get from city D to city F.

Finally, the edges in our graph represent a very simple relationship, *i.e.*, one city is connected to another. However, just as we can store information at vertices (*e.g.*, the city name), we can also store information at each edge. For example, we might want to store the distance between cities at edges or the time the trip takes or the cost of the ticket or all of those pieces of information.

To keep our example simple, however, we'll just store information at the vertices, and not at edges.

8.4 GRAPH OPERATIONS

As mentioned, graphs are pretty generic data structures in that they can be used to represent lots of things. Thus, exactly what operations we'll want for a graph will depend on what we want to do with it.

Suppose, we want the following operations :

`* AddVertex:`

Adding a new vertex to the graph.

For example, suppose there is a new city we want to add to our map of train routes. `AddVertex (graph, G)` would give :

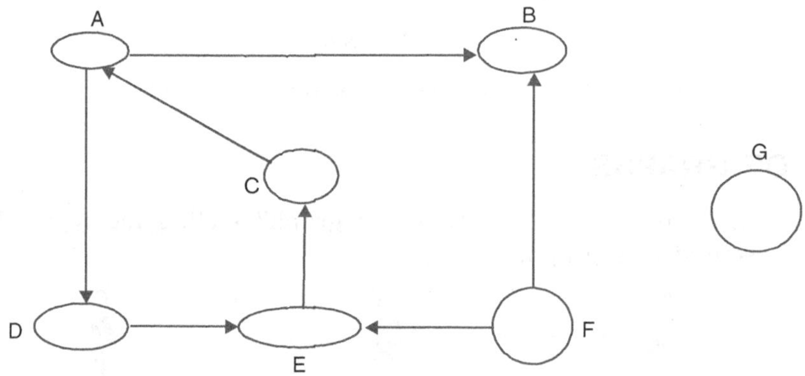

Fig. 8.8

`* AddEdge:` Adding a new directed edge to the graph. For example, adding the city was not enough, we also need to say how the rail lines connect it to other cities. Thus, we might

do an `AddEdge(graph, B, G)`, giving :

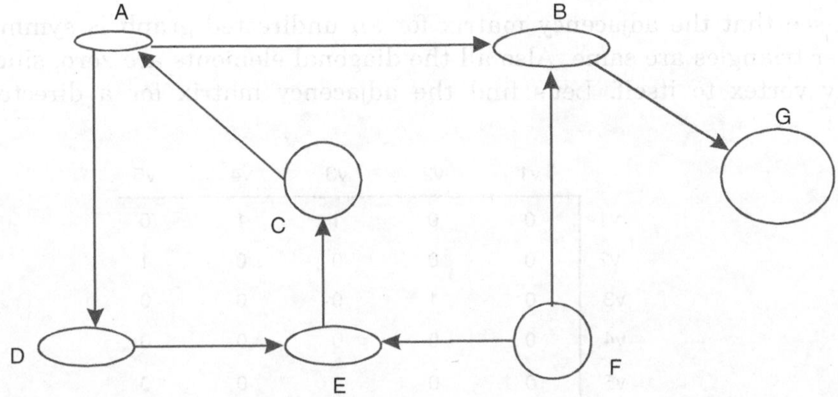

Fig. 8.9

An edge from B to G.

```
* IsReachable:
```

Reports whether we can get there from here.
For example, we might want to know whether we can get to city E from city A :

```
IsReachable(graph, E, A) would report a true value.
```

Again, we might want to know whether we can get to city D from city E :

```
IsReachable(graph, D, F) would report a false value.
```

There are many other operations we might want, but these will suffice for our example.

8.5 GRAPH REPRESENTATION

We need graph to solve our problems during project analysis but how we can store graphs inside a computer's memory?

There are two ways to do so.

1. *Adjacency Matrix Representation*
2. *Adjacency List Representation.*

8.5.1 Adjacency Matrix Representation

The adjacency matrix A for a graph G(V, E) with n vertices, is an n × n matrix of bits, such that A

A_{ij}=1, if and only if there is an edge from v_i to v_j.

A_{ij}=0, if there is no such edge.

Fig. 8.10 shows the adjacency matrix for the graph given in Fig. 8.2 :

	v1	v2	v3	v4	v5
v1	0	0	1	0	0
v2	0	0	1	0	0
v3	1	1	0	1	1
v4	0	0	1	0	0
v5	0	0	1	0	0

Fig. 8.10

You can see that the adjacency matrix for an undirected graph is symmetric as the lower and upper triangles are same. Also all the diagonal elements are zero, since there is no edge from any vertex to itself. Let's find the adjacency matrix for a directed graph given in Fig. 8.4 :

	v1	v2	v3	v4	v5
v1	0	0	1	1	0
v2	0	0	0	0	1
v3	0	1	0	0	0
v4	0	0	0	0	0
v5	0	0	1	0	0

Fig. 8.11

The number of 1's in each row tells the outdegree of the corresponding vertex. The adjacency matrix is a simple way to represent a graph but has two disadvantages.

1. It tacks $O(n^2)$ space to represent a graph with n vertices. (n is the number of vertices.)
2. It takes $O(n^2)$ time to solve a problem.

8.5.2 Adjacency List Representation

In this representation, we store a graph as a linked structure. We store all vertices in a list and then for each vertex, we have a linked list of adjacent vertices. If there are 5 vertices in a graph, then we need 5 linked lists. Consider the graph represented in Fig. 8.4.

Adjacency list representation of this graph is :

V1	⟶	V3	⟶	V4
V2	⟶	V5		
V3	⟶	V2		
V4				
V5	⟶	V3		

Fig. 8.12 Adjacency List Representation

Adjacent vertices may appear in the list in an arbitrary order.

Note. *However, since our graphs can have loops, we need to make sure that we don't enter an infinite cycle. Also, since there may be more than one way to get to a single vertex, we want to make sure we don't waste effort by exploring a vertex more than once. To solve both problems, we just need to make sure that we don't go to a vertex we've been to before. The easiest way to keep track of this is to add a field to each vertex that keeps track of whether it has been already visited or not.*

Data types for implementation

With our choice of graph implementation made, we are ready to define the types needed in the implementation of graphs in C. For each vertex, we need to store an element, its visited flag, its list of edges, and a link to the next vertex. Thus, we use the following type to store a vertex :

```
typedef struct vertexTag
{
   graphElementT element;
   int visited;
   struct edgeTag *edges;
   struct vertexTag *next;
}
   vertexT;
```

Note how we use the type "struct edgeTag" to refer to the edge nodes, which haven't been defined as yet.

For each edge, we need a link to the vertex it connects to and a link to the next edge. Thus, we use the following type to store an edge :

```
typedef struct edgeTag
{
   struct vertexTag *connectsTo;
   struct edgeTag *next;
}
   edgeT;
```

Finally, we need to define what information is needed to keep track of the whole graph :

```
typedef struct graphCDT
{
   vertexT *vertices;
}
 graphCDT;
```

which is just a pointer to the initial vertex.

8.6 GRAPH TRAVERSAL

As you know graph is used to store non-linear collection of elements. We need to write some algorithms to traverse from one node to another in a way so that vertices should not be visited again. There are two methods to write an algorithm for Reachable Operation. (Reachable Operation : whether a vertex is reachable by any other vertex.)

8.6.1 Depth First Search (DFS)

In graphs, we do not have any starting vertex or any special vertex singled out to start traversal. Therefore, the traversal may start from any arbitrary vertex. But if it is asked whether a vertex is reachable from a specified vertex, then traversal will be started from specified vertex only. At any instant, children of a node are visited first and then siblings are visited. Let us consider the following algorithm as an example :

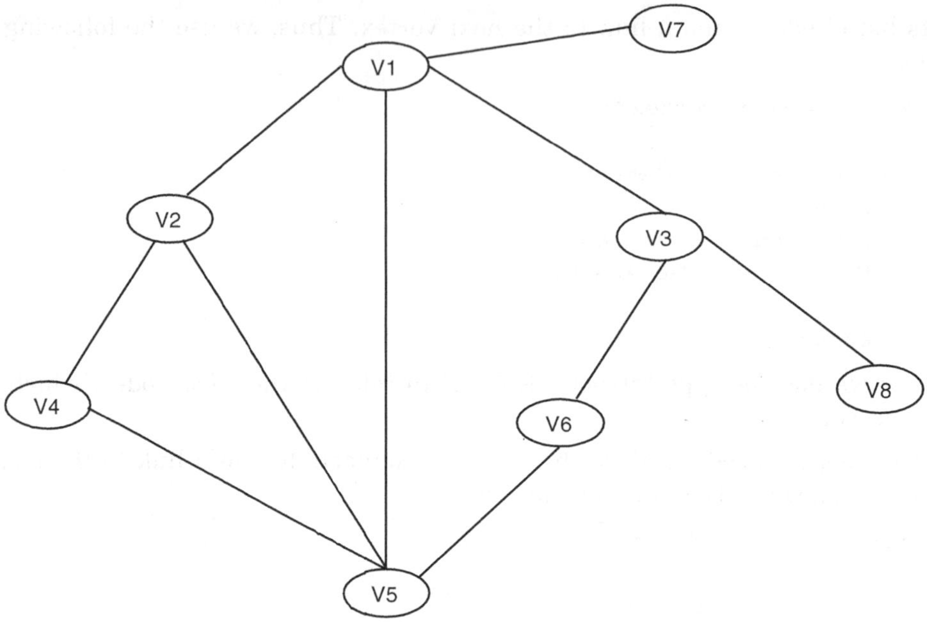

Fig. 8.13

Algorithm 8.1 : *To search a node using depth first search (DFS)*

START

1. Set all the vertices flags to false and x=0.
2. Go to the start vertex.
3. If vertex you are at has been visited, don't pursue this route again. Go back to where you came from, returning false.
4. else If x=total nodes traverse completed, so return true.
5. else Set its visited flag to true and increment x by 1.
6. Go through each of the edges.

   Go to the vertex an edge connects to (new starting location).

   Go to step 3.

STOP.

Algorithm 8.2 : *To traverse whole graph using depth first search (DFS)*

START

1. Set all vertices flags to false and create an empty stack.
2. Go to the start vertex.
3. If vertex you are at has been visited,

   go to step 4.

   Else

   Set its visited flag to true and put all of its adjacent nodes in stack.
4.

   if stack is empty

OUT PUT"traversal is completed"
Exit.
Else
Start vertex=pop(stack)
Go to step 3.
STOP.

Steps required to traverse in the graph are shown in Fig 8.13 :

Let us start with v1.
Its adjacent vertices are v2, v3, v5, v7, so push v7, v5, v3, v2 in stack.
Start vertex=Pop stack that is v2
Its adjacent vertices are v1, v4, v5, so push v1, v4, v5 in stack
Start vertex=v4(pop).
Its adjacent vertices are v2, v5, so push v5, v2 in stack.
Start vertex=v2 (pop)
but it is already visited.
Start vertex=v5 (pop)
Adjacents to v5 are v1, v2, v3, v4, v6, so push them in stack.
v1, v2, v4 are already visited(pop three times).
Set start vertex= v3 (pop)
Its adjacents are v1, v5, v6, v8, so push them in stack.
v1, v5 are already visited(pop 2 times).
Set start vertex=v6(pop).
Adjacents to v6 are v3, v5, so push them in stack.
Both v3 and v5 have already visited(pop 2 times).
We backtrack and keep poping.
Now set start vertex=v8.
Push v3 in stack.
Start vertex=v3 (pop) but it is already visited.
Traverse back and reach at v7 and set start vertex=v7 (last pop).

We have used stack to push all unvisited vertices adjacent to the one just visited. And poped vertex becomes start vertex.

8.6.2 Breadth First Search(BFS)

In BFS, we first visit all the adjacent vertices of the start vertex and then visit all the unvisited vertices adjacent to these and so on. Let's consider the same example for graph shown in Fig. 8.13. We start with v1(you may start from any other vertex). It's adjacent vertices are v2, v3, v5, v7.

These vertices will be visited sequentially and then adjacent vertices of v2 are visited which are v4, v5 but v5 is already visited, so v4 is visited and similarly adjacent vertices to v3, v5 and v7 are visited.

The final path would be v1, v2, v5, v3, v7, v4, v6, v8.

Algorithm 8.3 : *To reach a node using breadth first search (BFS)*

START

STEP 1
   Set all vertices visited flag=false
   AND create empty queue.

STEP 2
   Point at any vertex and refer it as start_node

STEP 3
   Insert this vertex in queue.

STEP 4
   V=Retrieve front vertex of queue

STEP 5
   Visit the adjacency vertices of v one by one and
   Insert in queue.

STEP 6
   Delete vertex from front of queue.

STEP 7
   If QUEUE IS EMPTY
   Then
      Output" Traversal completed"

STEP 8
   Else go to step 4.

STOP

8.7 SHORTEST PATH PROBLEM

One of the important uses of graphs is to find shortest path and the minimum spanning tree. This application of graphs is very useful for the air force of a country to hit targets with minimum cost(travelling minimum distance and hitting all targets) during a war. Shortest path from vertex v to vertex u is a path for which the sum of the weights of the edges on the path is minimum. We will discuss three algorithms to find shortest path in a graph.

1. *Kruskal's Algorithm*
2. *Prim's Algorithm*
3. *Dijkstra's Algorithm.*

8.7.1 Kruskal's Algorithm

This algorithm creates a forest of trees initially the forest consists of n single node trees (and no edges). At each step, we add one (the cheapest one) edge so that it joins two trees together. If it forms a cycle, then this edge is dropped. There should not be any cycle. And final result will be **minimum spanning tree.**

Before further discussion on minimum spanning tree, let us understand the forest of trees (or vertices). Consider the following figure of graph. (An individual vertex can also be called *a tree*).

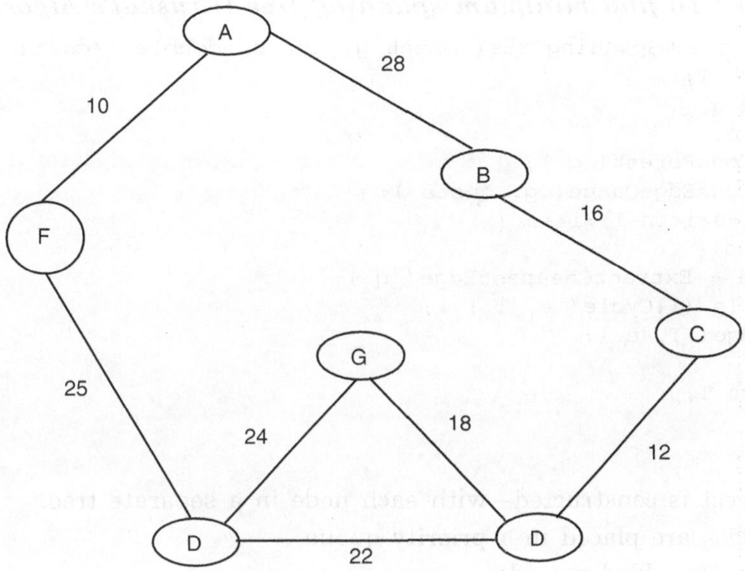

Fig. 8.14

This graph can be converted in a forest of trees as follows.

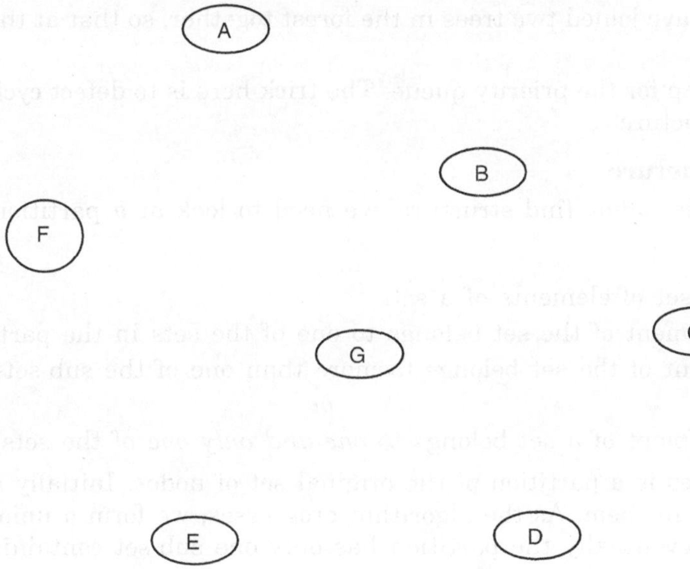

Fig. 8.15 Forest of vertices

We are interested to find out a path which touches all the vertices in forest and cost for constructing such a path should be minimum. Initially the forest consists of n single node trees. At each step, we add one (cheapest one) edge so that it joins two trees together. If it were to form a cycle, it would simply link two nodes that were already part of a single connected tree, so that this edge would not be needed. Hence this edges should be dropped. The basic algorithm looks like this :

Algorithm 8.4 : *To find minimum spanning tree (Kruskal's Algorithm)*

```
Forest MinimumSpanningTree( Graph g, int n, double **costs ) {
    Forest T;
    Queue q;
    Edge e;
    T = ConsForest( g );
    q = ConsEdgeQueue( g, costs );
    for(i=0;i<(n-1);i++) {
        do {
        e = ExtractCheapestEdge( q );
    } while ( !Cycle( e, T ) );
    AddEdge( T, e );
    }
    return T;
    }
```

The steps are :

1. The forest is constructed—with each node in a separate tree.
2. The edges are placed in a priority queue.
3. Until we've added n-1 edges.
   (*i*) Extract the cheapest edge from the queue.
   (*ii*) If it forms a cycle, reject it.
   (*iii*) Else add it to the forest. Adding it to the forest will join two trees together.

Every step will have joined two trees in the forest together, so that at the end, there will only be one tree in T.

We can use a heap for the priority queue. The trick here is to detect cycles. For this, we need a union-find structure.

Union-find structure

To understand the union-find structure, we need to look at a partition of a set.

Partitions

A partition is a set of elements of a set.

- Every element of the set belongs to one of the sets in the partition.
- No element of the set belongs to more than one of the sub-sets.

or

- Every element of a set belongs to *one and only one* of the sets of a partition.

The forest of trees is a partition of the original set of nodes. Initially all the sub-sets have exactly one node in them. As the algorithm progresses, we form a union of two of the trees (sub-sets), until eventually the partition has only one sub-set containing all the nodes.

A partition of a set may be thought of as a set of *equivalence classes*. Each sub-set of the partition contains a set of equivalent elements (the nodes connected into one of the trees of the forest). This notion is the key to the cycle detection algorithm. For each sub-set, we denote one element as the *representative* of that sub-set or equivalence class. Each element in the sub-set is, somehow, equivalent and represented by the nominated representative.

As we add elements to a tree, we arrange all the elements' point to their representative. As we form a union of two sets, we simply arrange that the representative of one of the sets now points to any one of the elements of the other set.

So the test for a cycle reduces to : for the two nodes at the ends of the candidate edge, find their representatives. If the two representatives are the same, the two nodes are already in a connected tree and adding this edge would form a cycle. The search for the representative simply follows a chain of links.

Each node will need a representative pointer. Initially, each node is its own representative, so the pointer is set to NULL. As the initial pairs of nodes are joined to form a tree, the representative pointer of one of the nodes is made to point to the other, which becomes the representative of the tree. As trees are joined, the representative pointer of the representative of one of them is set to point to any element of the other. (Obviously, representative searches will be somewhat faster if one of the representatives is made to point directly to the other.)

Let's find minimum spanning tree of the graph shown in Fig 8.14.

From Figs. 8.16 to 8.21 we have selected one cheapest edge to connect two vertices in a forest.

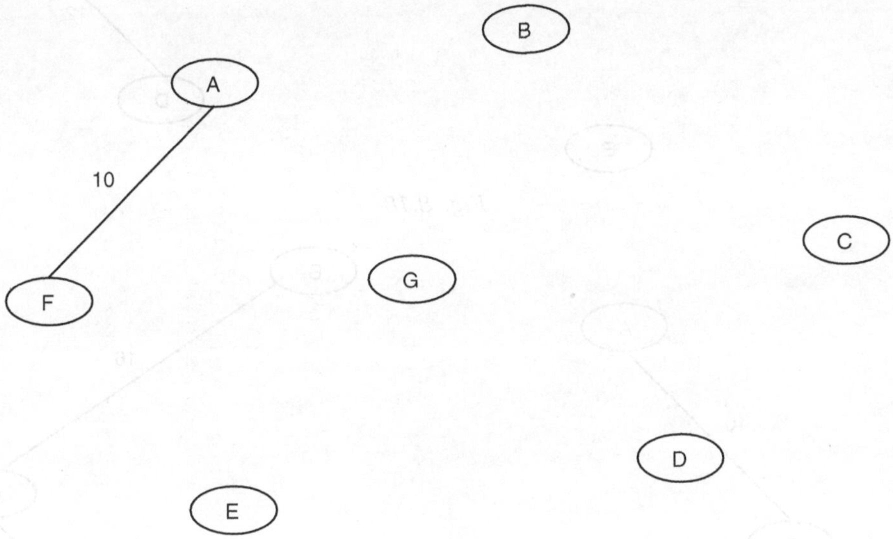

Fig. 8.16

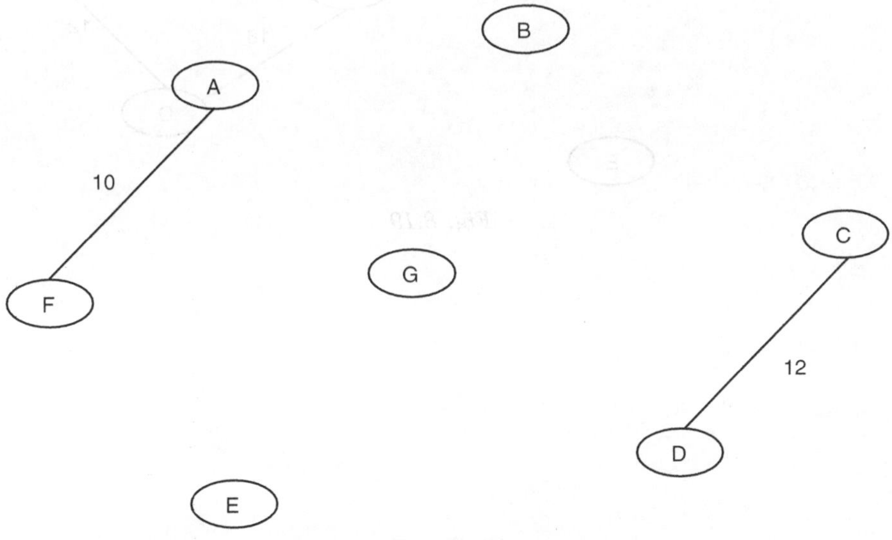

Fig. 8.17

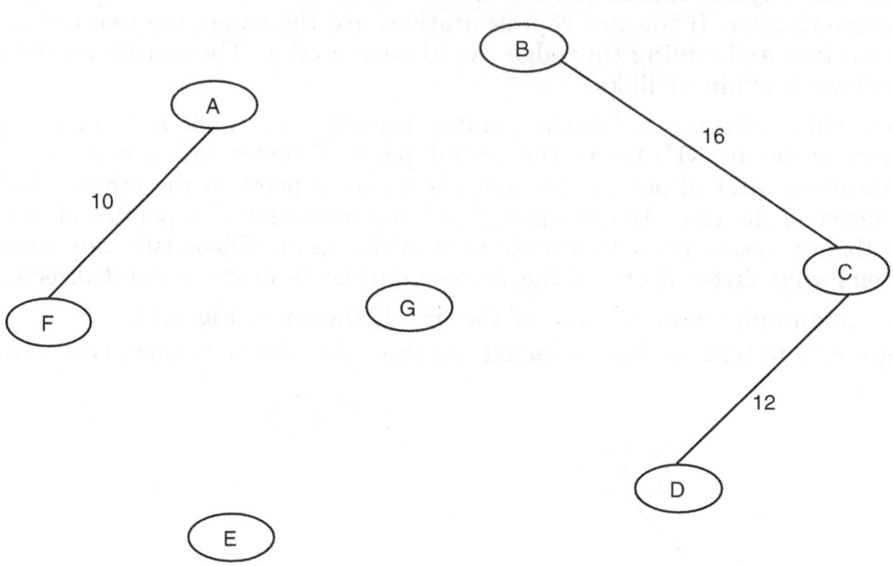

Fig. 8.18

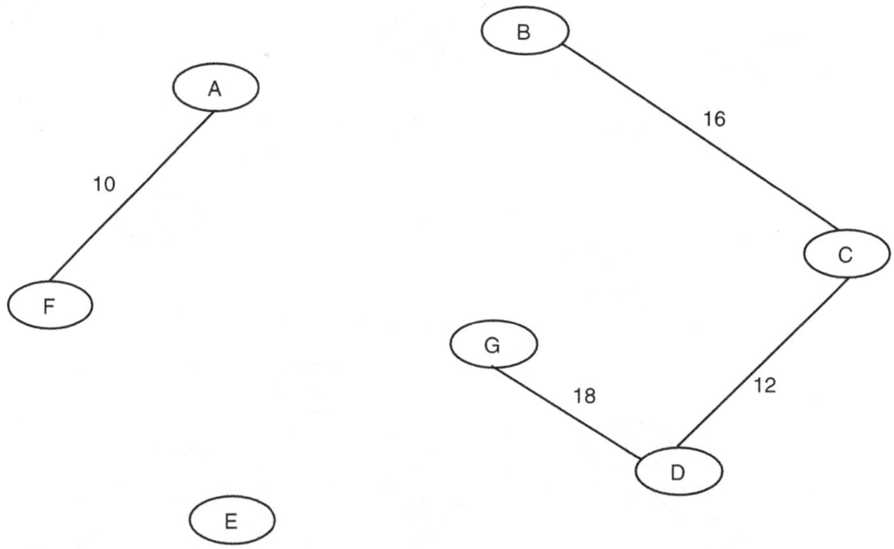

Fig. 8.19

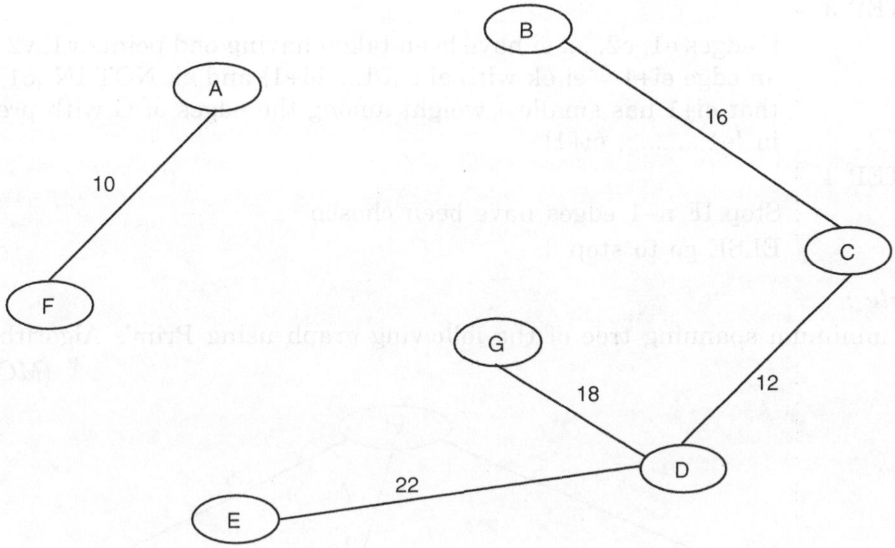

Fig. 8.20

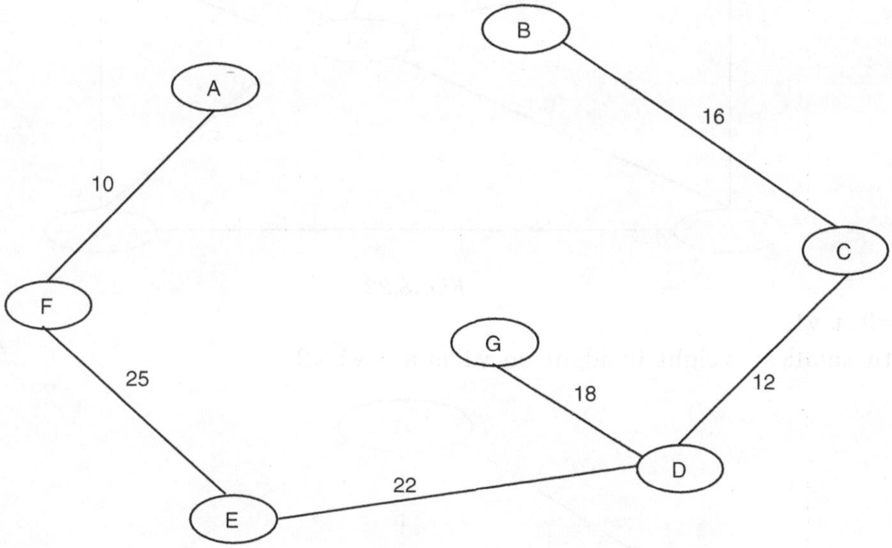

Fig. 8.21

Thus, the minimum spanning tree is found.

After connecting ED in Fig. 8.20, next cheapest edge is EG. But adding this edge to our tree, we get a cycle and cycles are not allowed in trees, so we skip this edge and consider next cheapest edge. And finally, we get a Minimum spanning tree.

8.7.2 Prim's Algorithm

STEP 1

Select a vertex v1.

STEP 2

Select an edge e=v1v2 of G such that v2 ≠ v1 and e has smallest weight among the edges of G incident with v1.

STEP 3

If edges e1, e2,..... ei have been taken having end points v1, v2..... vi+1..Select an edge ei+1 = ej ek with ej ε {e1,... ei+1} and ek NOT IN {e1,....., ei+1} such that ei+1 has smallest weight among the edges of G with precisely one end in {e1,.........., ei+1}

STEP 4

Stop IF n–1 edges have been chosen
ELSE go to step 3.

Example :
Find a minimum spanning tree of the following graph using Prim's Algorithm.

(MCA, June 1999)

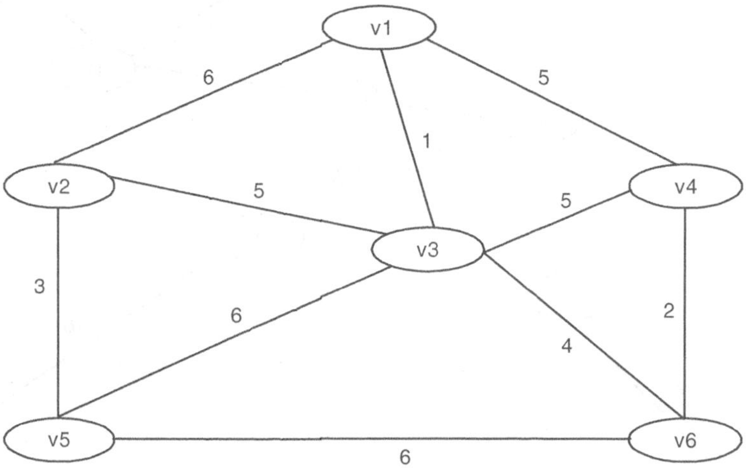

Fig. 8.22

Let us select v1.
Edge with smallest weight incident on v1 is e = v1 v3.

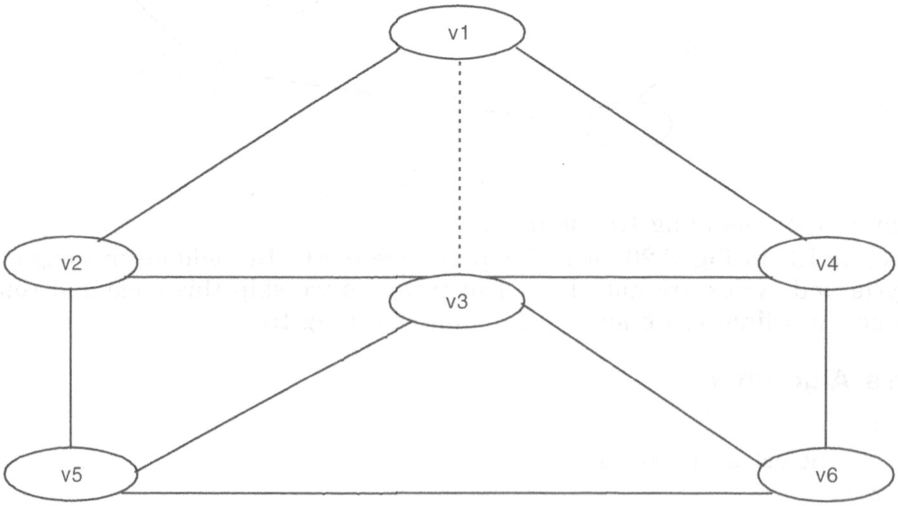

Fig. 8.23

Now weights of edges incident on v1 and v3 are as follows :

W (v1, v2)= 6

W (v1, v4)= 5

W (v3, v5)= 6

W (v3, v2)= 5

W (v3, v4)= 5

W (v3, v6)= 4

The smallest weight edge is e= v3, v6

Now our path extends to :

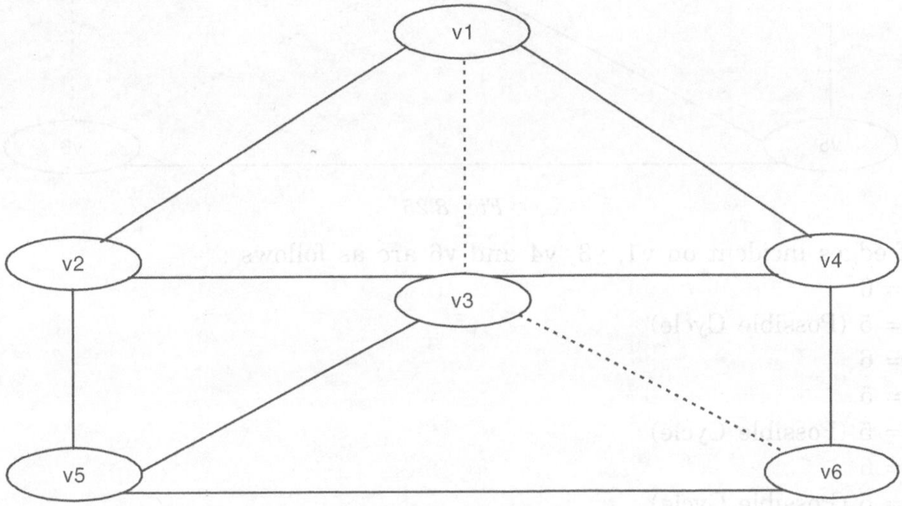

Fig. 8.24

Weights of edges incident on v1, v3 and v6 are as follows :

W (v1, v2)= 6

W (v1, v4)= 5

W (v3, v5)= 6

W (v3, v2)= 5

W (v3, v4)= 5

W (v6, v4)= 2

W (v6, v5)= 6

Smallest weighted edge is e= v6, v4 :

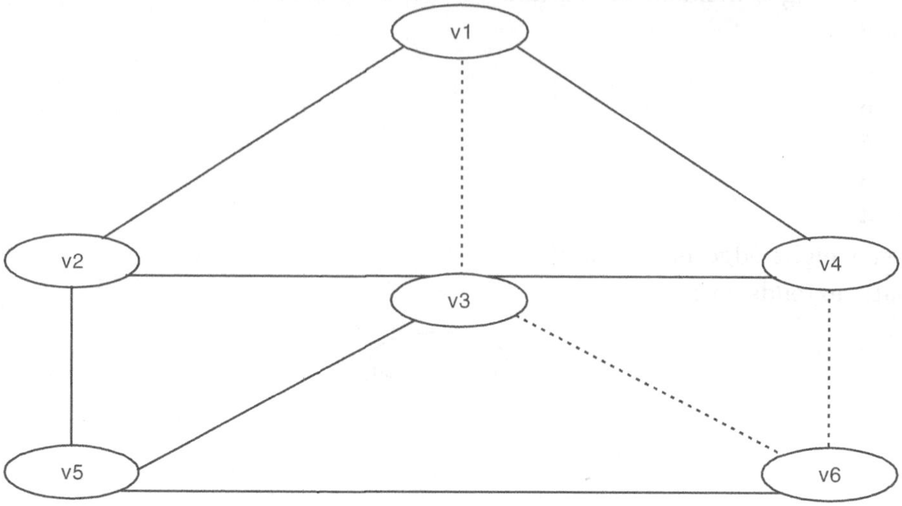

Fig. 8.25

Weights of edges incident on v1, v3, v4 and v6 are as follows :
W (v1, v2)= 6
W (v1, v4)= 5 (Possible Cycle)
W (v3, v5)= 6
W (v3, v2)= 5
W (v3, v4)= 5 (Possible Cycle)
W (v6, v5)= 6
W (v4, v1)= 5 (Possible Cycle)
W (v4, v3)= 5 (Possible Cycle)

We will not consider the edges with possible cycles.

Now smallest edge is e= v3, v2.

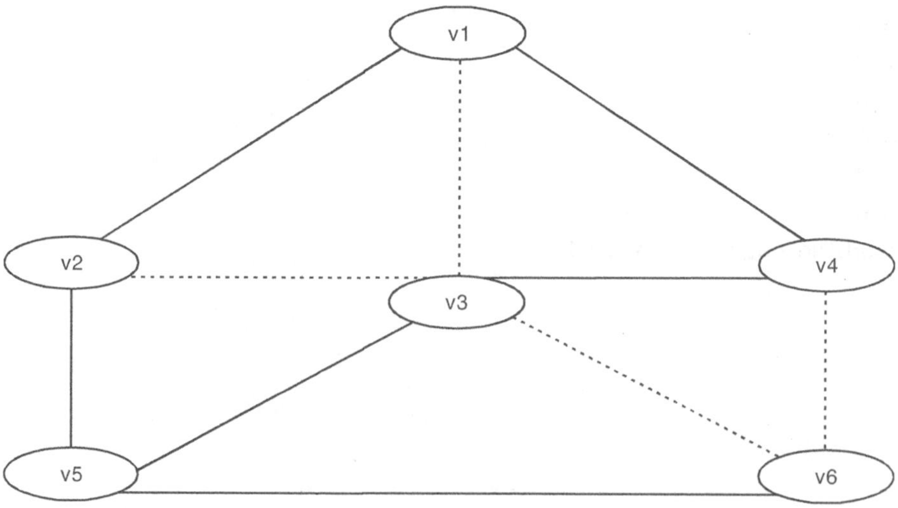

Fig. 8.26

Weights of edges incident on v1, v3, v4 and v6 are as follows :

W (v1, v2)= 6 (Possible Cycle)

W (v3, v5)= 6

W (v6, v5)= 6

W (v2, v5)= 3

We will not consider the edges with possible cycles.

Select e= v2, v5.

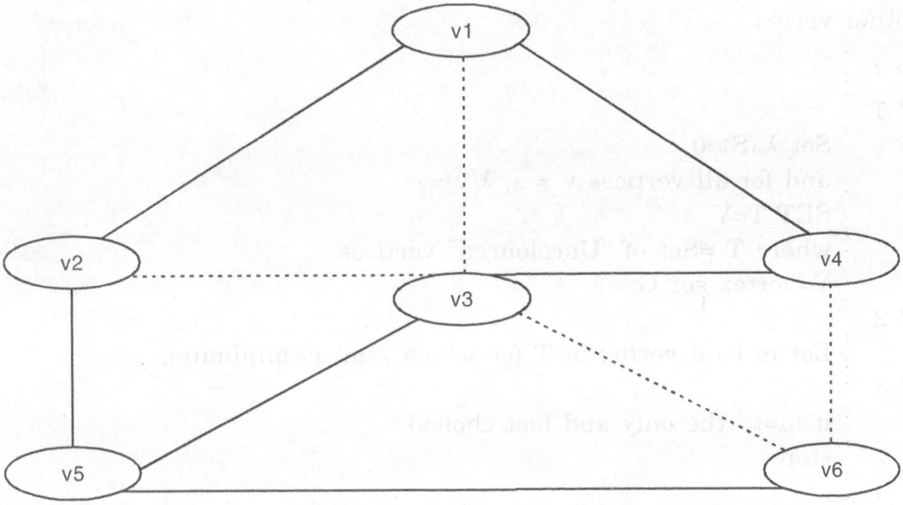

Fig. 8.27

Total number of edges of our path=5
which is equal to n–1 (n=total vertices)
Hence Minimum spanning tree is found and represented as

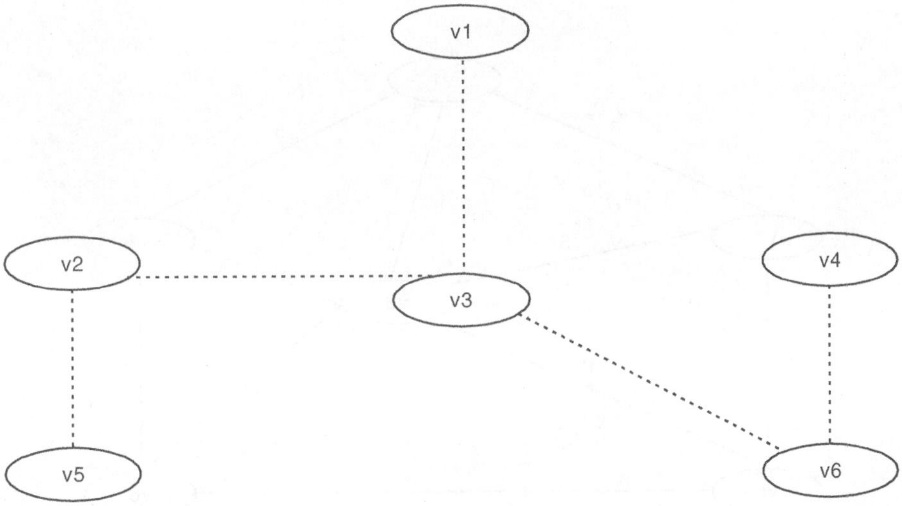

Fig. 8.28

8.7.3 Dijkstra's Algorithm

Djikstra's algorithm solves the problem of finding the shortest path from a point in a graph (the source) to a destination. It turns out that one can find the shortest paths from a given source to all points in a graph in the same time. Hence, this problem is sometimes called the **single-source shortest paths** problem.

This problem is related to the spanning tree one. The graph representing all the paths from one vertex to all the others must be a spanning tree—it must include all vertices. There will also be no cycles as a cycle would define more than one path from the selected vertex to at least one other vertex.

Algorithm :

STEP 1

Set $\lambda.(S)=0$
and for all vertices $v \neq s$, $\lambda(v)=\infty$
SET T=V
where T =Set of "Uncoloured" vertices.
V=vertex set G.

STEP 2

Let m be a vertex in T for which $\lambda(m)$ is minimum.

STEP 3

if m=t, (the only and last choice)
stop.

STEP 4

For every edge e=mv, incident with m, if $v \varepsilon T$ *i.e.* v is from uncoloured set of vertices, change $(\lambda(v))$ to min $(\lambda(v), \lambda(m) + \omega(e))$.

STEP 5

Change T to T–{u} (Colour u) and go to step 2 to find an uncoloured vertex with minimum distance from source vertex.

Example :

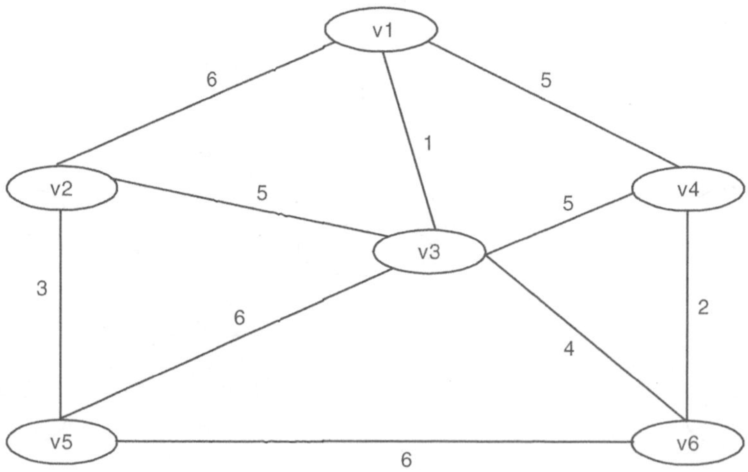

Fig. 8.29

Initialization :

Vertex V	v1	v2	v3	v4	v5	v6
λ(v)	0	∝	∝	∝	∝	∝
T	v1	v2	v3	v4	v5	v6

Iteration 1 :

for m= v1, λ(m)=0. (distance from v1 to v1).
Three edges incident with v1 are v1v2, v1v3 and v1v4.
Vertices v2, v3, v4 are in T(Uncoloured).
λ(v2)= ∝ >6=0+6=λ(v1) + ω(v1, v2)
Now λ(v2) becomes 6. Similarly λ(v3) = 1 and λ(v4)=5.
T becomes T–{v1} (We colour v1).

Vertex V	v1	v2	v3	v4	v5	v6
λ(v)	0	6	1	5	∝	∝
T		v2	v3	v4	v5	v6

Iteration 2 :

Assign m= v3 because λ(v3) is minimum and v3 ε T.
There are four edges incident on v3 where v ε T.
v2, v4, v5, v6.
λ(v2)=6=1+5=λ(v3)+ω(v3 v2). So, λ(v2) remains 6.
λ(v4)=4<1+5=λ(v3)+ω(v3 v4)
=> λ(v4) remain 4.
For λ(v5)=∝ > 1+6=λ(v3)+ ω(v3 v5)

Assign λ(v5)=7.
Similarly,
Assign λ(v6)=5
Now T becomes T–{v3}

Vertex V	v1	v2	v3	v4	v5	v6
λ(v)	0	6	1	5	7	5
T		v2		v4	v5	v6

Iteration 3 :

(We can select any one of v4 and v6 beause λ(v4), λ(v6) are same and minimum.)
Let, Assign m= v4, because λ(v4) is minimum and v4 ε T.
There only one edges incident on v3 where vεT.
v4 v6.
λ(v6)=5<5+2=λ(v4)+ω(v4 v6).
So, λ(v6) remains 5.

Now T becomes T–{v4}

Vertex V	v1	v2	v3	v4	v5	v6
λ(v)	0	6	1	5	7	5
T		v2			v5	v6

Iteration 4 :

Assign m=v6, because λ(v6) is minimum and v6 ε T.
There only one edges incident on v5 where v ε T.
v6 v5.
λ(v5)=7<5+6=λ(v6)+ω(v6 v5).
So, λ(v5) remains 7.
Now T becomes T–{v6}

Vertex V	v1	v2	v3	v4	v5	v6
λ(v)	0	6	1	5	7	5
T		v2			v5	

Iteration 5 :

Assign m=v2, because λ(v2) is minimum and v2 ε T.
There only one edges incident on v2 where v ε T.
v2 v5.
λ(v5)=7<6+3=λ(v2)+ω(v2 v5).
So, λ(v5) remains 7.

Vertex V	v1	v2	v3	v4	v5	v6
λ(v)	0	6	1	5	7	5
T					v5	

v5 is the only choice
hence we stop.
Our final table becomes.

Vertex V	v1	v2	v3	v4	v5	v6
λ(v)	0	6	1	5	7	5
T						

CONCEPTUAL PROBLEMS

Problem 8.1 : *Consider the following diagraph :*

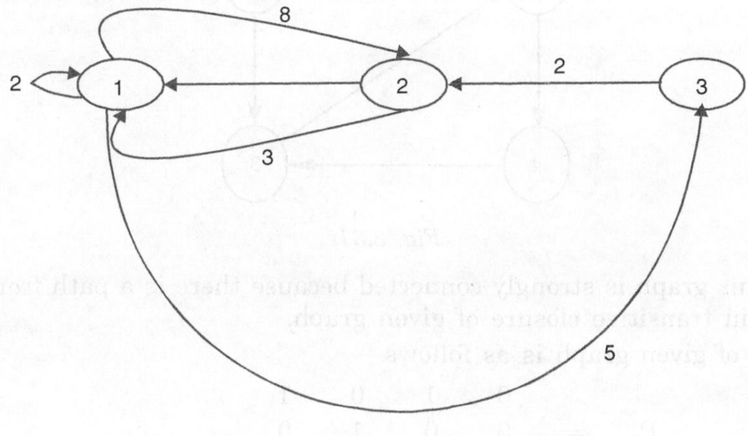

Fig. 8.30

Compute transitive closure of adjacency matrix representation by above diagraph.

(BCA June, 1999)

Solution :

Transitivity property of diagraph states that if there exists a path from vertex v1 to v2 and v2 to v3, then there exits a path from vertex v1 to vertex v2.

Adjacency matrix of given graph is as follows :

$$P_0 = \begin{matrix} 1 & 1 & 1 \\ 1 & 0 & 0 \\ 0 & 1 & 0 \end{matrix}$$

To compute transitive closure, we are using Warshall's algorithm as follows :

for(k=1;k<=n;k++)
for(i=0;i<n;i++)
for(j=0;j<n;j++)
$P_k = P_{k-1}[i][j]$ OR ($P_{k-1}[i][k-1]$ AND $P_{k-1}[k-1][j]$)

Applying above algorithm to P_0 :

$$P_1 = \begin{matrix} 1 & 1 & 1 \\ 1 & 1 & 1 \\ 0 & 1 & 1 \end{matrix}$$

$$P_2 = \begin{matrix} 1 & 1 & 1 \\ 1 & 1 & 1 \\ 1 & 1 & 1 \end{matrix}$$

$$P_3 = \begin{matrix} 1 & 1 & 1 \\ 1 & 1 & 1 \\ 1 & 1 & 1 \end{matrix}$$

Hence P_3 is the transitive closure (Path matrix) of the adjacency matrix P_0.

Note. *When path matrix is a unit matrix, then that graph is called strongly connected graph.*

Problem 8.2 : *Is the directed graph below strongly connected ?*
List all the simple paths. (MCA December, 2001)

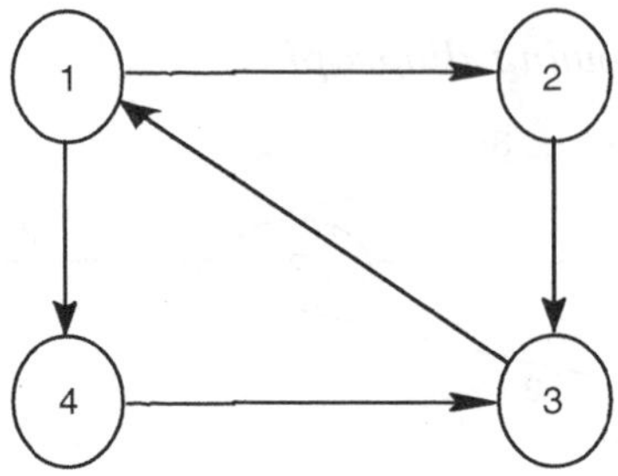

Fig. 8.31

Solution : Yes, this graph is strongly connected because there is a path from any vertex to any other vertex in transitive closure of given graph.
Adjacency matrix of given graph is as follows :

$$P_0 = \begin{matrix} 0 & 1 & 0 & 1 \\ 0 & 0 & 1 & 0 \\ 1 & 0 & 0 & 0 \\ 0 & 0 & 1 & 0 \end{matrix}$$

Path matrix of given graph can be computed by Warshall's algorithm and result is given below :

$$P_4 = \begin{matrix} 1 & 1 & 1 & 1 \\ 1 & 1 & 1 & 1 \\ 1 & 1 & 1 & 1 \\ 1 & 1 & 1 & 1 \end{matrix}$$

Problem 8.3 : *Consider the graph of the following figure :*

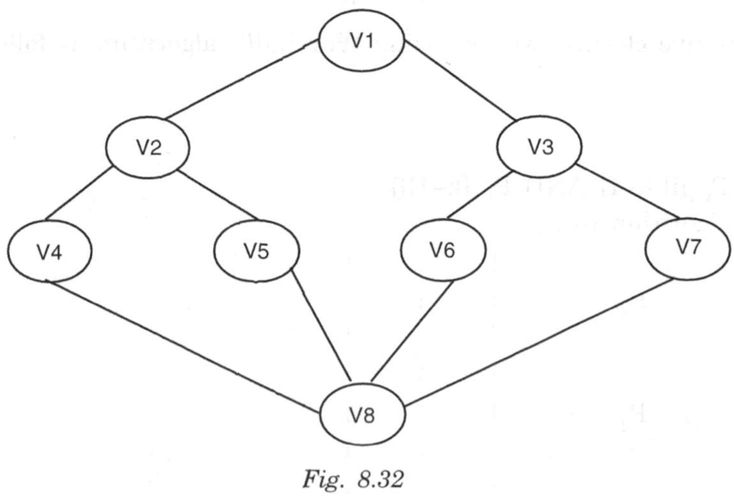

Fig. 8.32

Perform a Breadth-First Search beginning at vertex V1. List the vertices in the order which are visited. (MCA December, 2001)

Solution : Let Q be an empty queue. Following steps are performing BFS for given figure.

STEP 1

Insert V1 in Q.
Q={V1}

STEP 2

dequeue(Q)
ReadV1.
Insert vertices adjacent to V1 in Q.
Q={V3, V2}

STEP 3

dequeue(Q)
Read V2.
Insert vertices adjacent to V2 in Q.
Q={V5, V4, V3}

STEP 4

dequeue(Q)
Read V3.
Insert vertices adjacent to V3 in Q.
Q={V7, V6, V5, V4}

STEP 5

dequeue(Q)
Read V4.
Insert vertices adjacent V4 in Q.
Q={V8, V7, V6, V5}

STEP 6

dequeue(Q)
Read V5.
Insert vertices adjacent to V5 in Q.
Q={V8, V8, V7, V6}

STEP 7

dequeue(Q)
Read V6.
Insert vertices adjacent to V6 in Q.
Q={V8, V8, V8, V7}

STEP 8

dequeue(Q)
Read V7.
Insert vertices adjacent to V7 in Q.
Q={V8, V8, V8, V8}

STEP 9

dequeue(Q)
Read V8.
Q={V8, V8}

STEP 10

dequeue(Q)
V8 is already visited
Q={V8}

STEP 11

dequeue(Q)
V8 is already visited.
Q={ }Empty queue.

STEP 12

BFS traversal is completed and result is as follows :
V1, V2, V3, V4, V5, V6, V7, V8.

Problem 8.4 : *Consider the graph of following figure :*

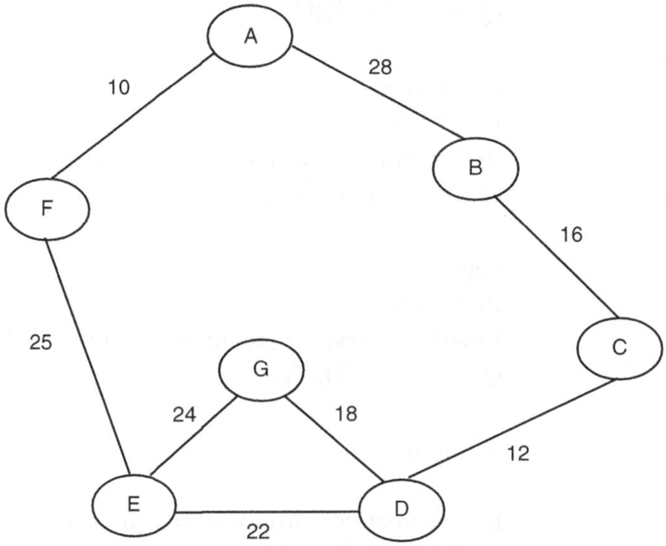

Fig. 8.33

Find the Minimum Cost Spanning Tree of the above graph. (MCA June, 2001)

Solution : Minimum cost tree is graph in which all vertices are connected in such a way that the total cost to connect all vertices is minimum.

To find minimum cost, let us start from forest of tree and add edges one by one. We will test two conditions while adding new edges :

(*i*) Edge with minimum cost is selected.

(*ii*) There must not be any cycle.

Minimum spanning tree for the graph is shown in Fig. 8.34.

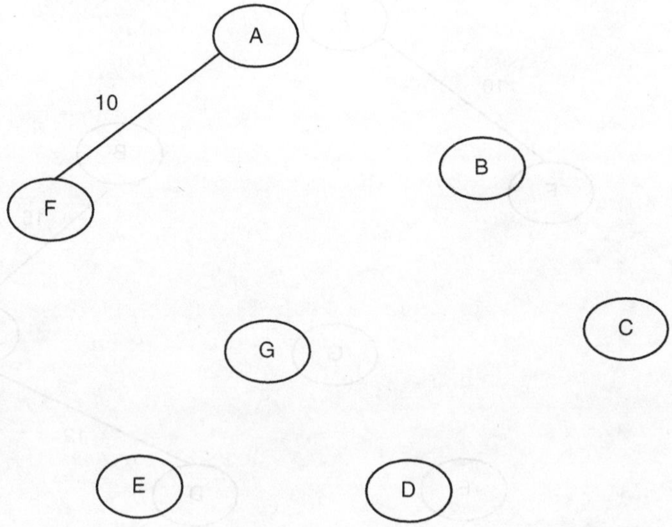

Fig. 8.34

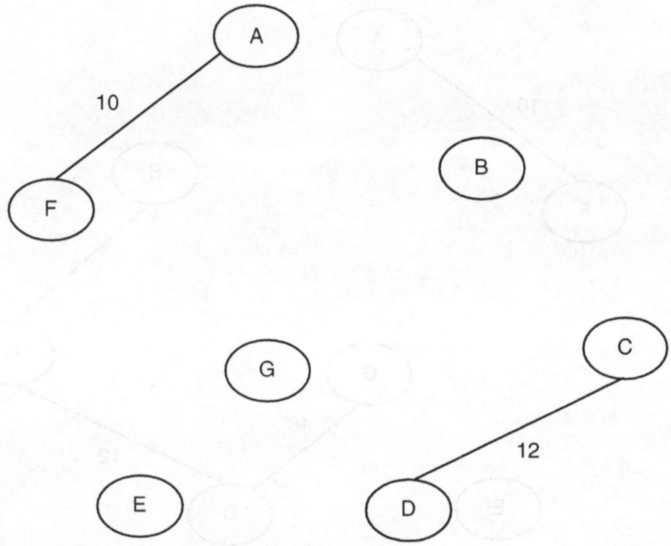

Fig. 8.35

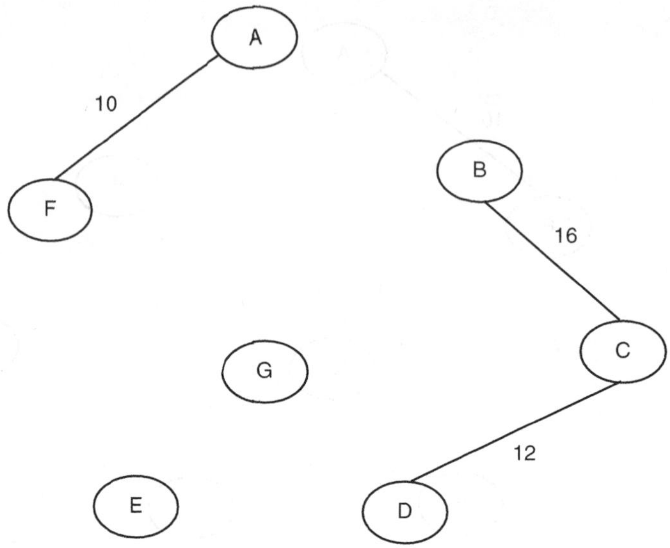

Fig. 8.36

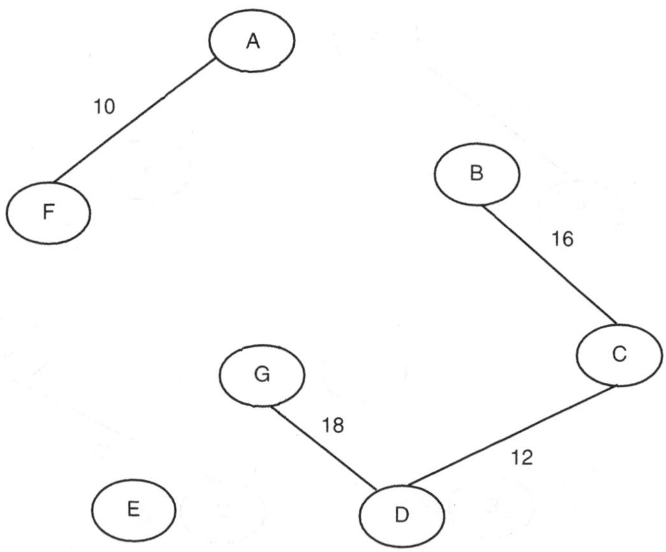

Fig. 8.37

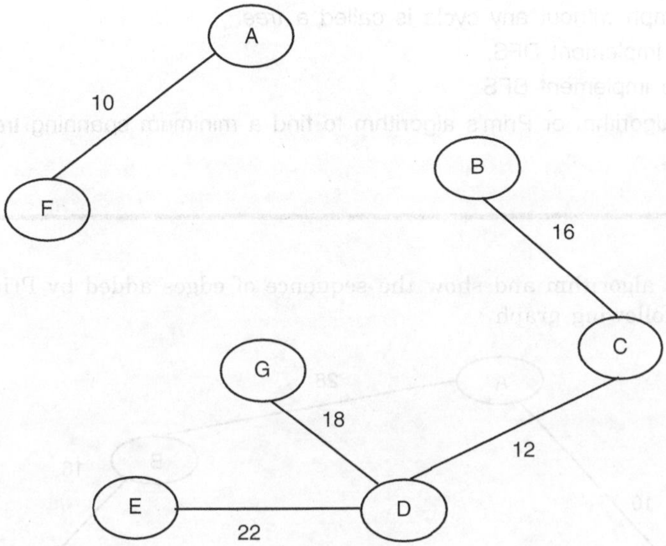

Fig. 8.38

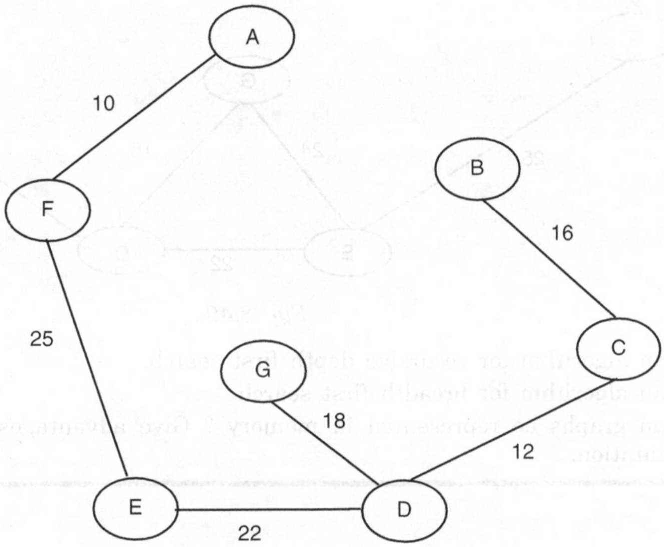

Fig. 8.39

Minimum spanning tree is found.

KEY POINTS

- A graph G is defined as a ordered set (V, E), where V(G) represents the set of all elements called vertices and E(G) represents the edges between these vertices.
- A path between any two vertices is a sequence of vertices between these two vertices.
- A cycle is the path in which first and last vertices are same.

- A connected graph without any cycle is called a *tree.*
- Use a stack to implement DFS.
- Use a queue to implement BFS.
- Use Kruskal's algorithm or Prim's algorithm to find a minimum spanning tree.

EXERCISE

1. Design Prim's algorithm and show the sequence of edges added by Prim's algorithm in constructing for following graph :

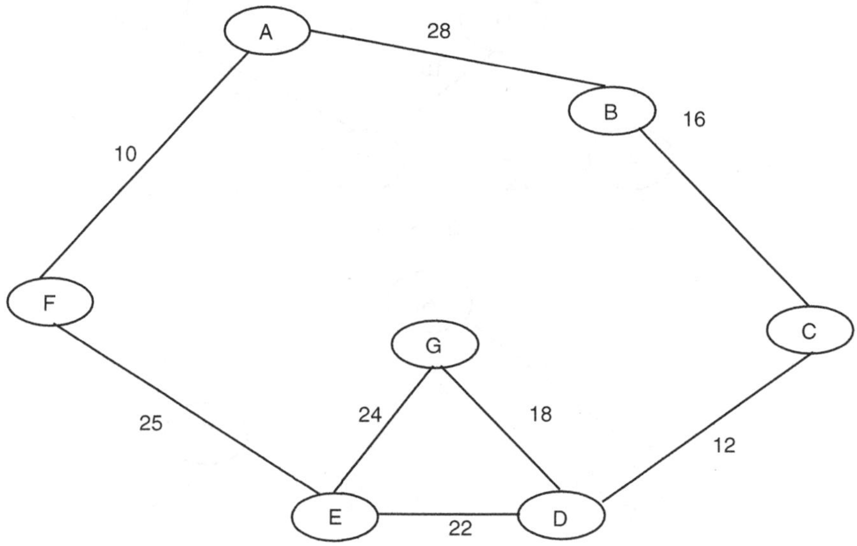

Fig. 8.40

2. Write an algorithm for recursive depth first search.
3. Write an algorithm for breadth first search.
4. How can graphs be represented in memory ? Give advantages and disadvantages of each representation.

9

TREE

9.1 INTRODUCTION

The term "tree" is used in Computer Science to denote a particular type of abstract data structure. Trees contain data in structures called *nodes*, which are in turn linked to other nodes in the tree. Every tree has a primary node called a root from which all other branch nodes in the tree descend. The nodes that have no descendents are called leaf nodes. Additionally, each node is the parent of subtrees. Every node in a tree has 0 or more children. One or more of the subtrees may have no elements and are called **empty** subtrees. In this way a tree can be described as being made up of multiple subtrees.

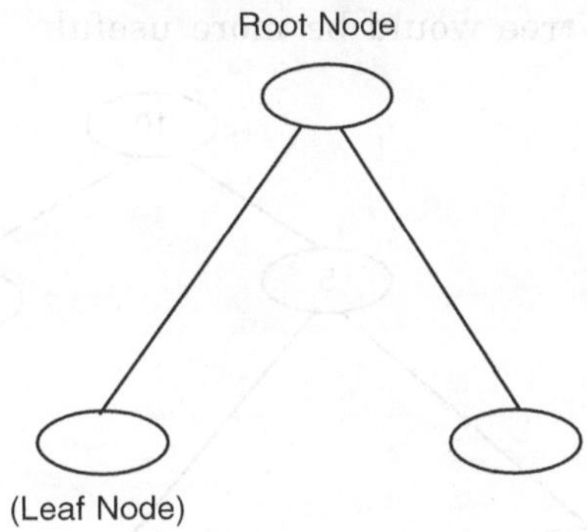

Fig. 9.1

KEY TERMS

Root. A tree contains a unique first node which is shown at the top of the tree structure, this node is called *root* of the tree.

Leaf nodes. The nodes which do not have children are called *leaf nodes.*

Interior nodes. The nodes which have children nodes are called *interior nodes.*

Siblings. If two or more nodes have same parent, then these nodes are called siblings to each other.

Ancestor. A node is called *ancestor* of another node if either it is the parent of that node or it is the parent of some other ancestor of that node.

Descendent. A node is called *descendent* of another node if it is the child of that node or the child of some other descendent of that node.

Depth of tree. The length of the longest path from root to any other node is known as the *depth of the tree.* (Path is the number of edges from root to any node.)

Degree of an node. The degree of a node is the number of children it has. Degree of leaf is zero.

Degree of tree. The degree of a tree is the maximum of its node degree.

Why should you use trees ?

Why do we use trees as data structures ? Primarily, trees are useful for organizing data in a manner that makes it efficient to retrieve it. To illustrate this, picture a collection of data organized in a linked list structure.

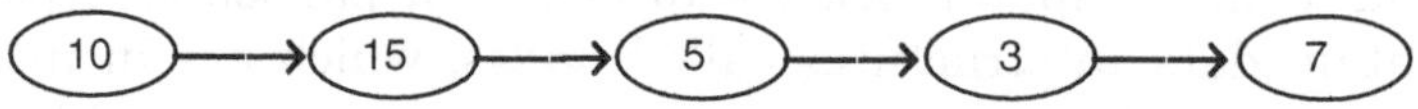

Fig. 9.2 Linked list

To find a single item in the list one's only option is to traverse the entire list from one end to the other until the item is found. This is not efficient for a large amount of data. A better approach in this case would be to use a tree structure to organize the data. A special type of tree known as a binary search tree would be more useful.

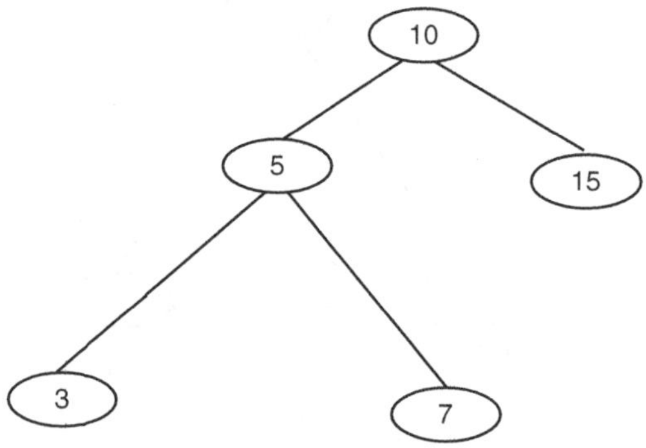

Fig. 9.3 Binary tree

The binary search tree is organized in such a way that all of the items less than the item in a chosen node are contained in the left subtree and all the items greater than the chosen node are contained in the right subtree. In this manner, one does not have to search the entire tree for a particular item in the manner of linked list traversals.

Binary trees can, therefore, be considered a *(self-sorting)* data structure. Consequently, search times through the data structure are, on average, greatly reduced. Good designers, conscious of this obvious benefit, are careful to keep their trees well balanced, as balanced trees produced better search times for the average case.

Different Types of Tree

Tree can be divided in different classes as follows :

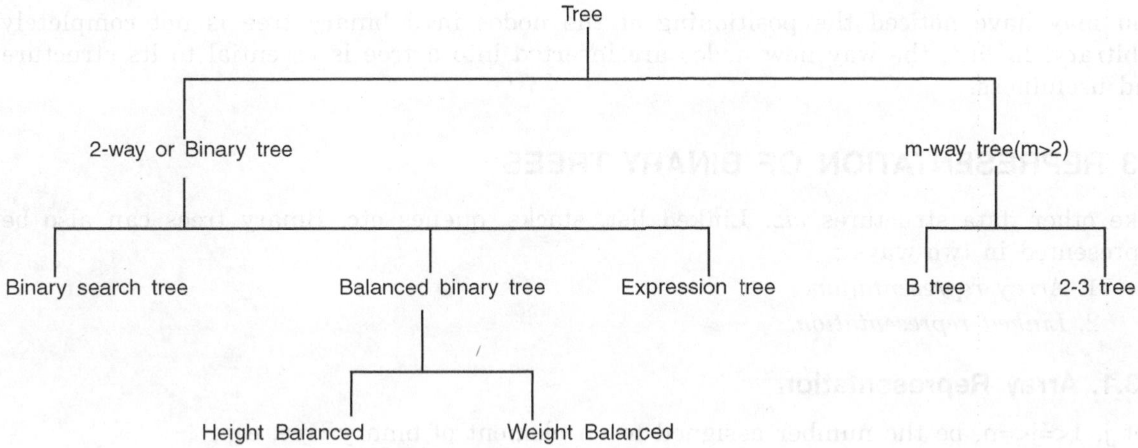

Fig. 9.4 Tree classes

9.2 BINARY TREES

To begin with, we will describe the most common type of tree, the binary tree. The binary tree is so named because each node can have at most two descendents. Typically, these descendents are described as "left" and "right" children of the parent node. Each node can have one child, two children or no children.

Perhaps, the most commonly used types of tree data structures are *binary trees*. They are the simplest type to implement and can be very efficient if used properly. A Binary Tree is made of nodes that can have at most two offspring *(children)*. The root node is the node that is not a child of any other node, and is found at the "top" of the tree structure. A node with no children is referred to as a leaf node. Nodes that are not a root node or a leaf node are often referred to as non-leaf nodes.

A node is constructed of a left pointer ***(LP)***, a right pointer ***(RP)***, and a data field ***(DATA)***.

A **balnced binary tree** is one for whom the longest path through the left subtree is the same length as the longest path of the right subtree, from root to leaf. Unbalanced binary trees lead to longer search times and should be avoided. Rebalancing techniques such as that for the **Height Balanced Tree** could be used, or the information can be sorted prior to the building of the tree.

While the definition of a binary tree may seem abstract, it is really quite simple. Consider the following real world examples. You may be surprised to learn that you are the root node of a binary tree. Every person has two parents, who also have two parents and so on. This reverses the parent-child relation as described earlier, but it gives the general idea. An example which relates more closely to the software data type is cell division. A parent cell divides into two child cells through varying generations. If you were to graph the reproduction of several generations you would begin to notice a perfect binary tree.

Each node also contains some data. This data may be any type of record with arbitrary complexity provided certain conditions are met. Each record must have what is referred to as a key. Of course, each record's key must be distinct. Also, you must be able to compare the keys using the operations greater-than, less-than, and equal. Good examples of key types are integer, character and string.

You may have noticed the positioning of the nodes in a binary tree is not completely arbitrary. In fact, the way new nodes are inserted into a tree is essential to its structure and usefulness.

9.3 REPRESENTATION OF BINARY TREES

Like other data structures *viz.* Linked list, stacks, queues etc. Binary trees can also be represented in two ways :

1. *Array representation.*
2. *Linked representation.*

9.3.1. Array Representation

Let j, 1<=j<=n, be the number assigned to an element of binary tree, *e.g.,*

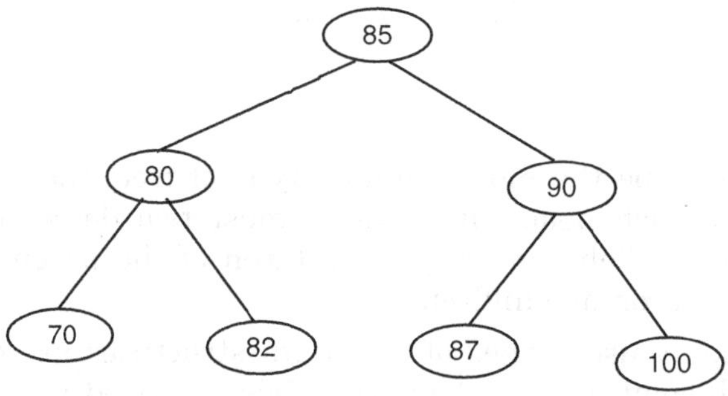

Fig. 9.5 Binary tree

In this representation, a binary tree having *n* elements may require a array of size (2^n – 1) in the worst case. Array representation for Fig. 9.5.

85	80	90	70	82	87	100

Fig. 9.6 Array representation of elements.

Let's consider some more examples :

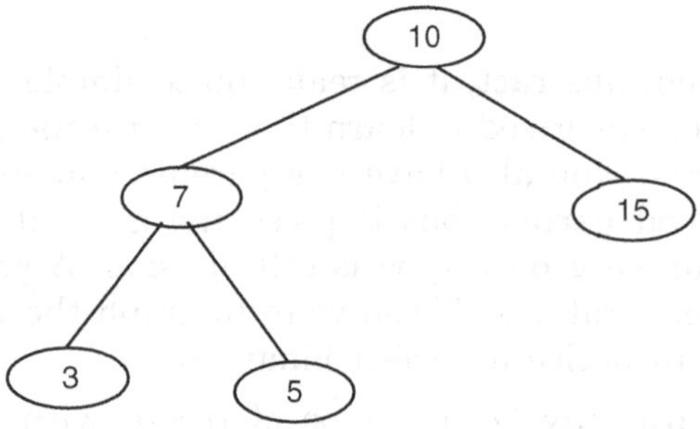

Fig. 9.7 (a)

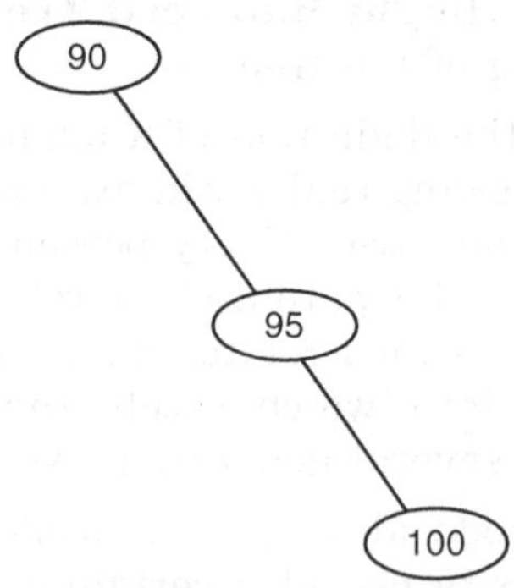

Fig. 9.7 (b) Right skewed binary tree

10	7	15	3	5		

Fig. 9.8 Array representation for Fig. 9.7(a)

90		95				100

Fig. 9.9 Array representation for Fig. 9.7(b).

This scheme of representation is quite wasteful of space when the binary tree is skewed or if the number of elements is small as compared to its height. Hence, array representation is useful when the binary tree is full or complete.

9.3.2. Linked Representation

In linked representation, each element is represented by an anode that has exactly two link fields. Let's call these fields left pointer (lp) and right pointer (rp). In addition to these two link fields, each node has a data field called *info*.

Declaration of binary tree :

```
typedef  struct  binarytree
{
        int  info;
        struct  binarytree   *lp;
        struct  binarytree   *rp;
}tree;
tree  *t;
```

linked representation for Fig. 9.7(*a*).

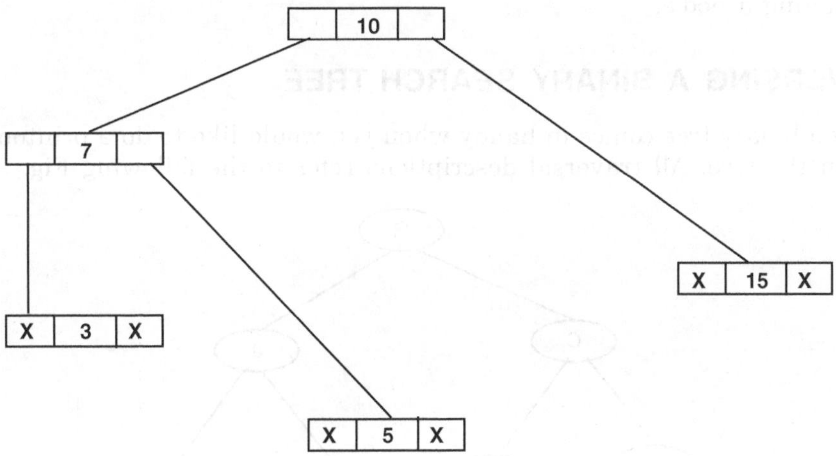

Fig. 9.10 Linked representation.

X represents NULL values inside nodes pointer fields. Each edge in the drawings of a binary tree is represented by a pointer from the parent node to child node. This pointer is placed in the appropriate link field of the parent node. Since a n-element binary tree has exactly n–1 edges, there will be 2n–(n–1)=n+1 link fields that have NULL values (×). In some applications it is better to use a pointer to parent in place of × (NULL) fields. It means in Fig. 9.10, we can replace x by reference of parent node. If there are two × (nodes in Fig. 9.10 have pair of NULL *values*) inside a node, then anyone can hold reference of parent node. Such a tree is called *threaded binary tree.*

9.4 BINARY SEARCH TREES

A binary search tree is a binary tree that may be empty. A non-empty binary search tree satisfies the follwing properties :

1. All keys are unique (keys are the data inside the nodes).
2. The left key is always smaller than the right key.
3. The left and the right subtrees of the root are also binary search trees.

Operations Applicable to Binary and Binary Search Trees

Operations applicable on both binary trees and binary search trees :

1. Creating an empty tree
2. Traversing
3. Counting internal nodes (non leaf nodes)
4. Counting extrnal nodes (leaf nodes)
5. Counting total nodes
6. Finding mirror image
7. Finding height of tree.

Operations Applicable to Only Binary Search Trees

1. Inserting a new node
2. Searching an element
3. Finding smallest element
4. Finding largest element
5. Deleting a nod e.

9.5 TRAVERSING A BINARY SEARCH TREE

Traversing a binary tree comes in handy when you would like to do a printout of all the data elements in the tree. All traversal descriptions refer to the following Fig. 9.11.

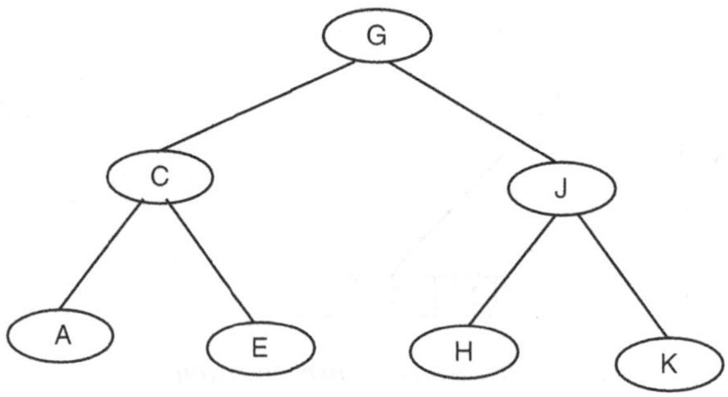

Fig. 9.11 Binary search tree

These three types are as follows :

9.5.1. Pre Order Traversal

A Pre order traversal prints the contents of a sorted tree, in Pre order. In other words, the contents of the root node are printed first, followed by left subtree and finally the right subtree. So in Fig. 9.11, an in order traversal would result in the following string :

GCAEJHK

Algorithm 9.1 : ***To traverse pre order (recursive)***

```
START
            Void PreOrder (tree *t)
STEP 1
            If t < > null
            Then print (t–>data)
            Else
            Print ('empty tree')
STEP 2
            If t–>1p < > null
            Then PreOrder (t–>1p)
STEP 3
            If t–>rp < > null
            Then PreOrder (t–>rp)
            End.
STOP
```

9.5.2. In Order Traversal

An in order traversal prints the contents of a sorted tree are in order. In other words, the lowest in value first and then increasing in value as it traverses the tree. The order of a traversal would be 'a' to 'z' if the tree uses strings or characters, and would be increasing numerically from 0 if the tree contains numerical values. So in Figure 9.11, an in order traversal would result in the following string :

ACEGHJK

Algorithm 9.2 : ***To traverse in order (recursive)***

```
START
            Void InOrder (tree *t)
STEP 1
            If t < > null
            Print ('empty tree')
STEP 2
            If t–>1p < > null
            Then InOrder (t–>1p)
            Print (t–>data)
STEP 3
            If t–> rp < > null
            Then InOrder (t–>rp)
            End
STOP
```

9.5.3. Post Order Traversal

A post order traversal prints the contents of a sorted tree, in post order. In other words, the contents of the left subtree are printed first, followed by the contents of the right subtree and finally the root node. So in Fig. 9.11, an in order traversal would result in the following string :

AECHKJG

Algorithm 9.3 : ***To traverse in post order (recursive)***

```
START
            Void PostOrder (tree *t)
STEP 1
            If t = null
            Then print ('empty tree')
STEP 2
            If t–>1p < > null
            Then PostOrder (t–>1p)
STEP 3
            If t–> rp < > null
            Then PostOrder (t–>rp)
            Print (t–>data)
            End.
STOP
```

Algorithm 9.4 : ***To search a node in a binary search tree (BST)***

```
START
            tree * Search (tree *t, info)
STEP 1
            If t = = NULL {into is not in the tree}
            then print ('sorry tree is empty')
            returns NIL
STEP 2
            else if info = t–> info then print ('item found'; t–>info)
            returns t
STEP 3
            else if into <t–> info and t–>lp < > NULL, then
            Search (t–>lp, info)
STEP 4
            else if info >t–> info and t–>rp< > NULL, then
            Search (t–>rp, info)
STOP
```

9.6 INSERTION OF A NODE IN A BINARY SEARCH TREE

The General Steps of Insertion

A binary search tree is constructed by the repeated insertion of new nodes into a binary search tree structure. Insertion must maintain the order of the tree. That is, values to the left of a given node must be less than that node, and values to the right must be greater.

The Technical Details of Insertion

Inserting a node into a tree is actually two separate operations. First, the tree must be searched to determine where the node is to be inserted. Second, on the completion of the search, the node is inserted into the tree. Two cases must be considered when constructing a binary search tree.

1. *Inserting a node into an empty tree.*

Before insertion of 5 After insertion of 5

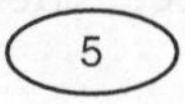

Fig. 9.12

In this case, the node inserted into the tree is considered as the root node.

2. *Inserting a node into a non-empty tree.*

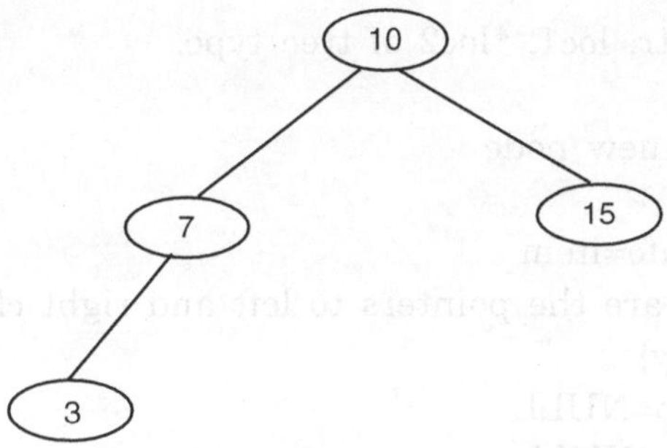

Fig. 9.13. Before insertion of 5

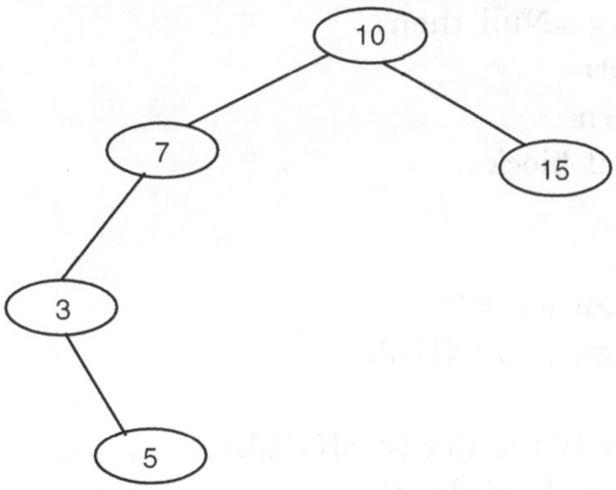

Fig. 9.14. After insertion of 5

The tree must be searched, as was noted above, to determine where the node is to be inserted. The new node is compared first to the root node of the tree.

If the value of the new node is less than the value of the root node, the new node is :

- appended as the left leaf of the root node, if the left subtree is empty,
- else, the search continues down the left subtree.

If this search procedure finds that the insertion node already exists in the tree, the procedure terminates as it cannot insert it again.

Note that careful consideration of the above algorithm reveals that the searching procedure described is actually a modified In Order traversal of the tree.

Complexity

Average case is $O(\log_2 n)$.

Worst case is $O(n)$.

Insertion General Steps

1. If this is the first insertion, then create a node and set its fields.
2. If the name is not already in the tree, then attach the new mode to the existing tree else write ('Item already there').

Algorithm 9.5 : *To insert a node in a binary search tree (BST)*

```
START
        Void insert (tree **t, item)
STEP 1
        Declare *ptr, loc1, *loc2 of tree type.
STEP 2
        ptr=create new node
STEP 3
        Set Ptr->info=item
        {lp and rp are the pointers to left and right child
        respectively}
        Set ptr->1p=NULL
        Set ptr->rp=NULL
STEP 4
        If *t= =Null then
        *t=ptr
        return
        end if block
STEP 5
        Else
        Assign loc2=*t
        Assign loc1=NULL
STEP 6
        Loop While (loc2< >NULL)
        Assign Loc1=loc2
STEP 7
        If item<loc2->info
```

Then
Loc2=loc2->1p
Else
Loc2=loc2->rp
End if

STEP 8

End while loop

STEP 9

If loc1->info>item
Loc1->1p=ptr

STEP 10

Else
Loc1->rp=ptr
End if

STOP

Algorithm 9.6 : *To search an element in a binary search tree (BST)*

START

Tree * search (tree *t, int item)

STEP 1

If (t–>info= =item OR tree= = (tree *) NULL)
Return tree
End if block

STEP 2

Else if (item<t–>info)
Return search (t–>lp, item)
End else if block

STEP 3

Else return search (t–>rp, item)
End else block

STOP

Following listing covers all operations on a Binary Search Tree

LISTING 9.1

```
#include<stdio.h>
#include<conio.h>
#include<alloc.h>
typedef struct binarytree
        {
              int info;
              struct binarytree *lp; \\pointer to left subtree
              struct binarytree *rp; \\pointer to right subtree
        }tree;
        void create_empty_tree(tree **t)
        {
        *t=(tree *)NULL;
        }
```

```
void insert_node(tree **t,int item)
{
tree *ptr,*loc1,*loc2;
ptr=(tree *)malloc(sizeof(tree));
ptr->info=item;
ptr->lp=(tree *)NULL;
ptr->rp=(tree *)NULL;
if(*t= =(tree *)NULL)
*t=ptr;
else
{
     loc1=(tree *)NULL;
     loc2=*t;
     while(loc2!=(tree *)NULL)
     {
          loc1=loc2;
          if(item<loc2->info)
          loc2=loc2->lp;
          else if(item>loc2->info)
          loc2=loc2->rp;
          else if(item= =loc2->info)
          {
          print("item already exist")
          getch();
          return;
          }
     }
     if(item<loc1->info)
     loc->1p=ptr;
     else
     loc1->rp=ptr;
}
}

     void inorder(tree *t)
     {
     if((t!=(tree*)NULL))
     {
     inorder(t->lp);
     printf("%d",t->info);
     inorder(t->rp);
     }
     }
     void preorder (tree *t)
     {
     if(t!=(tree *)NULL)
          {
                printf("%d",t->info);
                preorder(t->lp);
                preorder(t->rp);
          }
     }
     void postorder(tree *t)
```

```
{
if(t!=(tree  *)NULL)
     {
          postorder(t->lp);
          postorder(t->rp);
          printf("%do",t->info);
     }
}

int  total_nodes(tree  *t)
{
     if(t!=(tree  *)NULL)
     return(total_nodes(t->lp)+total_nodes(t->rp)+1);
     else
     return  0;
}
int  internal  (tree *t)
{
     if((t==(tree*)NULL)||((t->lp==(tree  *)NULL)&&(t
     ->rp==(tree*)NULL))
     return  0;
     else
     return(internal(t->lp)+internal(t->rp)+1);
}
int  external(tree  *t)
{
if(t==(tree  *)NULL)
return  0;
else  if( (t->lp==(tree  *)NULL)&&(t->rp==(tree  *)NULL))
return  1;
else
return(external(t->1p)+external(t->rp));
}
tree  *search(tree  *t,int  item)
{
if((t->info==item)||(t==(tree  *)NULL))
return  t;
else  if(item<t->info)
return  search(t->1p,  item);
else
return  search(t->rp,item);
}

void  mirror(tree  *t)
{
tree  *loc;
     if(t!=(tree  *)NULL)
     {
     mirror(t->lp);
     mirror(t->rp);
     loc=t->lp;
     t->1p=t->rp;
     t->rp=loc;
     }
}
```

```
void tree_height(tree *t,int *height)
{
     int lh,rh;
     if(t==(tree *)NULL)
     *height=0;
     else
     {
     tree_height(t->lp,&lh);
     tree_height(t->rp,&rh);
     if(lh>rh)
     *height=lh+1;
     else
     *height=rh+1;
     }
}

tree *smallest(tree *t)
{
     if((t==(tree *)NULL)||(t->lp==(tree *)NULL))
     return t;
     else
     return smallest(t->lp);
}
tree *largest(tree *t)
{
     if((t==(tree *)NULL)||(t->rp)==(tree *)NULL))
     return t;
     else
     return largest(t->rp);
}
void delete_node(tree **t,int item)
{
     tree *loc;
     if(*t==(tree *)NULL)
     {
     printf("\nElement does not exist");
     return;
     }
     if(item<(*t)->info)
     delete_node(&((*t)->lp),item);
     else if(item>(*t)->info)
     delete_node(&(*t)->rp),item);


     else if( (*t)->lp&&(*t)->rp)
     {
          loc=largest((*t)->lp);
          (*t)->info=loc->info;
          delete_node(&((&t)->1p),loc->info);
     }
     else
     {
     loc=*t;
```

```
        if((!(*t)->lp)&&(!(*t)->rp))
        *t=(tree *)NULL;
        else if(!(*t)->rp)
    *t=(*t)->lp;
    else
    *t=(*t)->rp;
    free(loc);
        }
    }

    void main()
    {
    tree *t,*loc;
    int item,element,choice,total,leaf,nonleaf,hig;
    create_empty_tree(&t);
    while(1)
    {
    clrscr();
    printf("\n1.insert");
    printf("\n2.traverse in order");
    printf("\n3.traverse pre order");
    printf("\n4.traverse post order");
    printf("\n5.Counting total nodes");
    printf("\n6.Counting Internal nodes");
    printf("\n7.Counting external nodes");
    printf("\n8.Finding smallest item");
    printf("\n9.Finding largest item");
    printf("\n10.search an item");
    printf("\n11.Hight of tree");
    printf("\n12.finding Mirror Image");
    printf("\n13.delete a node from tree");
    printf("\n14.Exit");
    printf("\nenter your choice");
    scanf("%d",&choice);
    switch(choice)
    {
    case 1:
            print("\nenter a no");
            scanf("%d",&item);
            insert_node(&t,item);
            break;
    case 2:
            inorder(t);
            getch();
            break;
    case 3:
            preorder(t);
            getch();
            break;
    case 4:
            postorder(t);
            getch();
            break;
```

```
case 5:
        total=total_nodes(t);
        printf("Total no. of nodes in this tree are
            %d",total);
        getch();
        break;
case 6:
        nonleaf=internal(t);
        printf("Number of Internal nodesare %d",nonleaf);
        break;
case 7:
        leaf=external(t);
        print("Number of external nodes are %d",leaf);
        break;
case 8:
        loc=smallest(t);
        if(loc!=(tree *)NULL)
        printf("\nSmallest element is %d",loc->info);
        else
        printf("\ntree is empty");
        getch();
        break;
case 9:
        loc=largest(t);
                if(loc!=(tree *)NULL)
                printf("\nLargest Elementis %d",loc->info);
            else
            printf("\ntree is empty");
            getch();
            break;
case 10:
        printf("\nEnter element to search");
        scanf("%d",&element);
            loc=search(t,element);
        if(loc!=(tree *)NULL)
                printf("\nElement %d is found",loc->info);
            else
            printf("\nelement does not exist in tree");
            getch();
            break;

case 11:
            tree_height(t&hig);
        printf("\n height of trees is %d",hig);
        getch();
        break;
case 12:
        mirror(t);
        break;
case 13:
        printf("\nEnter element to delete from tree");
        scanf("%d",&element);
        delete_node(&t,element);
        break;
```

```
            case 14:
                    exit();
            }

        }
    }
```

9.7 THE GENERAL STEPS OF DELETION

The algorithm to delete an arbitrary node from a binary tree is deceptively complex, as there are many special cases. The algorithm used for the delete function splits it into two separate operations, searching and deletion. Once the node, which is to be deleted, has been determined by the searching algorithm, it can be deleted from the tree. The algorithm must ensure that when the node is deleted from the tree, the ordering of the binary tree is kept intact.

Special cases that have to be considered :

1. *The node to be deleted has no children*
   In this case, the node may simply be deleted from the tree.

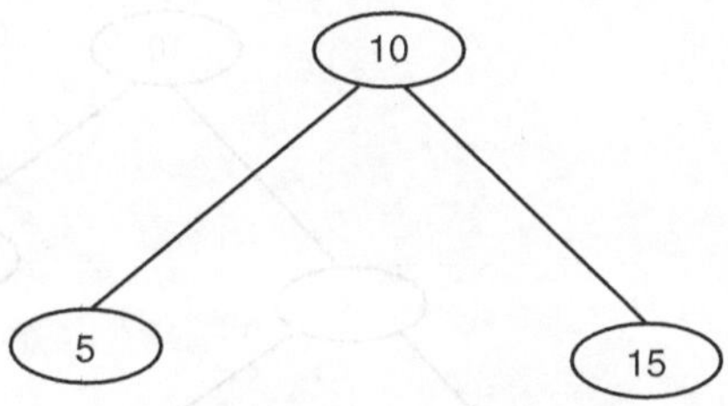

Fig. 9.15 (a) Before deletion of 5

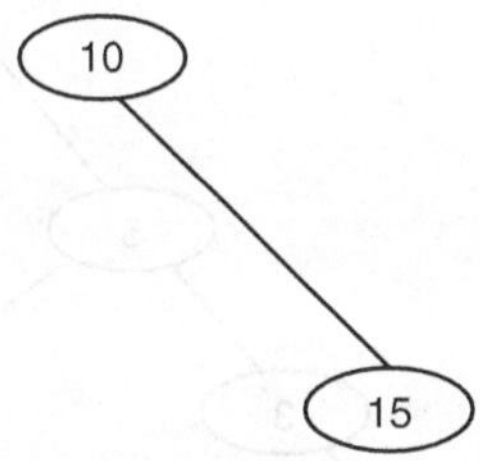

Fig. 9.15 (b) After deletion of 5

2. *The node has one child*
   The child node is appended to its grandparent. (The parent of the node to be deleted.)

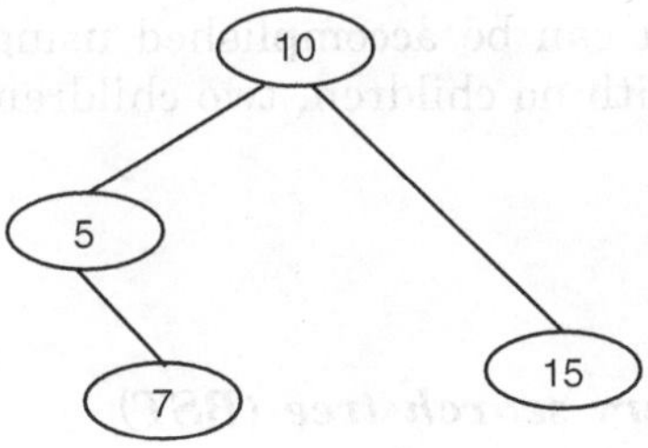

Fig. 9.16 (a) Before deletion of 5

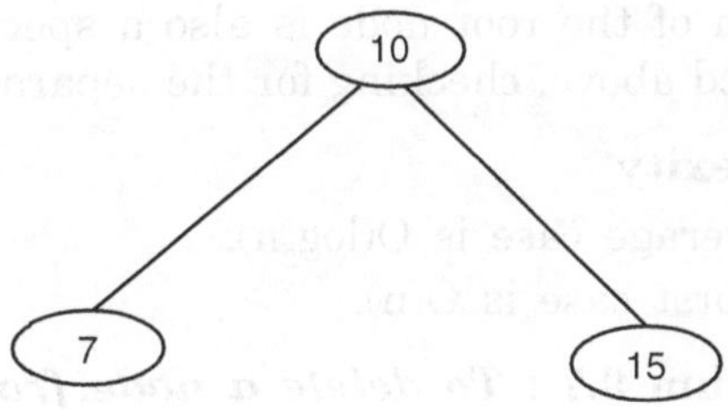

Fig. 9.16 (b) After deletion of 5

3. *The node to be deleted has two children*
   This case is much more complex than the previous two, because the order of the binary tree must be kept intact. The algorithm must determine which node to use in place of the node to be deleted.

(*i*) Use the inorder successor of the node to be deleted.

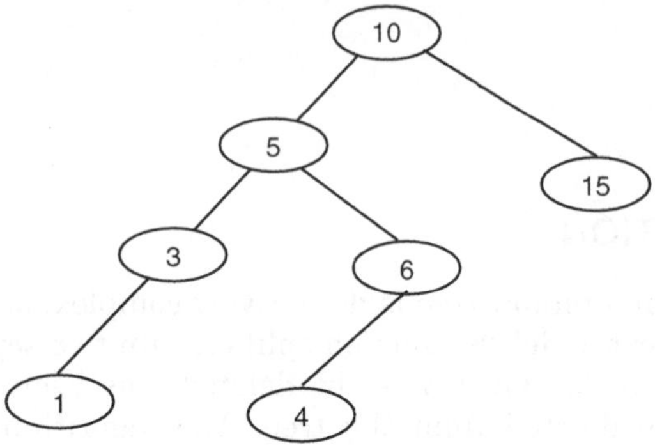

Fig. 9.17 (a) Before deletion of 5

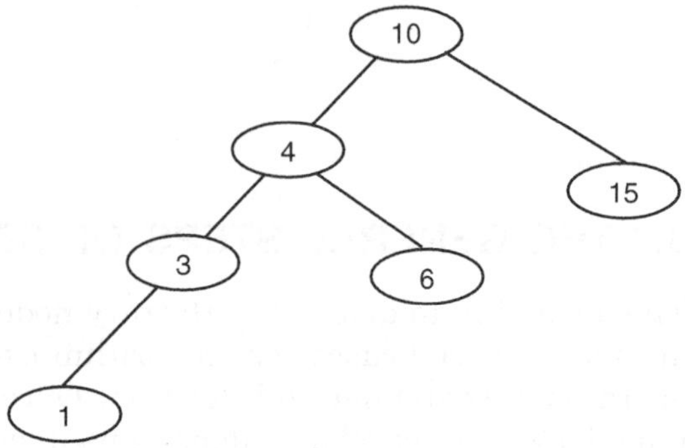

Fig. 9.17 (b) After deletion of 5

(*ii*) Else if no right subtree exists, replace the node to be deleted with its left child.

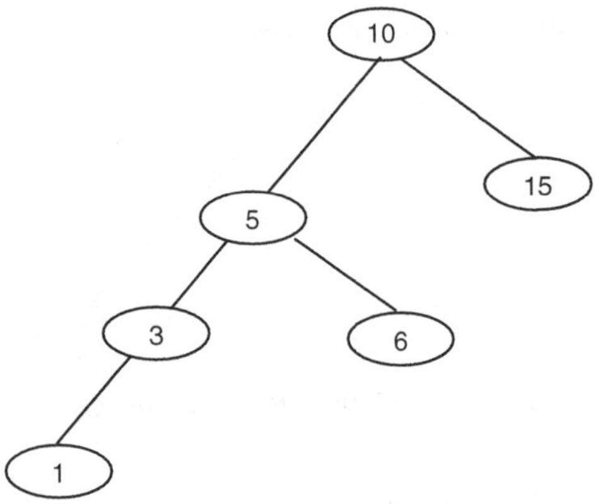

Fig. 9.18 (a) Before deletion of 5

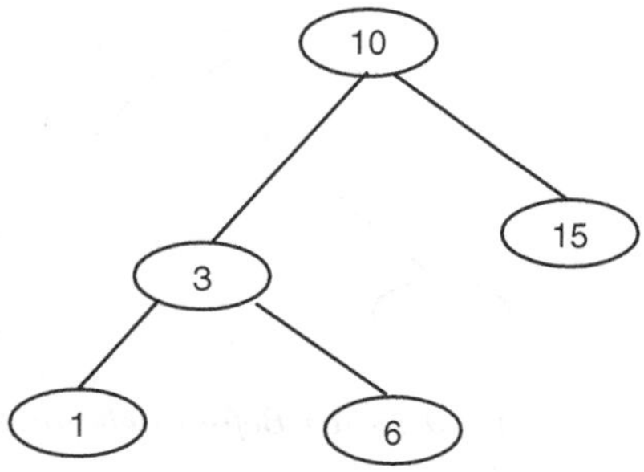

Fig. 9.18 (b) After deletion of 5

Deletion of the root node is also a special case. It can be accomplished using the methods described above, checking for the separate cases with no children, two children, or one child.

Complexity

Average case is $O(\log_2 n)$.

Worst case is O(n).

Algorithm 9.7 : *To delete a node from a binary search tree (BST)*

There are different methods to write a algorithm, to delete a node from a tree. One of the easy methods is considered in following algorithm :

START

Void delete_node(tree **t,item)

STEP 1

Declare ***loc**, *del, *ptr of type tree

STEP 2

```
*t=search(*t,item)
If *t= =NULL
Then
OUTPUT "node does not exist"
Return
End if block
```

STEP 3

```
{if left subtree is empty}
Else If ((*t)->lp= =NULL)
    Then
    loc=*t
    *t=(*t)->rp
    free(loc)
    end else if block
```

STEP 4

```
Else if((*t)->rp= =NULL)
loc=*t
* t=(* t)->lp
free (loc)
end else if block
```

STEP 5

```
Else if ((*t)->lp !=NULL && (*t)->rp!=NULL)
loc=(*t)->rp
```

STEP 6

```
Loop while(loc->lp!= NULL)
loc=loc->lp
End while
```

STEP 7

```
loc->lp=(*t)->lp
loc->rp=(*t)->rp
del=ptr
```

STEP 8

```
Ptr=loc
```

STEP 9

```
free(loc 2)
```

STOP

Algorithm 9.8 : *To count internal nodes*

START

```
Int internal(tree *t)
```

```
STEP 1
        If ((t= =NULL) OR (t–>lp= =NULL)AND(t–>rp= =NULL))
        Return 0
        End if block
STEP 2
        Return (internal(t–>lp)+internal(t–>rp)+1)
STOP
```

Algorithm 9.9 : *To count external nodes*

```
START
        Int external (tree *t)
STEP 1
        If (t= =NULL)
        Return 0
        End if block
STEP 2
        Else if((t–>lp= =NULL) AND (t–>rp= =NULL))
        Return 1;
        End else if block
STEP 3
        Else
            Return(external(t–>lp)+external(t–>rp))
STOP
```

Algorithm 9.10 : *To find a mirror image of a tree*

```
START
        Void mirrorimage(tree *t)
STEP 1
        Declare *loc of type tree
STEP 2
        If (t !=NULL)
        Then
        mirrorimage(t->lp)
        mirrorimage(t->rp)
STEP 3
        loc=t->lp
        t->lp=t->rp
        t->rp=loc
STEP 4
        End if
STOP
```

9.8 BINARY EXPRESSION TREE

A binary tree used to represent a binary expression is called a *binary expression tree*. Root node of BET contains operator and two children node contains operands. For example, x+y can be represented as follows :

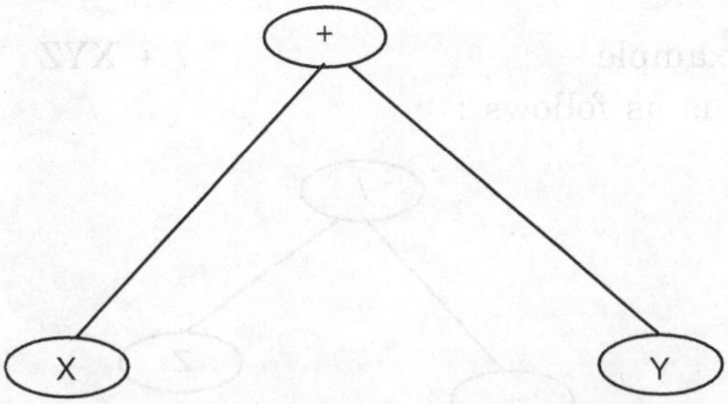

Fig. 9.19

If we have an expression with more operators and operands like:

(X+Y) / (U–V)

Here we will construct two sub trees and then these sub trees will be added to root node which will be /

Sub tree 1: for X+Y

This tree will be same as shown in Fig. 9.19.

Sub tree 2: for U–V

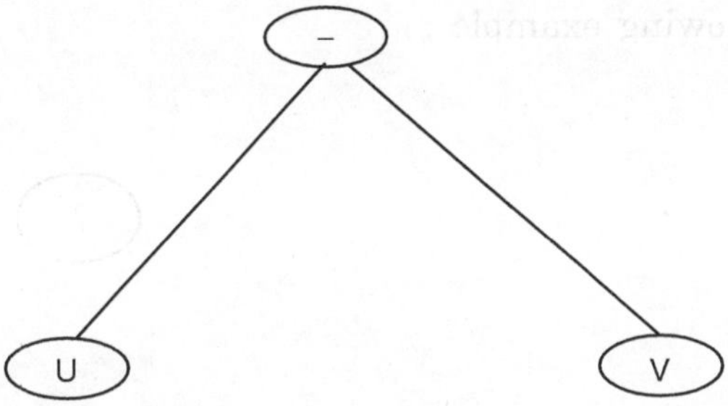

Fig. 9.20

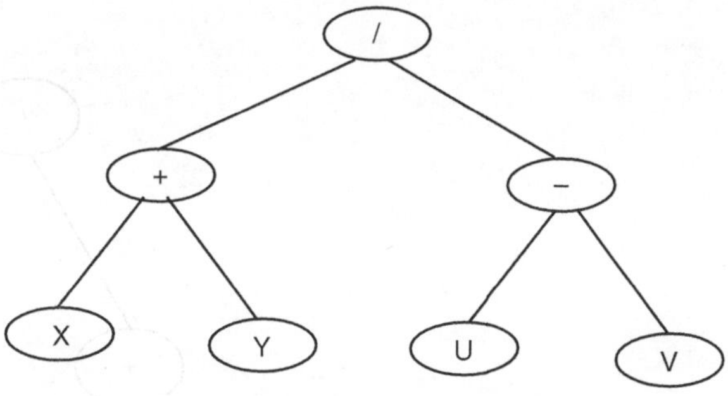

Fig. 9.21

The operations present at higher levels of the tree are evaluated after those present at lower levels.

Constructing a BET for Prefix Expression

We have done an example to construct a BET for infix expression. Now we will discuss a prefix expression :

Let us consider an example / + XYZ

BET for above expression is as follows :

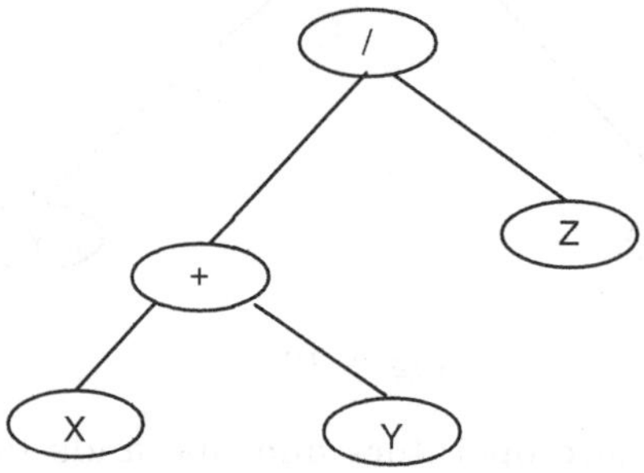

Fig. 9.22

The method followed here is to keep inserting operator nodes to the left until we encounter an operand node. This operand node is also set on left side and next operand node is set as right sibling.

Now we backtrack to the last operator, and the next node is set in its right. To find last operator node, a stack is used.

Let's consider the following example :

/ + XY–UV

stack

Fig. 9.23

Push(Op2)

Fig. 9.24

Fig. 9.25

Pop(Op2)

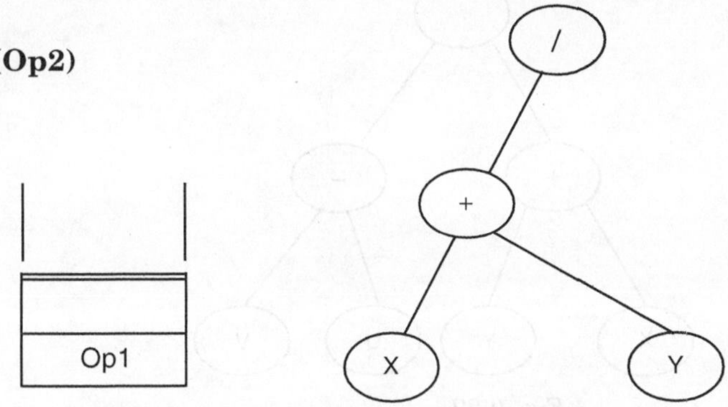

Fig. 9.26

Pop(Op1) and push (Op3)

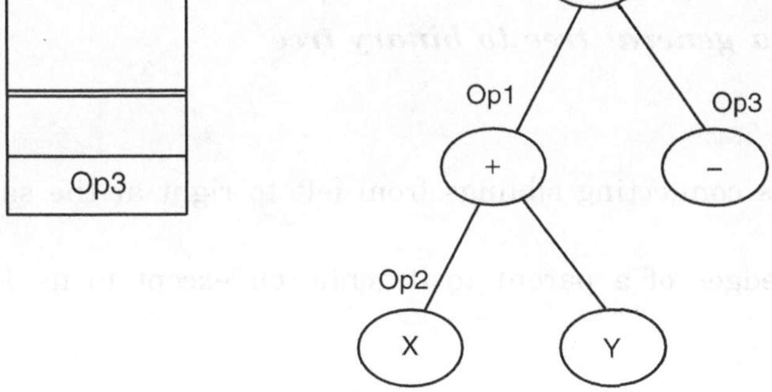

Fig. 9.27

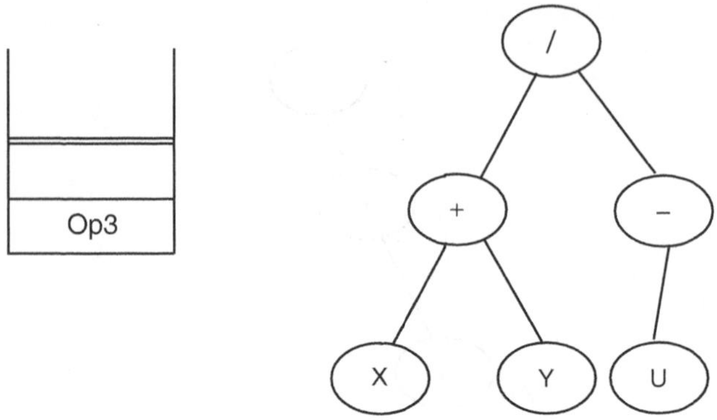

Fig. 9.28

Pop(Op3)

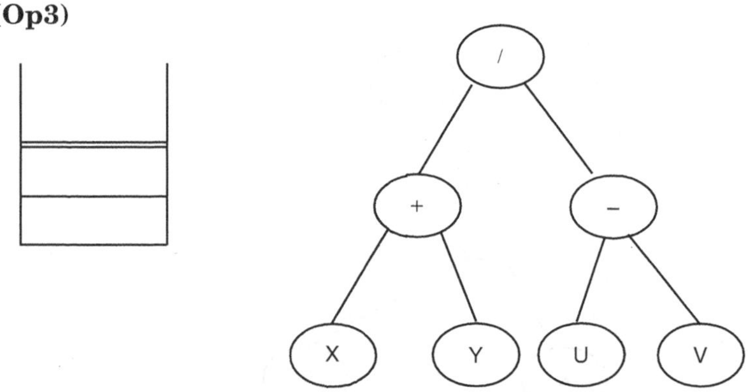

Fig. 9.29

9.9 CONVERSION OF GENERAL TREES TO BINARY TREES

As we know that binary trees are far better than general trees for searching and traversing. It is interesting to convert a general tree to a binary tree.

Algorithm 9.11 : ***To convert a general tree to binary tree***

START

STEP 1

Insert edges connecting siblings from left to right at the same level.

STEP 2

Delete all edges of a parent to its children except to its leftmost offspring.

STEP 3

Rotate the resultant tree by the angle of 45° to make clearly left and right subtrees.

STOP

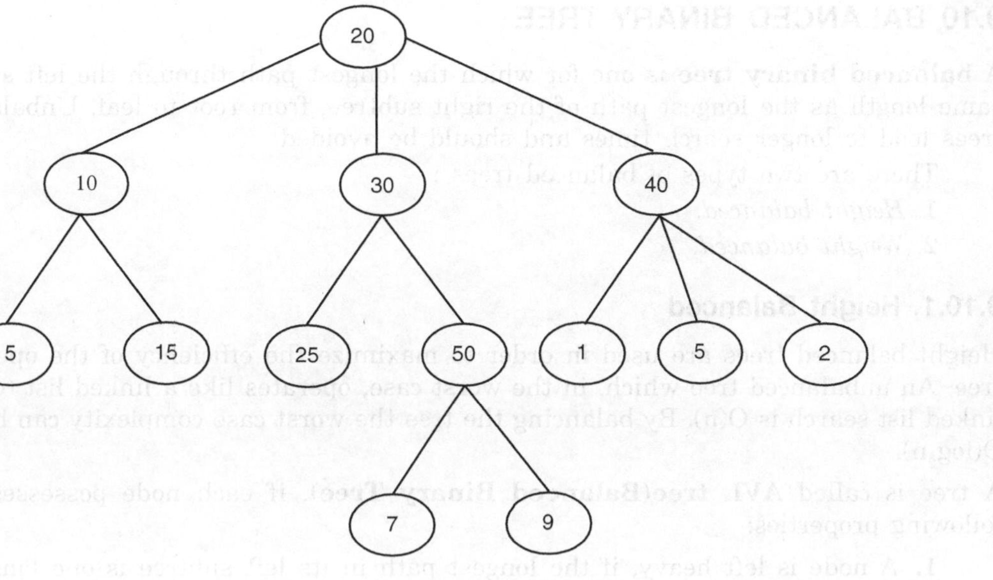

Fig. 9.30

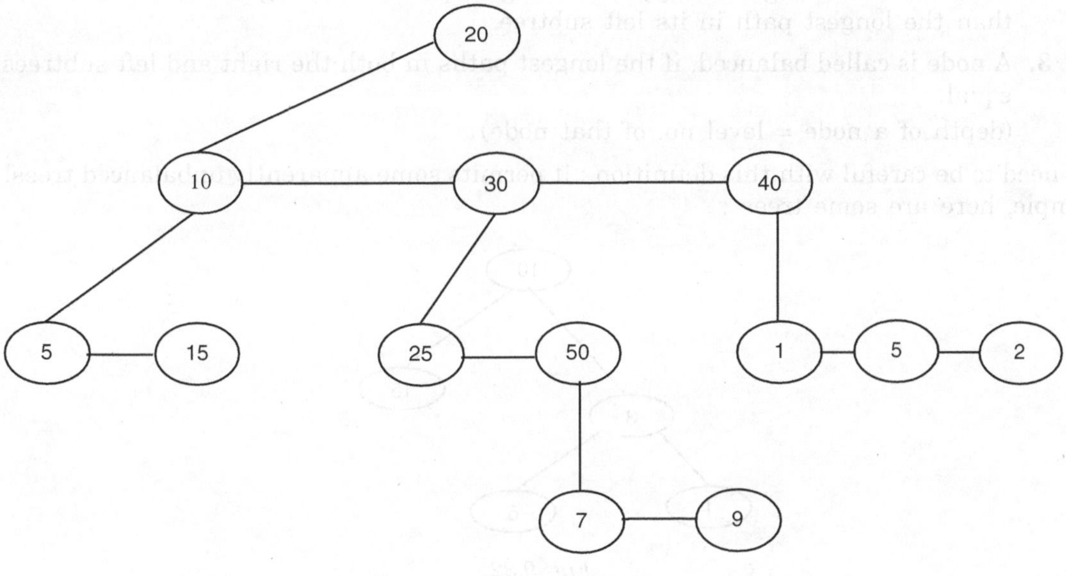

Fig. 9.31 Binary tree

You can rotate this tree to give a good look. Well even if you don't rotate, it is still a Binary tree. (You must notice that we have converted a general tree to a binary tree and not to a binary search tree).

9.10 BALANCED BINARY TREE

A **balanced binary tree** is one for which the longest path through the left subtree is the same length as the longest path of the right subtree, from root to leaf. Unbalanced binary trees lead to longer search times and should be avoided.

There are two types of balanced trees :

1. *Height balanced.*
2. *Weight balanced.*

9.10.1. Height Balanced

Height balanced trees are used in order to maximize the efficiency of the operations on a tree. An unbalanced tree which, in the worst case, operates like a linked list (complexity of linked list search is O(n). By balancing the tree the worst case complexity can be reduced to $O(\log_2 n)$.

A tree is called **AVL tree(Balanced Binary Tree)**, if each node possesses one of the following properties:

1. A node is left heavy, if the longest path in its left subtree is one longer than the longest path of its right subtree
2. A node is called right heavy, if the longest path in the right subtree is one longer than the longest path in its left subtree.
3. A node is called balanced, if the longest paths in both the right and left subtrees are equal.

   (depth of a node = level no. of that node)

You need to be careful with this definition : it permits some apparently unbalanced trees! For example, here are some trees :

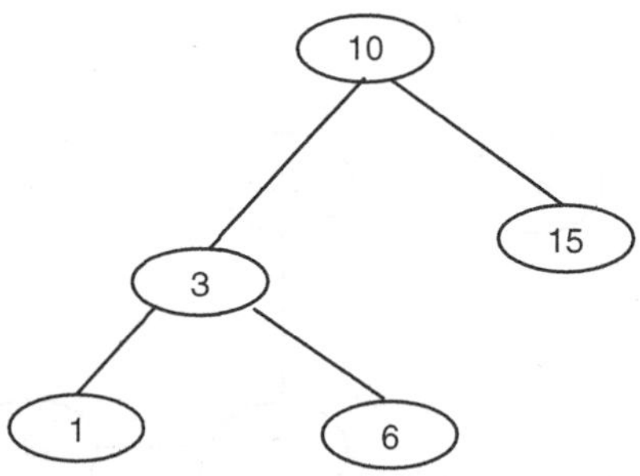

Fig. 9.32.

Level number of root is 1, hence root (10) in Fig. 9.32 is at depth 1. Longest path of left subtree is equal tomaximum depth of leaf node in left subtree which is 3 in Fig. 9.32. Similarly, longest path of right subtree is equal to maximum dept of leaf node in right subtree which is 2 in Fig. 9.32. Now, 3-2=1. Hence, tree is a height balance tree.

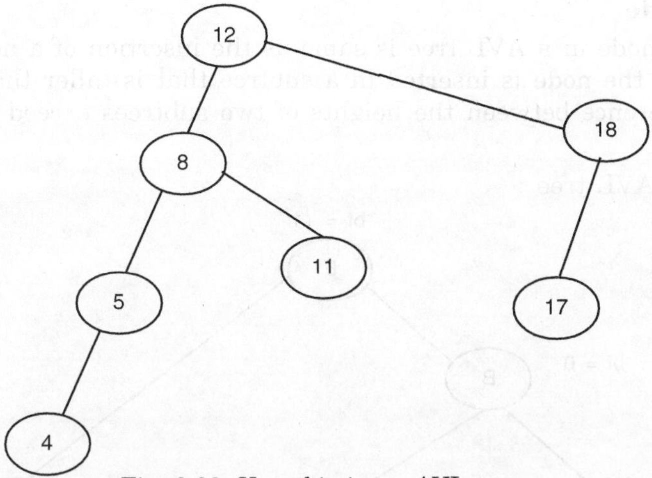

Fig. 9.33. Yes, this is an AVL tree

Examination shows that *each* left subtree has a height 1 greater than each right subtree.

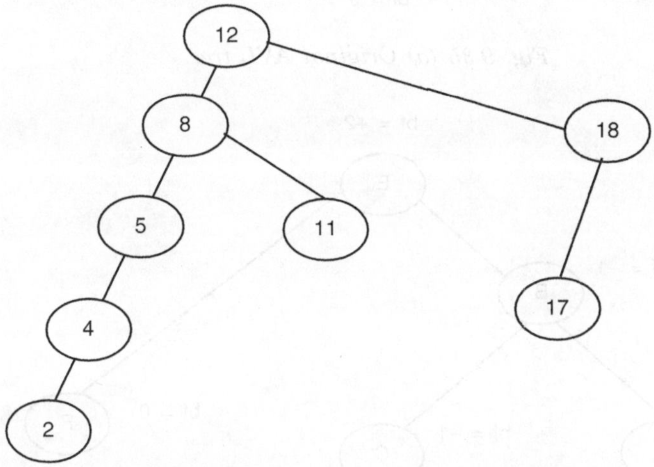

Fig. 9.34. No, this is not an AVL tree

Subtree with root 8 has height 4 and subtree with root 18 has height 2. An AVL tree can be represented by a struct as follows :

```
typedef struct avl_tree
{
        struct node *lp;
        int info;
        int bf;
        struct node *rp;
}avl;
```

bf is the balance factor field.

Insertion of a node

Insertion of a new node in a AVL tree is same as the insertion of a node in BST. But in a special case, when the node is inserted in a subtree that is taller than the other subtree. In such a case difference between the heights of two subtrees exceed the range of balance factor.

Consider following AVL tree :

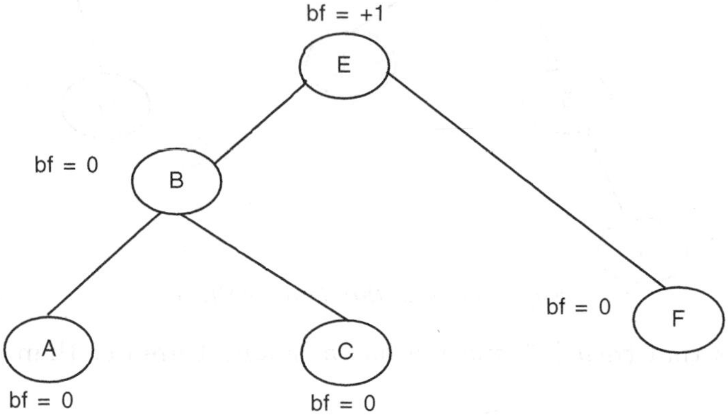

Fig. 9.35 (a) Original AVL tree.

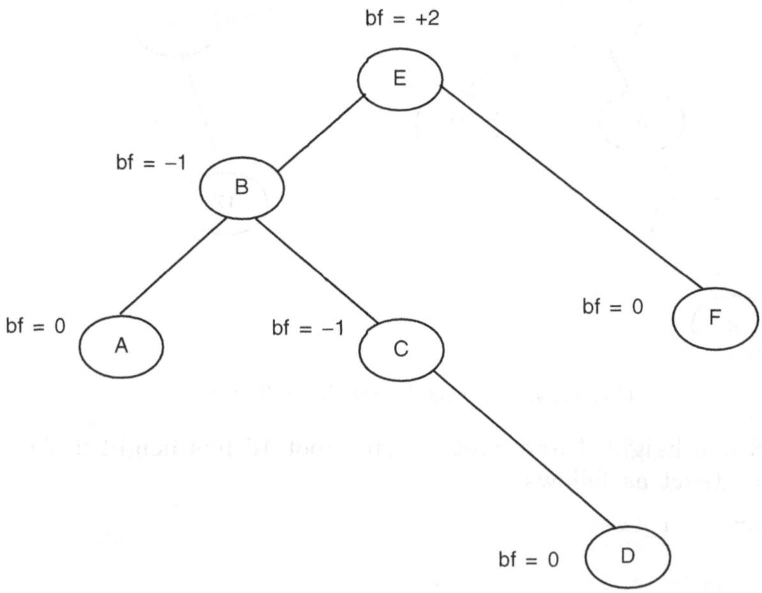

Fig. 9.35 (b) After inserting value D. (Balance factor at root gets changed).

Now, we will discuss some techniques to balance a binary tree.

- *Left rotation*

  To balance a tree, we can rotate it in either left or right direction. If balance factor of unbalanced node is −2, then we use left rotation.

  Let's consider an unbalanced tree.

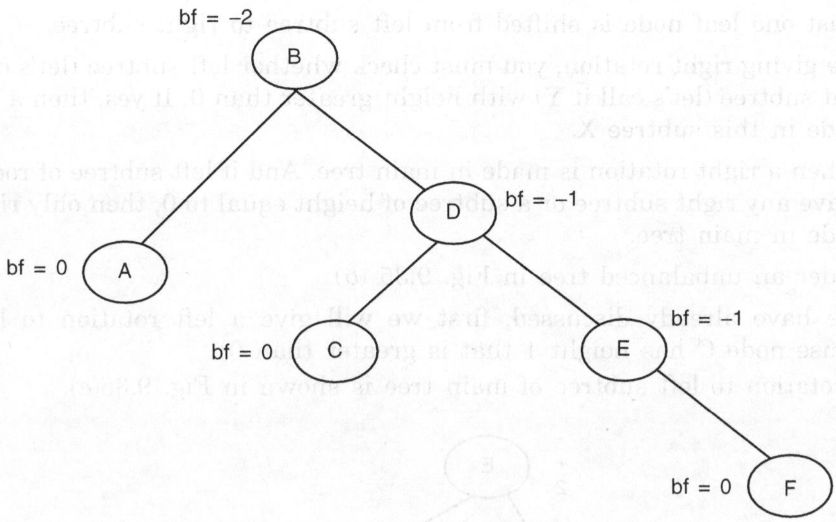

Fig 9.35 (c)

After left rotation:

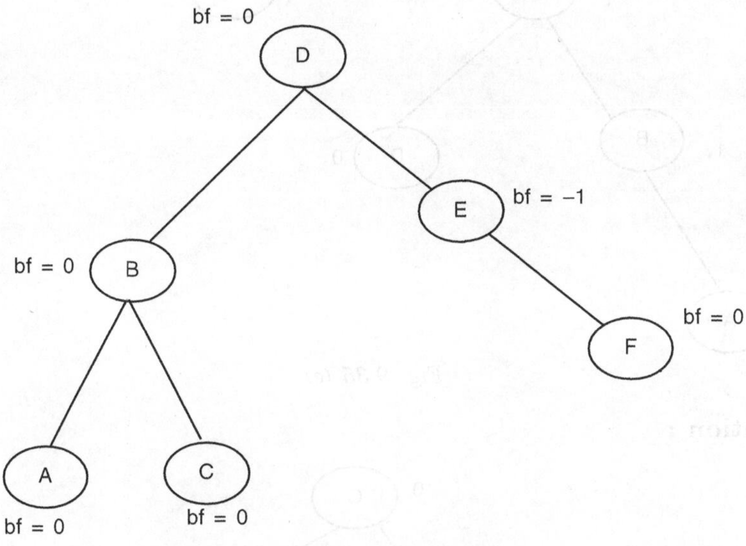

Fig. 9.35 (d)

You must note that if a tree needs left rotation for balancing, then at least one leaf node from right subtree is shifted to left subtree, as we have done with C in above figure.

If right subtree (let's call it X) of an unbalanced node has a left subtree (let's call it Y) and Y has height more than zero, then a right rotation is made in X and then left rotation is made in Y.

- *Right rotation*

  If the balance factor is +2, then tree needs right rotation.

At least one leaf node is shifted from left subtree to right subtree.

Before giving right rotation, you must check whether left subtree (let's call it X) has a right subtree (let's call it Y) with height greater than 0. If yes, then a left rotation is made in this subtree X.

And then a right rotation is made in main tree. And if left subtree of root node does not have any right subtree or a subtree of height equal to 0, then only right rotation is made in main tree.

Consider an unbalanced tree in Fig. 9.35 (*b*).

As we have already discussed, first we will give a left rotation to left subtree. (Because node C has height 1 that is greater than 0).

Left rotation to left subtree of main tree is shown in Fig. 9.35(*e*).

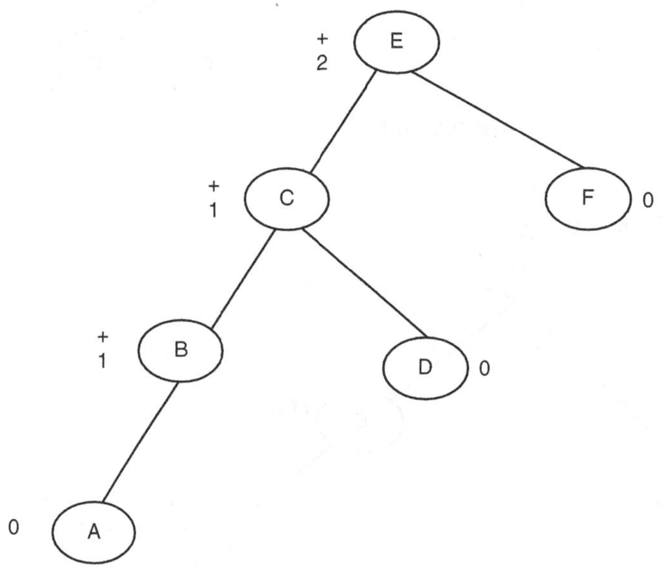

Fig. 9.35 (e)

Right rotation :

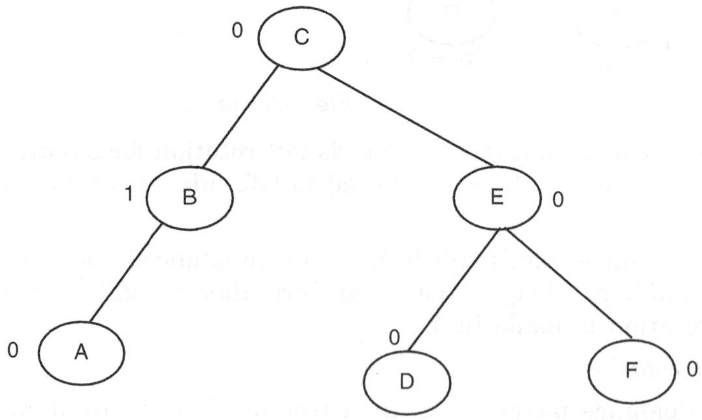

Fig. 9.35 (f)

Deletion of a node in a AVL tree. Follow similar steps as insertion of a node (left or right rotation). First of all, required node is searched and then it is deleted by the algorithm which is used in binary search tree to delete a node. And after deletion of a node if there is unbalanced node, then balancing is done.

9.10.2 Weight Balanced

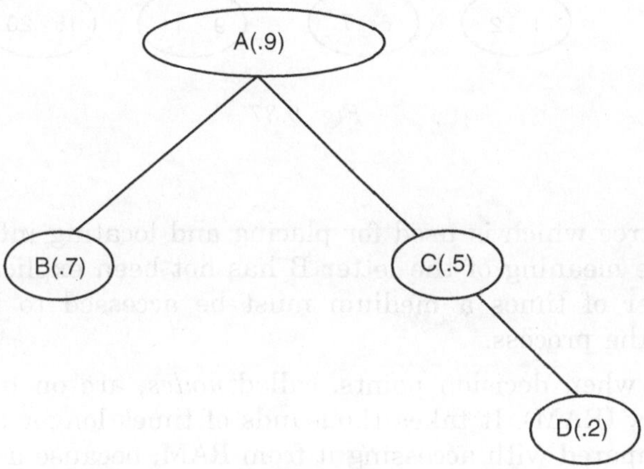

Fig. 9.36

The nodes of a weight balanced tree contain a data element, a left and a right pointer, and a probability or weight field. The data element and left and right pointers are essentially the same as any other node. The probability field is a special addition for a weight balanced tree. This field holds the probability of the node being accessed again. There are many different ways of coming up with this number. A good example of such a data structure is computing the probability according to the number of times the node has been previously searched for. When the tree is set up, the nodes with the highest probability of access are placed at the top. That way the nodes that are most likely to be accessed have the lowest search time. The tree is balanced if the weights in the right and left subtrees are as equal as possible. The average length of a search in a weighted tree is equal to the sum of :

probability * depth for every node in the tree

The tree is set up with the highest weighted node at the top of the tree or subtree. The left subtree contains nodes whose data values are less than the current node, and the right subtree contains nodes that have data values greater than the current data value.

9.11 M-WAY SEARCH TREES

Trees having m-1 keys and m children (maximum children of any key) are called m-way search trees. A binary tree is a 2-way tree. It means it has m-1=2-1=1 key in every node and it can have maximum of two children. A *binary tree* is also called a *m-way tree* of order 2. Similarly a m-way tree of order 3 is a tree in which key values could be either 1 or 2 inside every node and maximum number of children could be 3. Example of a m-way tree of order (degree) 4 is shown in Fig. 9.37.

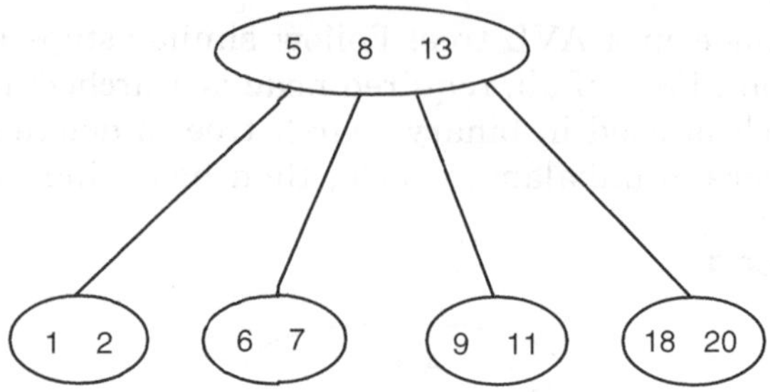

Fig. 9.37

9.11.1 B-tree

A B-tree is a m-way tree which is used for placing and locating information (called *records* or *keys*) in a file. (The meaning of the letter B has not been explicitly defined.) The B-tree minimizes the number of times a medium must be accessed to locate a desired record, thereby speeding up the process.

B-trees are preferred when decision points, called *nodes*, are on hard disk rather than in random-access memory (RAM). It takes thousands of times longer to access a data element from hard disk as compared with accessing it from RAM, because a disk drive has mechanical parts, which read and write data far more slowly than purely electronic media. B-trees save time by using nodes with many branches (called *children*), compared with binary trees, in which each node has only two children. But there are many children per node, a record can be found by passing through fewer nodes than if there are two children per node. A simplified example of this principle is shown below :

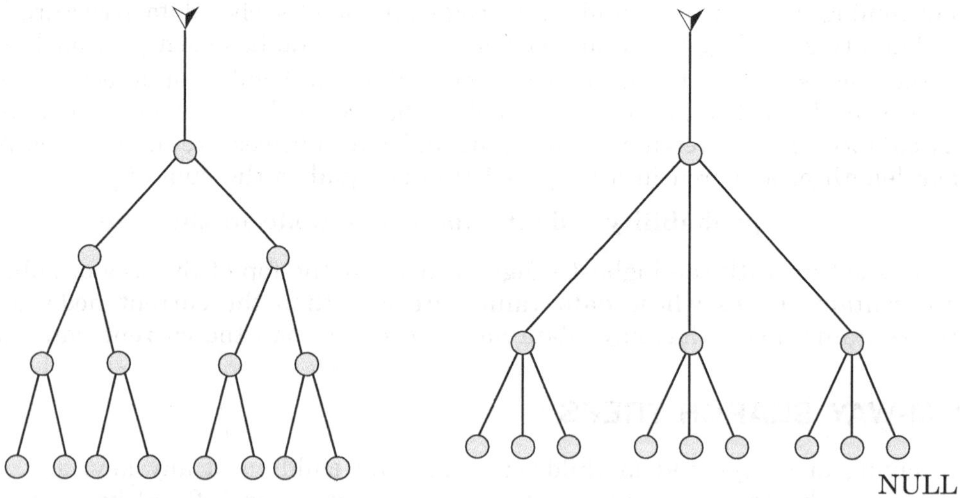

Fig. 9.38 (a) *Fig. 9.38 (b)*

In a tree, records are stored in locations called *leaves*. This name derives from the fact that records always exist at end points; there is nothing beyond them. The maximum number of children per node is called the *order* of the tree. The number of required disk accesses is called the *depth*. The image at left shows a binary tree for locating a particular record in a set of eight leaves. The image at right shows a B-tree of order three for locating a particular record in a set of eight leaves (the ninth leaf is unoccupied, and is called *a null*). The binary tree at left has a depth of four; the B-tree at right has a depth of three. Clearly, the B-tree allows a desired record to be located faster, assuming all other system parameters are identical. The tradeoff is that the decision process at each node is more complicated in a B-tree as compared with a binary tree. A sophisticated program is required to execute the operations in a B-tree. But this program is stored in RAM, so it runs fast.

In a practical B-tree, there can be thousands, millions, or billions of records. Not all leaves necessarily contain a record, but at least half of them do. The difference in depth between binary-tree and B-tree schemes is greater in a practical database than in the example illustrated here, because real-world B-trees are of higher order (32, 64, 128, or more). Depending on the number of records in the database, the depth of a B-tree can and often does change. Adding a large enough number of records will increase the depth; deleting a large enough number of records will decrease the depth. This ensures that the B-tree functions optimally for the number of records it contains.

B+ tree

It is a B-tree in which all leaves are linked to facilitate fast in order traversal.

9.11.2. 2-3 Tree

A 2-3 tree is a tree in which leaf nodes are the only nodes that contain values of stored data. All non-leaf nodes contain two values of the subtrees below, and two or three branches of other nodes. Also, all leaf nodes have the same path length from the root node. Look at Fig. 9.39 for a representation of a 2-3 tree.

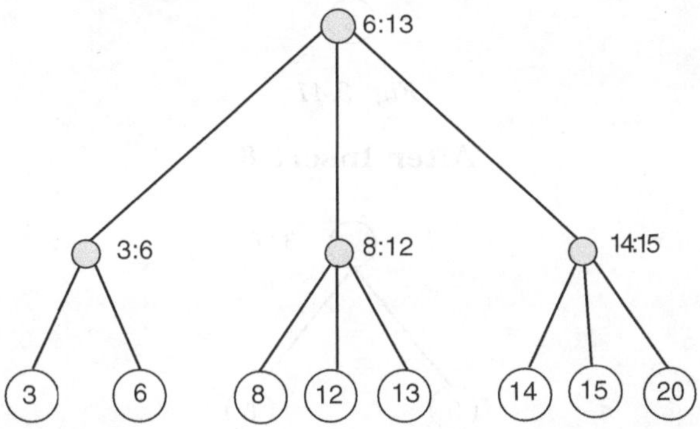

Fig. 9.39

Non-leaf nodes contain information that pertains to the path of a node. The first value in a non-leaf node is the maximum of all the leaf values in the left subtree. The second value contains the maximum value of the middle subtree. With this in mind, every leaf node in the left subtree of any non-leaf node is equal to or less than the first value. Every leaf node in the middle subtree is less than or equal to the second value and greater than the first value. And every leaf node in the right subtree is greater than the second value.

There are no complicated concepts involved, except when an insert is to take place. There are four cases which occur when inserting into a 2-3 tree. These cases are :

(i) The tree is empty

In this case the node to be inserted becomes the only node in the tree, and the root node points at this node.

Insert 3

Fig. 9.40

(ii) The tree contains just one node

In this case, a non-leaf node is created, with the left subtree pointing at the lesser of the two leaf nodes, and the middle subtree pointing at the greater of the two leaf nodes. Label the non-leaf node as <left node value> : <middle node value>.

> ***Note :*** *The next two cases deal with the tree when there are more than one nodes in the tree. In this case, we find the insertion point and then deal with one of these two cases.*

Before Insert 6

Fig. 9.41

After Insert 6

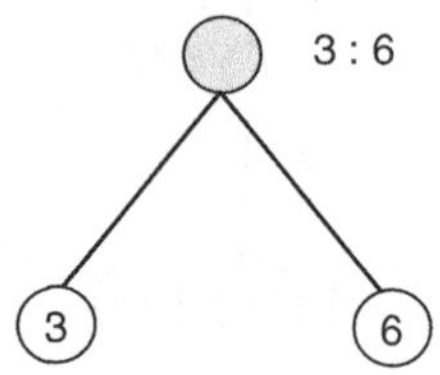

Fig. 9.42

(iii) The node to be inserted into tree having two children

Insert the new node below the parent and if

- It is less than the current leaf nodes in the tree, the new node then takes the left most position, and the other two nodes are moved over.
- The new node is less than only the middle second node, the new node takes the middle node's position, and moves the middle node left.
- The new node is greater than both the nodes, the node gets inserted into the right subtree.

The parent node then gets labelled as <greatest in left tree> : <greatest in right tree>.

Insert 2

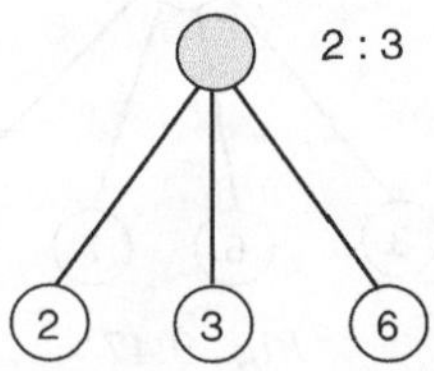

Fig. 9.43

Insert 8

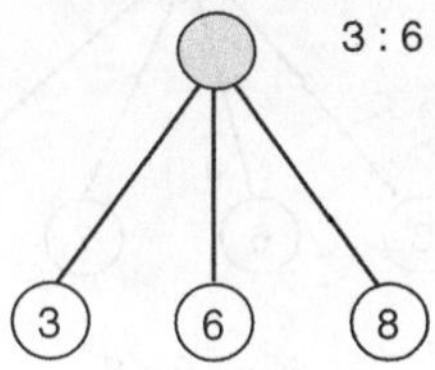

Fig. 9.44

Before Insert 7

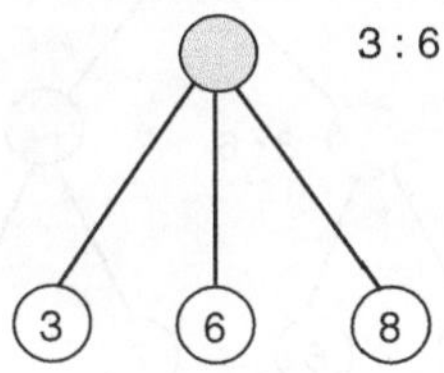

Fig. 9.45

(iv) The node to be inserted into having three children

If this is the case, then conceptually the new node becomes a fourth leaf in the tree and is inserted into the tree in order. However, there is only room for three nodes, so a new non-leaf node is created to the right of the parent. The two rightmost nodes of the four node subtree then become leaves of the new node. If this causes the node that has a new subtree to now have four subtrees, then the process is repeated.

Before Insert 7

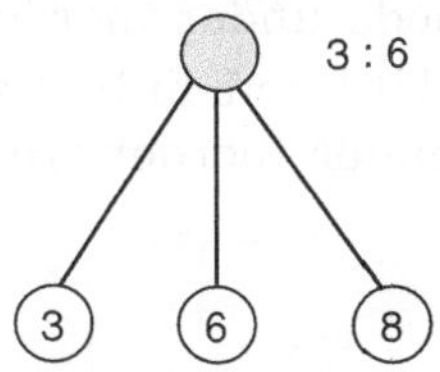

Fig. 9.46

Before Insert 7

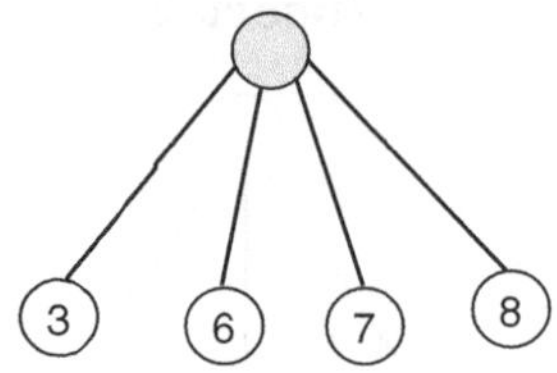

Fig. 9.47

Conceptual Step

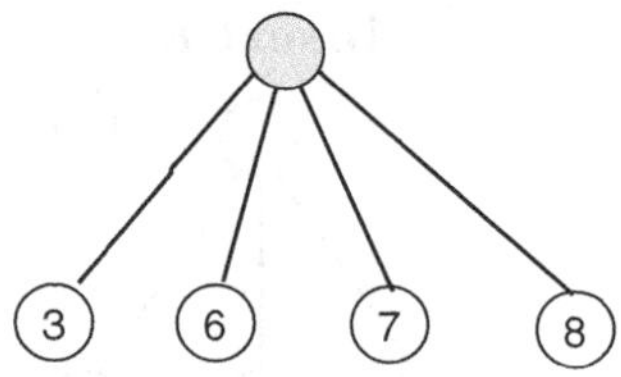

Fig. 9.48

After Inserting 7

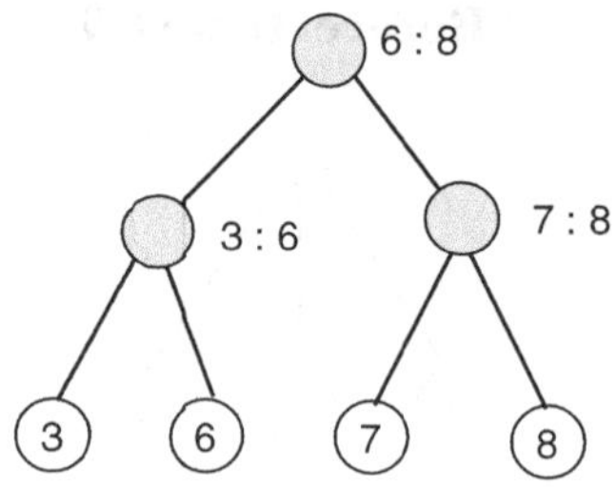

Fig. 9.49

9.12 THREADED BINARY TREES

The Binary tree algorithms, we have discussed so far use stack or recursion. So, it is worthwhile to write non-recursive algorithms to manipulate them. By changing the NULL links in a binary tree to special links called **threads**, it is possible to perform traversals, insertions, and deletions without using either a stack or recursion.

Right-threaded binary tree : Each NULL right link of a binary tree is replaced by a special link to the successor of that node under inorder traversal, called a *right thread.*

Left-threaded binary tree : Each NULL left link of a binary tree is replaced by a special link to the predecessor of that node under inorder traversal, called a *right thread.*

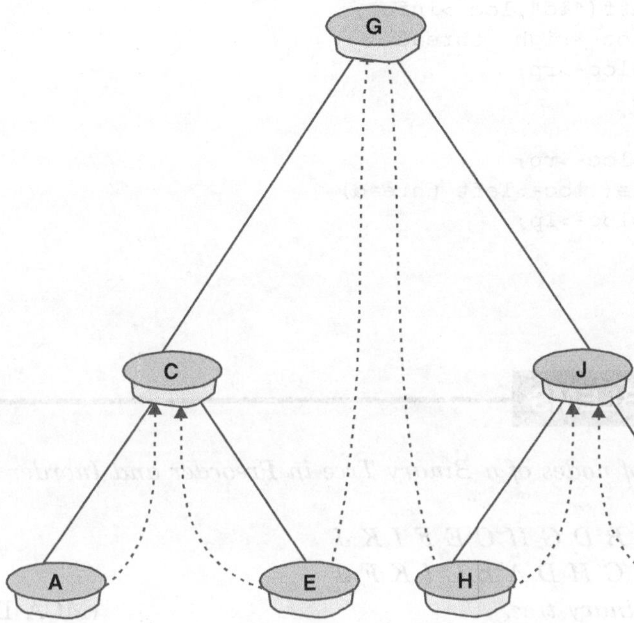

Fig. 9.50. A threaded binary tree.

The inorder traversal for above tree is :

A, C, E, F, H, J, K

First node A has no inorder predecessor so we leave left pointer as NULL and right pointer will be set to point to node C which is inorder successor of A.

Similarly threads of E, and H nodes are set to their in order predecessor and inorder successor respectively. Right thread of K remains NULL because there is no inorder successor of node K.

Declaration of TBT :

```
typedef  struct  TBT
{
int  left_thread,right_thread;
int  info;
struct  TBT*lp,*rp;
}tree;
```

LISTING 9.2

```
void  inorderTBT(tree *t)
{
tree *loc;
loc=t;
   while(!loc->left_thread)
loc=loc->lp;
   while(loc!=NULL)
   {
```

```
            printf("%d",loc->info);
            if(loc->right_thread)
            loc=loc->rp;
            else
            {
            loc=loc->rp;
            while(!loc->left_thread)
            loc=loc->lp;
            }
        }
    }
```

CONCEPTUAL PROBLEMS

Problem 9.1 : *The order of nodes of a Binary Tree in Preorder and Inorder traversal are as under :*

Preorder: *A B D G H C E F I K J*

Inorder: *B G H D A E C I K F J*

Draw the corresponding Binary tree. (MCA December, 2001)

Solution : Root node in Pre Order traversal = A

STEP 1

Pre Order :	*A*	*B D G H*	*C E F I K J*
	ROOT	Left Subtree	Right Subtree
In Order:	*B G H D*	*A*	*E C I K F J*
	LST	ROOT	RST

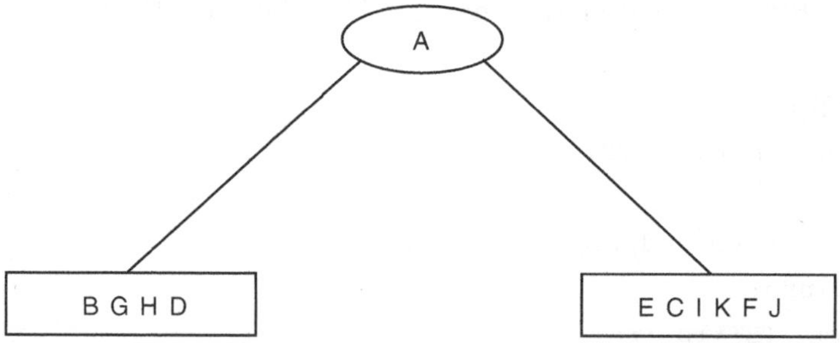

Fig. 9.51(a)

STEP 2

FOR LST

Pre Order : B D G H

In Order : B G H D

ROOT=B

Pre Order :	*B*	*D G H*
	ROOT	*RST*
In Order :	B	G H D
	ROOT	RST

FOR RST

Pre Order : C E F I K J
In Order : E C I K F J
ROOT=C

Pre Order :	*C*	*E*	*F I K J*
	ROOT	LST	RST
In Order :	*E*	*C*	I K F J
	LST	*ROOT*	*RST*

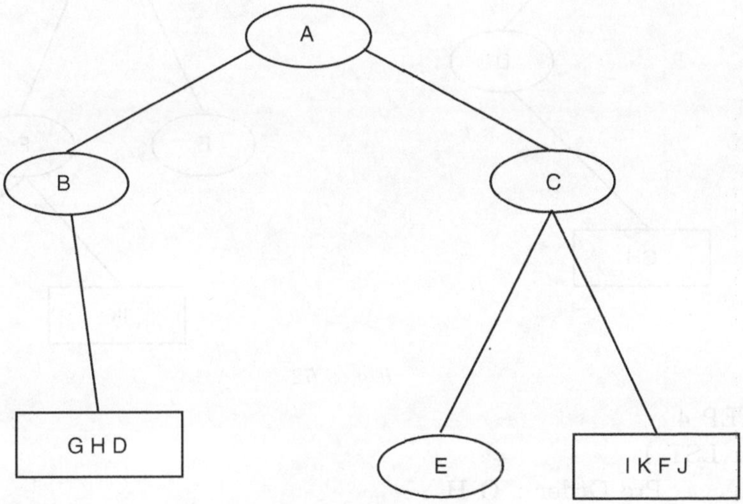

Fig. 9.51(b)

STEP 3

FOR LST

Pre Order : D G H
In Order : G H D
ROOT=D

Pre Order :	*D*	*G H*
	ROOT	LST
In Order :	*G H*	*D*
	LST	*ROOT*

FOR RST :

Pre Order : F I K J
In Order : I K F J
ROOT=F

Pre Order :	*F*	*IK*	*J*
	ROOT	*LST*	*RST*
In Order :	*IK*	*F*	*J*
	LST	*ROOT*	*RST*

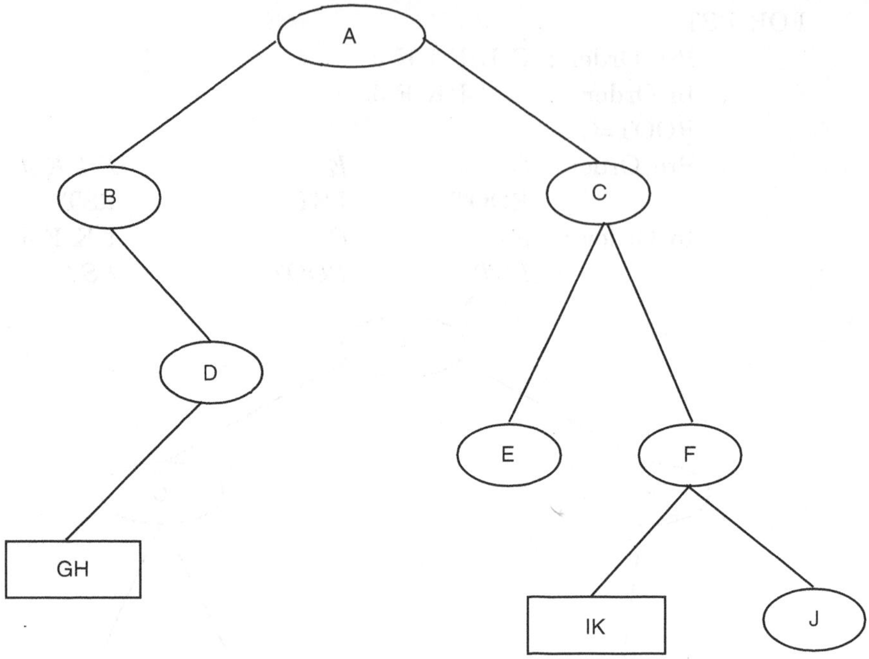

Fig. 9.52

STEP 4

For LST 1

Pre Order :	G H	
In Order :	G H	
ROOT=G		
Pre Order :	*G*	*H*
	ROOT	*RST*
In Order :	*G*	*H*
	ROOT	*RST*

For LST 2

Pre Order :	I K	
In Order :	I K	
ROOT=I		
Pre Order :	*I*	*K*
	ROOT	*RST*
In Order :	*I*	*K*
	ROOT	*RST*

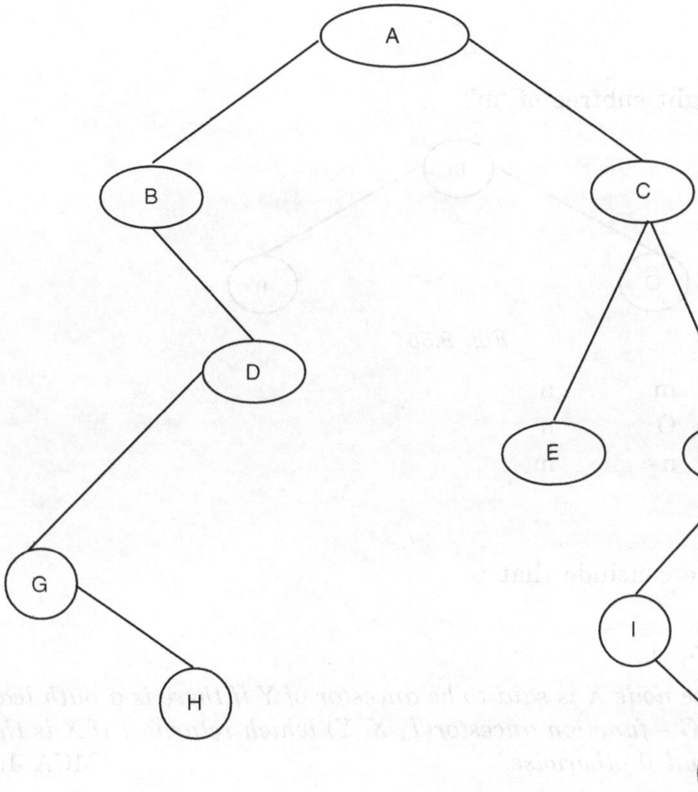

Fig. 9.53

Problem 9.2 : *We can test whether a node 'm' is a proper ancestor of a node 'n' by testing whether 'm' proceeds 'n' in X-order but follows 'n' in Y-order, where X and Y are chosen from {pre,post,in}.*
Determine all those pairs X and Y for which this statement holds.

(MCA December, 2001)

Solution : There are two cases when 'm' is a proper ancestor of a node 'n' in a binary tree.
Case 1 : 'n' is placed in left subtree of 'm'.
For example,

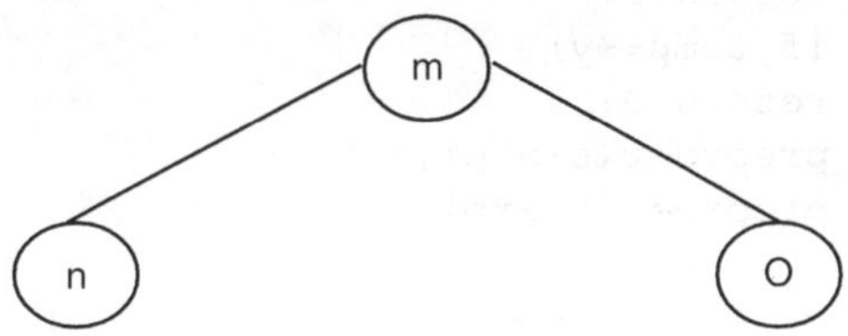

Fig. 9.54

In this case three different traversals are as follows :

In Order :	n	m	O
Pre Order :	m	n	O
Post Order :	n	O	m

Therefore X=pre order
Y={post,in}

Case 2 : 'n' is placed in right subtree of 'm'.

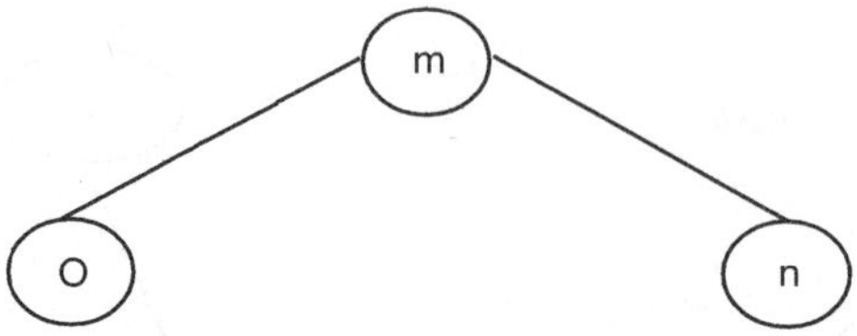

Fig. 9.55

In Order :	O	m	n
Pre Order :	m	O	n
Post Order :	O	n	m

Therefore X={in,pre}
Y=post

From case 1 and case 2, we conclude that :
X=In-Order OR Pre-Order.
Y=In-Order OR Post-Order.

Problem 9.3 : *In binary tree node X is said to be ancestor of Y if there is a path leading from Y upwards to X. Develop a C – function ancestor(T, X, Y) which returns 1 if X is the ancestor of Y in the binary tree T and 0 otherwise.* (MCA June, 1998)

Solution : We will use Pre-Order traversal to test given condition. As shown in the solution of Question 23 that Pre Order traversal reads ancestor before descendent. Listing for ancestor(T, X, Y) is as follows :

LISTING 9.3

```
int ancestor (tree *t,int x,int y)
{
    int temp;
    if(t!=(tree *)NULL)
        {
            temp=t->info;
            if(temp==x)
            return 1;
            if(temp==y)
            return 0;
            preorder(t->lp);
            preorder(t->rp);
        }
    }
```

Problem 9.4 : *Assume a linked representation for a Binary tree. Each node in the list is having two fields. One represents the data and the other represents the link to the next node. Now, write an algorithm to list the data fields of the nodes of the Binary tree by level. Within levels, nodes are to be listed left to right.* (MCA December, 2001)

Solution :

```
START
        void leveltraversal(tree *t)
STEP 1
        Declare *q of Queue type.
        Declare *loc of tree type.
STEP 2
        Create_empty_Queue(&q)
STEP 3
        enqueue(&q, t)
STEP 4  LOOP while Queue is not empty.
STEP 4.1
        loc=dequeue(&q)
STEP 4.2
        if(loc->left!=NULL)
        then
        enqueue(&q,loc->left)
        end if
STEP 4.3
        if(loc->right!=NULL)
        then
        enqueue(&q,loc->right)
        end if
STEP 4.4
        Print 1(oc->info)
        end loop.
STOP
```

Problem 9.5 : *Prove by induction that if T is a Binary tree with 'n' internal nodes, I its internal path length and E its external path length, then E=I + 2n, n>=0.*

(MCA December, 2001)

Note. *This problem holds incorrect statement. Correct form of above problem should be as follows :*

Problem : *Prove by induction that if T is a strictly binary tree with 'n' internal nodes, I its internal path and E its external path length, then E=I + 2n, n>=0.*

Solution :

Internal path length=sum of all paths of internal nodes.
External path length=sum of all paths of external nodes.
Strictly binary tree:-A binary tree in which each node either has 0 or 2 children.
We can prove E=I+2n by following steps :
STEP 1
n=1
In this case root node will have either zero or two children.

Case 1 : When root node has no child node, then

n=0

I=0

E=I+2n

=0+2*0

=0

which is true.

Case 2 : When root node has two children, then

n=1

I=0

E=I+2n

E=2

which is true.

STEP 2

Let this statement be true for n internal nodes, then we have to prove it for n+1

internal nodes as follows :

E=1+2n

for n=n+1

E=I+2(n+1)

=I+2n+2

=(I+2)+2n

which is true. Hence by the Induction, E=I+2N is true for n>=0.

Problem 9.6 : *Write an algorithm for preorder traversal of a Binary tree.*

(PGDCA June, 1996)

Solution : *Refer Algorithm 9.5.1 of Chapter 9.*

Problem 9.7 : *What are the maximum number of nodes in a Binary tree of height h?*

(BCA June, 1999)

Solution : A binary tree of height h has at least h and at most 2h–1 nodes.

Problem 9.8 : *Write short note on the following :*

AVL Trees and Balancing Techniques. (MCA June, 2001)

Solution : *Refer Section 9.10.1.*

Problem 9.9 : *Convert the following tree to binary tree.* (MCA, Dec. 2002)

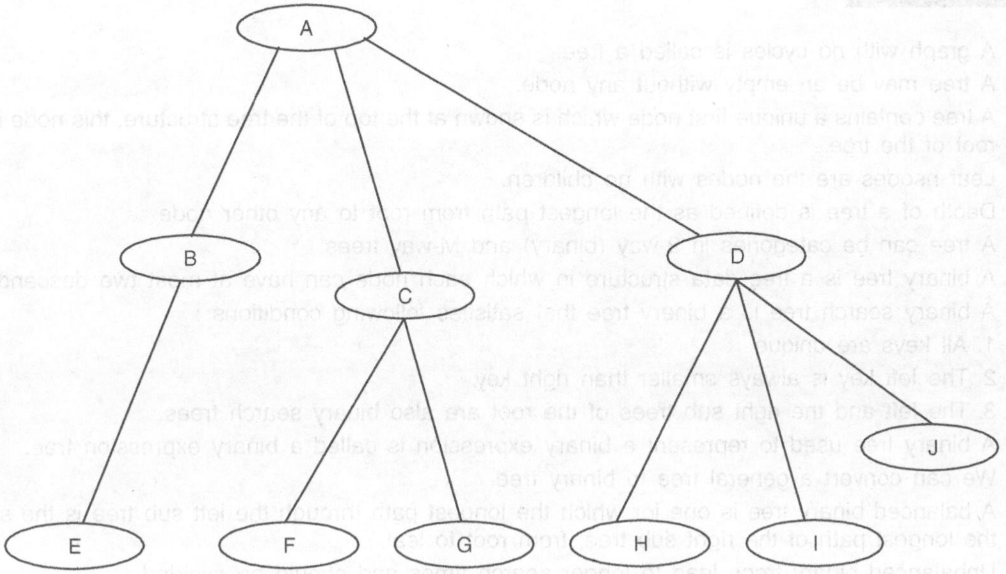

Fig. 9.56

Solution :

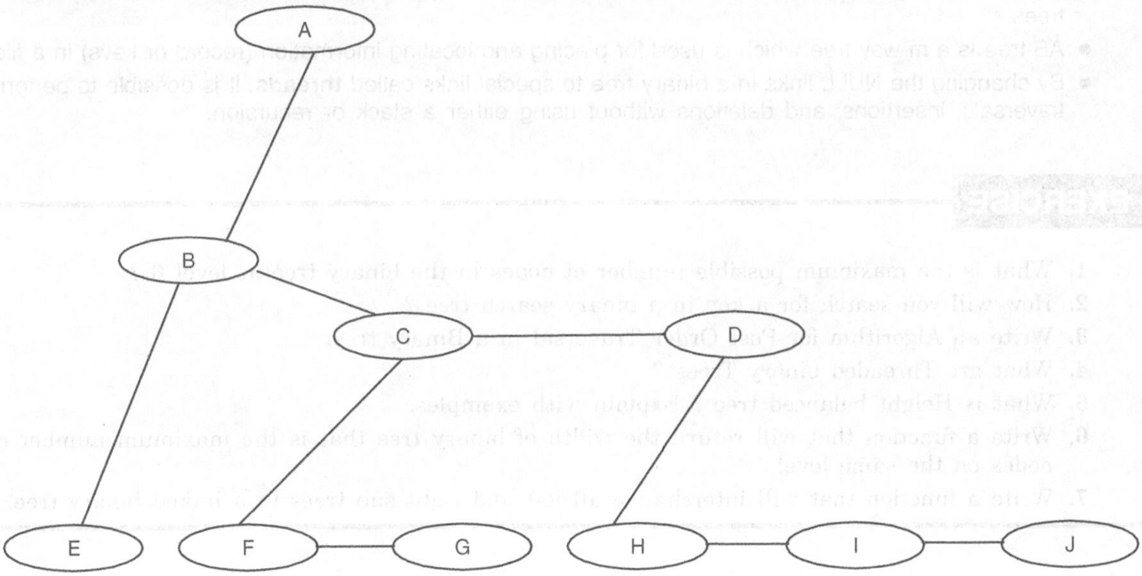

Fig. 9.57

KEY POINTS

- A graph with no cycles is called a tree.
- A tree may be an empty without any node.
- A tree contains a unique first node which is shown at the top of the tree structure, this node is called root of the tree.
- Leaf nsodes are the nodes with no children.
- Depth of a tree is defined as the longest path from root to any other node.
- A tree can be categories in 2-way (binary) and M-way trees.
- A binary tree is a tree data structure in which each node can have at most two descendents.
- A binary search tree is a binary tree that satisfies following conditions :
  1. All keys are unique.
  2. The left key is always smaller than right key.
  3. The left and the right sub trees of the root are also binary search trees.
- A binary tree used to represent a binary expression is called a binary expression tree.
- We can convert a general tree to binary tree.
- A balanced binary tree is one for which the longest path through the left sub tree is the same as the longest path of the right sub tree, from root to leaf.
- Unbalanced binary trees lead to longer search times and should be avoided.
- If the balance factor of every node of a tree is in the set {–1, 0+1}, then such a tree is called AVL tree.
- The tree having m–1 keys and m (maximum children of any key) children are called m-way search trees.
- AB-tree is a m-way tree which is used for placing and locating information (record or keys) in a file.
- By changing the NULL links in a binary tree to special links called **threads,** it is possible to perform traversals, insertions, and deletions without using either a stack or recursion.

EXERCISE

1. What is the maximum possible number of nodes in the binary tree at level 6 ?
2. How will you search for a key in a binary search tree ?
3. Write an Algorithm for Post Order Traversal in a Binary tree.
4. What are Threaded binary Trees ?
5. What is Height balanced tree ? Explain with examples.
6. Write a function that will return the width of binary tree that is the maximum number of nodes on the same level.
7. Write a function that will interchange all left and right sub trees in a linked binary tree.

10

FILE SYSTEM

10.1 INTRODUCTION

Files are the sequence of bytes. File may also be defined as named collection of records. File structure deals with writing algorithms to organize files in a required manner. We will not discuss the entire file structure in detail but discuss general types of files.

KEY TERMS

File organization. A technique for physically arranging the records of a file on secondary storage devices.

Sequential file organization. Records in the file are stored in sequence according to a primary key value.

Indexed file organization. Records are either stored sequentially or non-sequentially and an index is created that allows software to locate individual records.

Hashing file organization. The address for each record is determined using a hashing algorithm.

Denormalization. The process of transforming normalized relations into unnormalized physical record specifications. The transformation is done to improve the efficiency of access for certain transactions.

Index. A table or other data structure used to determine the location of rows in a file that satisfies some condition.

Secondary key. One or a combination of fields for which more than one record may have the same combination of values.

Data type. Each unit of a detailed coding scheme recognized by system software, such as a DBMS, for representing organizational data.

Bitmap index. A table of bits in which each row represents the distinct values of a key and each column is a bit, which when on indicates that the record for that bit column position has the associated field value.

Redundant Arrays of Inexpensive Disks (RAID). A set, or array, of physical disk drives that appears to the database user (and programs) as if they form one large logical storage unit.

Horizontal partitioning (Vertical partitioning). Horizontal partitioning is very similar to creating a supertype/subtype relationship because different types of the entity (where the subtype discriminator is the field used for segregating rows) are involved in different relationships, hence different processing. Neither horizontal nor vertical partitioning prohibits the ability to treat the original relation as a whole.

Indexed sequential; indexed nonsequential. An indexed sequential index structure is a nice compromise between a purely sequential file organization and an indexed nonsequential file organization, in which each data record may be stored anywhere on disk. Indexed sequential in comparison to indexed nonsequential allows more efficient use of space and faster sequential data processing without much of any sacrifice in random data record accessing speed.

Physical record; physical file. A physical file is a named portion of secondary memory (a magnetic tape or hard disk) allocated for the purpose of storing physical records. Physical records of several types can be clustered together into one physical file in order to place records frequently used together close to one another in secondary memory.

Page; physical record. Often a page will store multiple physical records. Depending on the computer system, a lengthy physical record may or may not be allowed to span two pages.

Secondary key; primary key. A secondary key is one or a combination of fields for which more than one record may have the same combination of values, while the primary key is one or a combination of fields for which every record has a unique value. Hence the primary key is a unique identifier for a row.

10.2 FILE ORGANIZATIONS

File organization deals with organizing data in physical media such that data can be accessed efficiently by end user. Time/space tradeoff factor plays an important role while organizing a file. There may be some systems where very fast response is expected and memory space does not matter; similarly there may be a system which seeks for efficient use of memory and secures data storage. So to deal with different needs of real life projects, there are different file organizations. Some factors involved in selecting a particular file organization for use are :

* Security
* Integrity
* Reliability
* Economy of storage
* Convenience of updates
* Retrieval time.

We can select a right file organisation according to our needs.
Following are various commonly used file organizations :

10.2.1. Sequential Files

Records are stored in some specific sequence *e.g.* order of arrival value of key field etc. Records of a sequential file cannot be accessed at random. To access the nth record, one must traverse the preceding (n-1)records. A sequentially organized file may be stored on either a serial—access or a direct-access storage medium. There must be a primary key which uniquely identifies a record. If there is no primary key, then a combination of two keys can be used to uniquely identify a record.
There are two algorithms which are applied on sequential files.

(*i*) Serial processing.
(*ii*) Sequential processing.

Serial processing is the accessing of records serially one after the other. Let us consider an example of university students database system. Now you have to search a record for a student named Raj Kumar. If processing is done serially, then all the records above the required record are read.

Sequential processing is the accessing of records, one after the other, in ascending order by a key of the record. In our example, key would be roll number. In most of cases, the records of a sequential file are arranged according to the value of some field in each record. Such a file is said to be a **sorted** file and the field which is used to determine the ordering is said to be the **sort key**. If we want to search a record by student name instead of roll number, then sequential processing becomes equivalent to serial processing.

If a query is made for a record of roll no. 200, then file pointer comes at the required record after reading all previous records. Now again a query is made for roll number 220. Then if file is sorted by roll no., file pointer will read only 19 records, before reading required record. But if serial processing is done, then every time file pointer will read all previous records before reading the required record.

The performance of a sequential file is determined by three major factors :

***(i)* Blocking factor**

The block size may be as large as possible. Further, it depends on main memory buffer space availability.

***(ii)* File length**

Sequential organization is the best choice for small volume of data. Sequential organization is not good for large number of records.

***(iii)* Key selection**

Key selection is an important factor for sequential files.In most of cases, a sort key is the primary key of the database. But if no primary key is available, then a combination of two keys is used.

Disadvantages of Sequential File Organization

- Records cannot be accessed randomly.
- All records must be homogeneous. If a new field is added, then every record must be rewritten to provide space for the new field.
- Continuous memory space is required to store records inside memory.
- Updates are not easily accommodated.

10.2.2 Relative Files

Records can be accessed directly. A transformation is made from the key of a record to the address of the storage location of that record. Records of a relative file do not necessarily appear physically in sorted order by their key values. Also, it is not necessary to access the records of a relative file in serial order. Relative files are processed directly (in most of cases). When a relative file is created, a transformation function is used to translate key value to physical address :

```
T(key value)=address.
```

Here T is a transformation function.

When a record is to be retrieved with a particular key value, then that key value is transformed into an address using function T. Hence, the record is found at pointed address. The records of the relative files can be updated in place without any need to recreate the entire file as in sequential file. There are many techniques to translate a key value to physical address.

- Direct transformation(mapping).
- Directory lookup
- Hashing

10.2.2.1 Direct Mapping

It is the fastest addressing technique. There are two types of direct mappings :

1. Absolute addressing. As we know that memory is divided in data blocks and one block is equal to one byte (usually). If a record requires four bytes to store, then it will be stored in four memory blocks. In such a case, we can logically divide memory in four byte, long blocks. Every record will have a unique address. We can store a record as a node (user defined) data type. Now, there will be a mapping of a key inside a record to its physical address. Let there be a program which keeps records of air passengers of an Airlines. Then ticket number could be mapped to physical address as follows :

```
T(key)=address.
=>T(ticket_no)=1001
=>ticket_no=1001
```

You must note that no index on this key is needed.

The key value is same as physical address.In this technique, searching will be fastest as compared to all other techniques. Disadvantage of this technique is that, if the storage device holding the file is changed, then address of records would be changed by file system. Hence, mapping will fail. So this technique is preferred if records are stored for a small period of time.

2. Relative addressing. This technique removes some of the disadvantages of absolute addressing, while retaining the advantages of the direct addressing. Transformation(mapping) function for relative addressing is as follows :

T(key)=Relative address(numeric position of record in the file). A relative address can then be translated to an absolute address.

10.2.2.2 Directory Lookup

It keeps a table or directory of key value and addresses.The table is searched for the key value and the address is used to access the record itself. The entries in the table may be sorted by key value so that efficient search is made. We may note that though the table is sorted, the relative file need not be in sorted order. Let's consider an example for storing records of the best students awarded in a university.

Physical Address	Roll_no	name	age
6000	1001	Ram	22
6010	1010	Raj	20
6020	1003	Rakesh	19
80008	22002	Sanjay	25

Fig. 10.1 Records of students inside a file

Key(roll_no)	Address
1001	6000
1003	6020
1010	6010
22002	80008

Fig. 10.2

Certainly, records of the toppers of a university would be present in different files.There may be a file containing all records of MCA students, and another file containing records of BCA students. Similary there may be another file containing records of M.tech students.Then if we required to store records of toppers from different courses then it is better to use a directory look up technique. In this way, we need not create a new file and we can just give references of records in different files from our directory lookup table. Hence, we can save the hard disc space and get a fast response.

Disadvantages

If a relative file is large, the directory may also be large. So lot of additional space is required to hold the directory.

10.2.2.3 Hashing

Hashing is discussed in Chapter 11. But we are giving a brief description of hashing. A hash function normally generates the same address for two or more unequal keys. Such a situation is called *collision*. A **bucket** may contain many records that have been mapped to the same address. If there are more colliding records for a given bucket than the bucket capacity, an overflow occurs. The overflow records can be handled using overflow handling techniques which are similar to collision resolution techniques used for handling hash tables. You should go through Chapter 8 for getting more about hashing.

10.2.3 Indexed Sequential Files

Indexed sequential files are the hybrid of sequential files and relative files. This means indexed sequential file organization organizes collection of records in such a way that it is possible to access the records sequentially by some key value and also to access the records individually by the same key.

Let us consider an example of search process for a word in language dictionary.The data in the dictionary is stored in a sequential manner. However, an index is provided in terms of thumb tabs. To search for a word, we do not search sequentially. We first access the index that is the appropriate thumb tab, locate an approximation location for word and then process to find the word sequentially.

An indexed sequential file has two parts : the index part and sequential data part. Index would be built as a tree of key values where each node contains a pointer to a sequential data file. Following figure shows an indexed sequential file whose index has been structured as a binary search tree. Here, the index is used to access every record of the file.

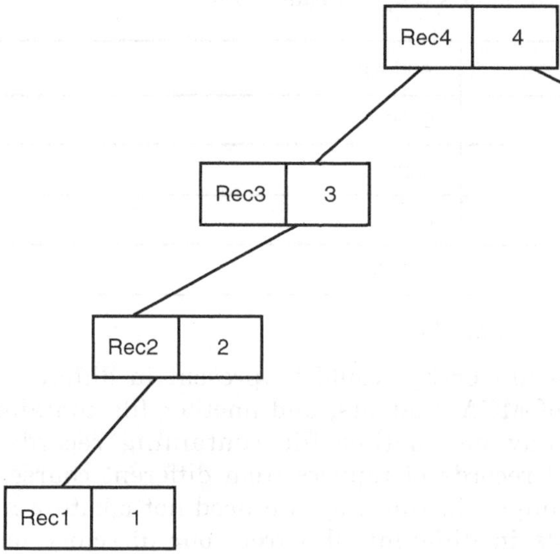

Fig. 10.3 Binary search tree as an index for a sequential file.

1	Rec1
2	Rec2
3	Rec3
4	Rec4
5	Rec5

Fig. 10.4 Sequential file

A B-tree may be used to build the index. And B-tree data structure is far better than Binary tree structure. We have already discussed B tree in Chapter 9. When the new records are inserted in the data file, the sequence of records need to be preserved and also the index is accordingly updated. Two approaches used to implement indexes are static indexes and dynamic indexes.

When changes are made in main data file, the static index contents may change but the structure does not change. In dynamic indexing approach, insertions and deletions in the main data file may lead to change in the index structure.

CONCEPTUAL PROBLEM

Problem 10.1 : *What are the different file organisations ? Explain them.*

(MCA December, 2001)

Solution : *Refer Section 10.2.*

KEY POINTS

- A technique for physically arranging the records of a file on secondary storage devices is called the **File Organization.**
- In sequential file organization, records are stored in sequence according to primary key value.
- An index is created that allows to locate individual records in indexed file organization.
- Denormalization is a process of transforming normalized relatoins into unnormalized physical records specifications.
- Primary key is one or a combination of fields for which every record has a unique value.
- In relative files, a transformation is made from a key record to the address of the storage location of that record.
- Records of a relative file do not necessarily appear physically in sorted order by their key values.
- Indexed files are considered as the hybrid of sequential files and relative files.

EXERCISE

1. What is file structure and how is it an important factor in programming ?
2. Can you create your own RDBMS like oracle or FoxPro in C language ? If yes, then explain in brief. What points will you consider to work on this project?
3. Write advantages and disadvantages of using sequential file organization.
4. Differentiate between Absolute addressing and Relative addressing.
5. Write down five differences between Sequential files and Relative files.
6. Why B+ trees are better to store records in indexed Sequential files ?

11

SORTING AND SEARCHING & HASHING AND COLLISION

SORTING AND SEARCHING

11.1 INTRODUCTION

Sorting is one of the most common tasks performed by computers today. It has been estimated that as much as one quarter of the running time of all the world's computers is spent on performing various types of sorting. Sorting is used to arrange names and numbers in meaningful ways. For example, it is relatively easy to look up the phone number of a friend because the names in the phone book have been sorted into alphabetical order. This example clearly illustrates that one of the main reasons for sorting large quantities of information is desirable. That is, sorting greatly improves the efficiency of **searching**. If we were to open a phone book and find that the names were not presented in any logical order, it would take an incredibly long time to look up someone's phone number!

Sorting can be performed in many ways. Over time, several methods have been devised to sort information, following specific algorithms. Some examples of these algorithms are the the Bubble Sort, Selection Sort, Quick Sort, the Merge Sort, the Heap Sort, the Binary Sort, and the Radix Sort. We will be exploring the Bubble Sort, the Selection Sort and the Quick Sort in depth in this chapter.

Some obvious questions that arise from the above discussion are: "Which sort method should I use? Is one sort algorithm clearly the best?" The answer to the second question is quite simple. There is no sort algorithm that is clearly better than all others in all circumstances. The answer to the first question, however, is difficult. The particular situations faced by people who need to sort information will invariably dictate what type of sort algorithm should be used. Some factors that will play an important part in the decision-making process are the complexity of the algorithm, the size of the data structure (an array, for example) to be sorted, and the time it takes for programmers to understand and implement various algorithms. For example, a small business that manages a list of customer names could easily use an algorithm such as the Bubble Sort. This algorithm is easy to understand and implement. Because of the fact that the data set to be sorted is relatively small, a simple algorithm such as the bubble sort will perform satisfactorily. However, a large corporation with millions of customers would experience horrible delays, while trying to sort their records with a bubble sort algorithm. They would be well advised to spend the extra time learning a more efficient algorithm, like the Quick Sort, to sort their data more efficiently. In actual practice, even the quick Sort may not be perfectly suited for this example.

Searching algorithms are used to read a perticular record from a collection of records. Different searching algorithms can be written for sorted or unsorted records. We will discuss Binary search, Linear search and Iterative deepening search in detail.

11.1.1 Bubble Sort

One form of sorting is the Bubble sort. Bubble sort works by repeatedly moving the largest element to the highest index position of the array. Rather than search the entire array to find the largest element, Bubble Sort focuses on successive adjacent pairs of elements in the array.

array[0]	array[1]			
8	5	7	3	9

Fig. 11.1

array[0] is greater than array[1] so switch the two elements.

5	8	7	3	9

Fig. 11.2

A General Algorithm to Bubble Sort

The Bubble Sort algorithm has many variations. However, the algorithm given here is the basis for all of them.

Procedure BubbleSort(item[1..n])

```
for j:=n downto 1 do {Each time through loop size reduced}
        for k:=1 to (j-1) {inner loop one less in length}
            if item[k] > item[k+1]
            then swap(item[k], item[k+1]);
                 {k:=k+1}
            {end for k}
        {j:=j-1}
 {end for j}
```

We will now examine how this algorithm works.

Main Loop

- ✻ compares two adjacent elements at index "k" and "k + 1"
- ✻ if the element at index "k" is greater than the element "k + 1", then swap the positions of the two values
- ✻ one iteration moves largest value to last position of array
- ✻ repeat loop

End Main Loop

A Bubble Sort algorithm can also be described step by step as follows :

1. Repeat Step 4 a total of n –1 times.
2. Repeat Step 3 for elements in the unsorted part of the array.
3. If the current element in the array is greater than the next element in the array, then exchange the elements.
4. If no changes were made, then return; otherwise, reduce the size of the unsorted array by one.

It compares the two elements, and then either swaps them (if the element with the smaller index number is larger than the other element) or leaves them alone (if the element with the smaller index is smaller than the other element). In either case, after such a step, the larger of the two elements will be in the higher index position.

The focus then moves to the next highest position, and the process is repeated. When the focus reaches the end of the array, the largest element will have "bubbled" from whatever its original position was, to the last or highest index position in the array. The procedure is then repeated, causing the next largest element to bubble up to the *highest index position -1*. This is repeated until all elements in the array have been sorted.

11.1.1.1 Bubble Sort Efficiency

Bubble Sort is comprised of two loops. The number of times the outer loop iterates (is repeated) is determined by the nature of the list which it is asked to sort. The inner loop is iterated one fewer times than there are elements in the list being sorted and is reentered (from the beginning) upon every iteration of the outer loop. Thus, the order of the inner loop is n-1 or O(n-1).

Best Case Situation

In this case, the list is already sorted when the Bubble Sort algorithm is called. The inner loop will iterate without the if condition evaluating true. The outer loop will terminate after one iteration. Thus in the best case situation the inner loop will iterate a total of n-1 times, the if statement never evaluates true, the swap procedure is never called and the number of swaps is 0.

Worst Case Situation

In this case, the analysis becomes a little more difficult. The worst case for the Bubble Sort algorithm occurs with an inverted list (9 8 7 ... 1). The largest element begins at the start of the list and thus has to move to the end in order for the list to be sorted. On the first iteration of the outer loop it will be swapped with the second element, on the second iteration of the loop it will be swapped with the third element. Continuing this argument, this element will move one position towards the end of the list on every iteration of the outer loop. For it to move from the start of the list to the end of the list, it will have to be swapped n-1 times.

Every other element in the list will also move one location towards the start or end of the loop on every iteration. As the elements at the start or end of the list have the farthest distance to move, all other elements will be in their correct place when the element which was at the end of the loop has moved to the start of the loop. One further iteration will be required to determine that the list is now sorted. Thus, the total number of iterations of the outer loop to sort an inverted list is n and the total number of iterations of the inner loop is n(n-1), which is approximately equal to n^2 or $O(n^2)$.

11.1.1.2 Advantages and Disadvantages of Bubble Sort

One of the primary advantages of the bubble sort is that it is fairly easy to write (about 5 lines of code). It is also fairly easy to understand in terms of a sorting algorithm.

Unfortunately, the bubble sort is also a relatively slow algorithm, taking $O(n^2)$ to complete sorting and therefore, it should not be used on large tables.

Let us discuss an example for bubble sort.

As an example, begin with the following array.

7	4	1	9	2

Fig. 11.3

The bubble sort focuses on the first two elements in the array (7 and 4) which are compared and swapped, if necessary. In this case, since the element at index 0 is larger than the one at index 1, the values are swapped.

4	7	1	9	2

Fig. 11.4

Then the focus moves to the elements at index 1 and 2 which are compared and swapped, if necessary. In our example, 7 is larger than 1, so the two elements are swapped. The result is that the largest of the first three elements is now at index 2.

4	1	7	9	2

Fig. 11.5

The process is repeated until the focus moves to the end of the array, at which point the largest of all the elements ends up at the highest possible index. In this case, the element 9 will be the last value of the array.

4	1	7	1	9

Fig. 11.6

Please note this result is after only one iteration. This loop will repeat itself until all values are sorted in increasing order.

11.1.2 Selection Sort

The selection sort is one of the easiest ways to sort data. Rather than swapping neighbours continuously like the Bubble Sort, this algorithm finds the smallest element of the array and interchanges it with the element in the first position of the array. After that, it re-examines the remaining elements in the array to find the second smallest element. The element which is found is interchanged with the element in the second position of the array. This process continues until all elements are placed in their proper order. The order would be defined by the user (*i.e.* descending or ascending).

The Selection Sort Algorithm is as follows :

```
on selection sort A, N
     put 1 into j, – – j is used to step through the array
     repeat until j > N
         put minimum(A[j]...A[N],N-j+1) into min
         swap A[j], A[min]
         add 1 to j
     end repeat
     return A
end selection sort
```

A Selection Sort algorithm can also be described step by step as follows :

1. Repeat Steps 1 through 5 a total of n-1 times.
2. Record the part of the array that has been already sorted.
3. Repeat Step 4 for the elements in the unsorted part of the array.
4. Record the location of the smallest element in the unsorted part of the array.
5. Exchange the first element in the unsorted array with the smallest element.

11.1.2.1 Selection Sort Efficiency

For a given number of data items, the selection sort always goes through a set number of comparisons and exchanges, so its performance is predictable. The number of element interchanges depends on how unsorted the array is. During each pass no more that one interchange is essential; thus, the maximum number of interchanges for this sort is n –1.

Thus, the total number of comparisons is proportional to n^2 or $O(n^2)$.

Worst Case

Selection Sort's worst case is $n^2/4$.

Average Case

$n^2/4$

11.1.2.2 Advantages and Disadvantages of Selection Sort

The selection sort is easy to understand and this makes it easy to implement the algorithm correctly and thus makes the sorting procedure easy to write. However, there are some reasons why programmers refrain from using this algorithm :

1. This method uses internal sorting. This means that it would require the entire array to be in main memory. This would require large amounts of memory and in the case of large commercial databases, more memory than is available.
2. This program's performance of $O(n^2)$ would become quite slow on large amounts of data. If you had an array with 100,000 elements, the selection sort would not be a wise choice.
3. At present many application databases have sorted lists of data and these lists are updated on a regular basis. Most times these databases are, for the most part, in order. An ideal method would be able to recognize this fact and would work only on the unsorted items. The selection sort is unable to do this.

Let us consider an example to better understand the Selection Sort.

As an example, begin with the following array :

7	4	1	9	2

Fig. 11.7

The Selection Sort marks the first element (7). It then goes through the remaining data to find the smallest number (1). It swaps with the first element (7) and the smallest element (1) which is placed in its correct position.

1	4	7	9	2

Fig. 11.8

It then marks the second element (4) and looks through the remaining data for the next smallest number (2). These two numbers are then swapped.

1	2	7	9	4

Fig. 11.9

Marking the third element (7) and looking through the remaining data for the next smallest number (4). These two numbers are now swapped.

1	2	4	9	7

Fig. 11.10

Lastly, it marks the fourth element (9) and looks through the remaining data for the next smallest number (7). These two numbers are then swapped.

1	2	4	7	9

Fig. 11.11

If we were not finished at this point, this sort would continue until n–1 passes have been made.

11.1.3 Quick Sort

The *Quick Sort* function sorts elements of data structures using a divide and conquer approach. This means the function resolves part of the problem and then recursively solves increasingly smaller partitions of the problem until eventually the whole problem is solved. This is part of the reason why the quick sort is also called **the Partition-Exchange Sort.**

Each time when function is called, a "key" value of the structure is selected to be positioned. The function then repeatedly scans through the structure from two directions. Values less than the key are passed to the left side of the structure and values that are greater than the key are passed to the right side of the structure. These "left to right" and "right to left" scans and swaps continue until a flag condition tells them to stop. This occurs when the structure can be divided into two sorted partitions. The key is then "switched into its final position". Next the quick sort function is called to sort the partition that contains the values that are less than the key. Then the *quick sort* function is called to sort the partition that contains the values that are greater than the key. This process continues until a condition indicates that the structure is sorted.

The Quick Sort Algorithm :

```
IF left < right THEN
    BEGIN
        pivot := partition (list, left, right);
        Quicksort (list, left, pivot-1);
        Quicksort (list, pivot + 1, right);
END
```

11.1.3.1 Quick Sort efficiency

Best Case Situation

Assuming that the list breaks into two equal halves, we have two lists of size N/2 to sort. In order for each half to be partitioned, (N/2)+(N/2) = N, comparisons are made. Also assuming that each of these lists breaks into two equal sized sublists, we can assume that there will be at the most log(N) splits. This will result in a best time estimate of O(N*log(N)) for Quick Sort.

Worst Case Situation

In the worst case, the list does not divide equally and is larger on one side than the other. In this case, the splitting may go on N-1 times. This gives a worst-case time estimate of $O(N^2)$.

Average Time

The average time for Quick Sort is estimated to be O(N*log(N)) comparisons.

11.1.3.2 Advantages and Disadvantages of Quick Sort

In theory, the Quick Sort is a very efficient algorithm needing n log n steps. However, in practice its performance depends on the pivot point. The farther we get from the median for the pivot value, the more lopsided the partitions become and the greater the depth of the recursion needs to be.

This algorithm also requires a higher level of knowledge on the part of the programmer. This is becuase this algorithm utilizes recursion which can be tricky to grasp for beginners.

Let's discuss an example for Quick Sort.

A Step Through Example

1. This is the initial array that you are starting the sort with

3	1	4	1	5	9	2	6	5	3	5	8

Fig. 11.12

2. The array is pivoted about its first element p =3

3	1	4	1	5	9	2	6	5	3	5	8

Fig. 11.13

3. Find first element larger than pivot (underlined) and the last element not larger than pivot (italicised)

3	1	<u>4</u>	1	5	9	2	6	5	***3***	5	8

Fig. 11.14

4. Swap those elements.

3	1	3	1	5	9	2	6	5	4	5	8

Fig. 11.15

5. Scan again in both directions

3	1	3	1	<u>5</u>	9	***2***	6	5	4	5	8

Fig. 11.16

6. Swap

3	1	3	1	2	9	5	6	5	4	5	8

Fig. 11.17

7. Scan

3	1	3	1	***2***	<u>9</u>	5	6	5	4	5	8

Fig. 11.18

8. The pointers have crossed : swap pivot with italicised.

2	1	3	1	**3**	9	5	6	5	4	5	8

Fig. 11.19

9. Pivoting is now complete : Recursively sorts the subarrays on each side of pivot.

1	1	2	3	3	4	5	5	5	6	8	9

Fig. 11.20

The array is now sorted.

11.1.4 Binary Search

A Binary Search can only be performed if the data is sorted—whether it is in the form of a tree, array, list or any other structure. This section will explain the concept of binary search using two examples. First, we will use an array and then for a more detailed example, we will use a binary tree.

To understand the concept of binary search, let us look at the analogy of a phone book. In order to look for a particular phone number, we estimate where in the phone book we expect it to be and then turn to a page that is located approximately, where we expect to find it. Sometimes the item is found right away and if not, then we have some idea which part of the book will contain the item. Thus, we repeat the process with just that part of the book. We can do this because a phone book is sorted. If it was not, we would have to start at the very first page and read every single entry in order to find a number.

The previous sorted phone book search implies that by splitting the data in half and then checking the middle item, we have halved the remaining items to check each time.

Algorithm

Below is a general algorithm for a sorted array and a binary tree.

Sorted Array

Compare X to the middle value of the array.

If X=Y (the middle element), we are done.

If X < Y, we continue our search, confine the search to first half only.

If X > Y, we continue our search, confine the search to second half.

Binary Tree

Compare X to the root of the tree.

If X=Y (the root), we are done.

If X < Y, recursively search for X in Y's left subtree.

If X > Y, recursively search for X in Y's right subtree.

If subtree is empty, we are done and X is not known to be in the tree.

Example :

Let us begin with an example of a searching for an element in an array.

Sorted array of integers (ascending order)

Index	1	2	3	4	5	6	7	8
Value	1	6	9	10	12	17	23	24

Fig. 11.21

Shown in the above picture is a sorted array of 8 elements. Let us say, you are looking for number 12. Following are the steps to search for 12.

Steps

- Compare the element you are looking* for *i.e.,* 12 to the middle element of the array. The middle element in this case is 10, which happens to be the fourth element since the array contains 8 elements.
- If 12 = A[4] *i.e.* the element at index 4 in the array, then we are done.
- If 12 < A[4], we continue our search but confine our search to the first half of the array and entirely ignore the second half of the array.
- If 12 > A[4], we confine our search to the second half of the array and completely ignore the first half.

In our example, since 12 > 10 (the element at index 4 - the middle element in the array), we confine our search to the second half of the array and look at higher indices. Index 6 is the middle of second half of the array - index 5 to index 8. We look at the value of the element at index 6 and it turns out to be 17. Now we compare the number that we are looking for (12) to 17 and since 12 < 17 (the element at index 6) and 12 > 10 (the element at index 4). Thus, if 12 is in the array, it must be at the index position 5 or A[5] = 12.

* We can take either 10 or 12 as the middle element.

Index	1	2	3	4	5	6	7	8
Value	1	6	9	10	**12**	17	23	24

Fig. 11.22

Thus, the element we are looking for is found.

Example for Binary Search on a Tree

Following is an example of a binary tree :

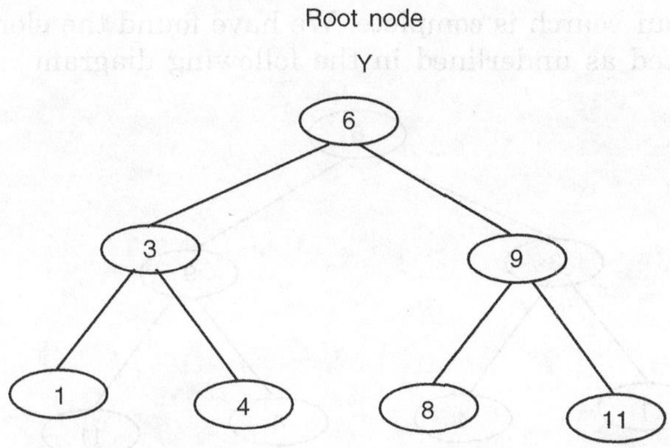

Fig. 11.23

There are two very important properties of a binary tree :

- Everything in a node's left subtree is smaller than the node's value.
- Everything in a node's right subtree is bigger than the node's value.

These two rules hold true for every single node in the tree. Thus, a tree with these above stated properties is called *a binary tree.*

We can search for a value in a binary tree containing N nodes in $O(\log_2 n)$ time. The algorithm that we use to search a node in a binary tree is same as the binary search algorithm used for lists or arrays. The only difference is that it is translated in terms of "root" and "subtrees".

Steps to search for a value in Binary Search tree :

We want to search a value X and Y is the value at the root node.

- Compare X to the root of the tree (Same as comparing the value to be found to the middle element in an array, as explained on the previous page).
- If X = Y, then we are done.
- If X < Y, we recursively search for X in the left subtree from the root node.
- If X > Y, we recursively search for X in the right subtree from the root node.
- If the subtree is empty (the item is not in the tree), then we are finished and the value X is not in the tree.

Now, let us look at an example which involves searching for different nodes in a binary tree. We have a binary tree represented in Fig. 11.23.

We want to find the element 6 in the tree. Now, the first thing that we need is a pointer to the root node.

We want to find a value X = 6.

Here are the steps that are followed to find the desired node value.

Steps

- Compare X = 6 to the root of the tree (Same as comparing the value to be found to the middle element in an array, as explained previously).
- If X = Y (the root value), then we are done. Since in this case the value is indeed equal to the root value, our search is complete. We have found the element we searched for and it is represented as underlined in the following diagram :

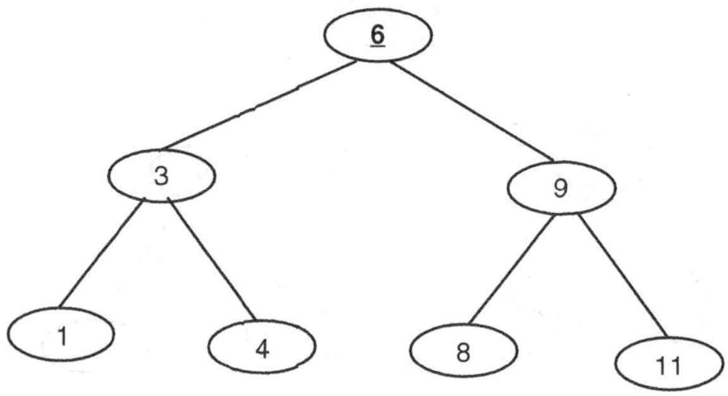

Fig. 11.24

Now we want to search for X=4. We follow the same algorithm as above and since X = 4 is not equal to the root node, we check to see if 4 is greater than or less than the root node :

If X < Y, we recursively search for X in the left subtree from the root node.

Now compare the value 4 with the left child (3) of the root node and find that 4 > 3, so we search the right subtree of the child node 3 and again repeat the above steps. We find that the right child node of 3 is equal to the value being searched for, thus our search is complete. We underline the element inside node to show that the value 4 is found. The elements inside the nodes that are visited in the process are Italicized.

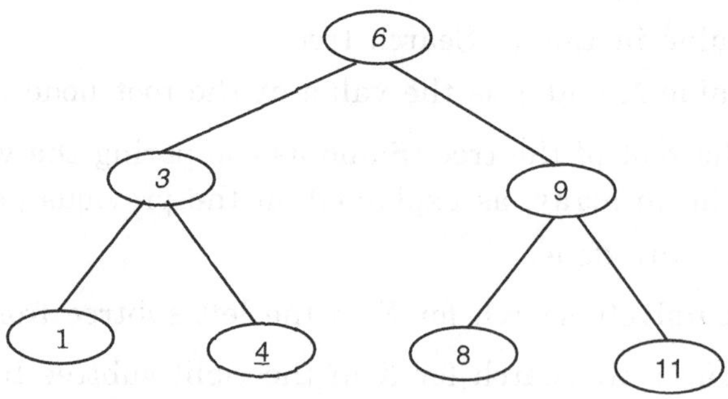

Fig. 11.25

You must note down the following points for Binary search :

- Binary search is performed on a sorted structure—a sorted array, sorted list ordered tree.

☞ Binary search for a particular element in a sorted array is performed by locating the middle entry of the array and its key value is examined. If the value to be searched is equal to the value at the middle element, then search is complete. If the value to be searched is less than the middle element, we confine our search to the first half of the array and the procedure is repeated on the first half until the required item is found. If the value is greater than the middle element, we confine our search to the second half and the procedure is repeated on the second half until the required item is found.

11.1.5 Linear Search

In the real world, searching is the process of finding an object among a group of objects. Amazingly, it is the same in the computing world. The simplest of these searches is the Linear Search.

A Linear Search is simply searching through a line of objects in order to find a particular item. This is similar to looking through a row of CD's to find your favorite. This leads to the possibility of two variations of a Linear Search, the Sorted Linear Search and the Unsorted Linear Search.

Algorithm for Linear Search

Unsorted Linear Search

```
SearchItem <- (Read Item to be searched for)

For N <- 1 to (# of Items in List)
    If (the Nth item in list) = SearchItem
    Return Success, Exit

Else
    Continue with next loop
If Loop exits
    Return Failure, Exit
```

Sorted Linear Search

```
SearchItem <- (Read Item to be searched for)

For N <- 1 to (# of Items in List)
    If (the Nth item in list) = SearchItem
        Return Success, Exit

    ElseIf (the Nth item in list) > SearchItem
        Return Failure, Exit
    Else
    Continue with next loop

If Loop exits
    Return Failure, Exit
```

Imagine instead of a row of CDs, we are dealing with a list of CD titles. This is a better description of how the computer represents information when using a Linear Search. This trivial task for a person is rather complicated for a computer. This is due to the computer's inability to see more than one title at a time. So where a person could instantly scan an entire list, a computer must go step by step through each item in the list.

The computer starts this stepping at the top of the list and compares each individual title on the list with the title it is trying to find. It goes through each item until one of two situations occurs, the CD is found or the bottom of the list is reached.

Item Found

An item is "found" when the computer compares that item with the item it is looking for, as is the case with our CDs, when the title on the CD list matches the title being searched for. Now that the item is found, the Linear Search is said to be successful.

Item Not Found

Sometimes the Linear Search will keep stepping through the entire list until it reaches the end of the list. This means that the item was not in the list to begin with, and the Linear Search is said to fail.

Now let's go back to the CD list. This time the CD list has been sorted by title, which is commonly called a sorted list. The Sorted Linear Search takes into account that it is working on a sorted list, and uses the fact that the item can only exist in one location in the list.

The **Sorted Linear Search** basically acts like the Unsorted Linear Search with one exception. The Unsorted Linear Search starts at the beginning of the list and steps through the entire list until it finds the item being searched for or it reaches the end of the list. The difference between the two searches is that the Sorted Linear Search will stop and fail if it hits an item in the list that is greater than the item being searched for.

Item Found

An item is "found" when the computer compares that item with the item it is looking for, as is the case with our CDs, when the title on the CD list matches the title being searched for. Now that the item is found, the Sorted Linear Search is said to be successful.

Item Not Found

Most times if the item is not in the list the Sorted Linear Search will find an item of greater value than the item being searched for. A few times the Sorted Linear Search will not find an item of greater value in the list and keep searching until it reaches the end of the list. In both cases, the Sorted Linear Search is said to fail. The advantage of this is that on average the search will take less time to report a failure, because it does not always traverse the entire list.

You must remember following key points about linear search :

- Linear search is the easiest of all searches.
- There are two different types of linear searches—The Sorted and the Unsorted Search.
- Both searches proceed linearly through a list.
- The sorted search requires a sorted list.
- A search is considered successful if the item is found or a failure if the item is not found.
- Both searches terminate with failure when the end of the list is reached.
- The sorted linear search will also terminate with failure when an item of greater value than the item being searched for is reached.

11.1.6 Iterative Deepening Search

It is recommended that you are familiar with both breadth first and depth first searching algorithms (discussed in Chapter 8), before attempting this iterative deepening discussion.

Iterative deepening is a graph search algorithm. It combines properties of depth first searching and breadth first searching. The basic idea is to implement a depth first search up to the Nth level. N should start at either 0 or 1 and be incremented after each search up to N is complete. This searching technique is complete and is guaranteed to return the desired node.

Starting with N=1 the nodes in a tree are searched as far as level N, N is then incremented (unless the desired node has been found) and the next level is searched. So with N=1, only three (if a binary tree is used) nodes will be searched. Assuming a balanced tree and more than 5 nodes, if N=2 the first three will be searched and then the immediate children of those (to a maximum depth of 2). This continues until the whole tree has been searched or time runs out.

Complexity

For depth d and branching factor b then iterative deepening has a time complexity **O(b^d)** and a space complexity of **O(bd)**.

Note : *The higher the branching factor, the lower the overhead of repeatedly expanded states, but even with a binary tree (b=2) iterative deepening search only takes about twice as long as a complete breadth first search.*

Optimality

The Iterative deepening search finds the highest quality solution when there are several different solutions.

Uses

In General, iterative deepening is the preferred search method when there is a large search space and the depth of the solution is not known.

HASHING

11.2 INTRODUCTION

A process whereby an item is placed into a structure based on a key-to-address transformation.

Hashing is a way of performing optimal searches and retrievals. Essentially, it increases speed, betters ease of transfer, improves retrieval, optimizes searching of data, reduces overhead. Thus, one objective of hashing is to optimize disk accesses and packing density. The packing density, roughly equivalent to a load factor, is simply how much of the table is filled (normally, 70% is sufficient). The ultimate goal, however, is to minimize disk space and access time by inserting and retrieving a record from the table in only one search. One way to minimize this time is to use small table sizes (say $m < 10$).

There are four key components involved in hashing :

- the hash table
- the hashing method
- collision
- collision resolution techniques

The hash table is a storage location in memory or on disk that records the hashed values created by the hashing algorithm. Some familiarity with the data to be stored is desirable. The hash table is normally created with a certain number of buckets or storage locations.

The number of buckets or size of the hash table is related to the quantity of data items that must be stored. It is ideal to choose hashing method that results in the *fewest collision* in a table, so you must take table size into consideration when choosing your hashing method.

Hashing differs from other types of data structures such as binary trees, stacks, or lists primarily because of the fact that the data in a hash table does not have to be reorganized before being retrieved or inserted. Also, in the aforementioned other data structures, the items are stored either in lists or trees. This tends to be a problem for larger data sets, where a search and retrieval must travel through all nodes of a tree or all elements of a list. With a hash table, the size is set, so inserting or searching for an item is limited, and not as cumbersome. One final note is that usually with lists, trees or even stacks, the time for storage and / or retrieval is related to the size of the data set.

The structure to which elements of data can be hashed is almost always a table (of size = m). These tables are stored in memory or on disk, and contain a set number of buckets.

11.2.1 Preconditioning

Converting a string to an integer using ASCII conventions.

When an item is a string, it has to be converted to an integer before a key can be found. This process is known as preconditioning.

Normally, ASCII conventions for converting characters are used. ASCII values are assigned to the 26 letters starting at 65. Thus, 'A' is 65, 'B' is 66, 'C' is 67, and so on until 'Z' is 90. All other numbers are assigned to 'special characters' such as +, –, =, /, * and so on. For example, "JOE" is converted to 747969 using J=74, O=79, and E=69.

Sometimes, after preconditioning an item, the resulting integer is too large to be stored in a table. For example, if we had an item that converted to 301522152618252415, then this would be too large to find a key. To solve this problem, we can use one hash method to achieve a usable number and a second method to map the result to the table.

11.2.2 Advantages and Disadvantages of Hashing

One advantage of hashing is that no index storage space is required, whereas inserting into other structures such as trees does normally require an index. Such an index could be in the form of a queue. In addition, hashing provides the advantage of rapid updates.

One disadvantage of hashing as an insert and retrieval tool is that it usually lacks locality and sequential retrieval by key. Consequently, insertion and retrieval are more random. Another disadvantage is the inability to use duplicate keys. This is a problem when key values are very small (*i.e.* one or two digits).

11.2.3 Application of Hashing

Database Indexing

☞ Some database systems have a separate file of files known as indexes. When a request is made for data, the key information is first found in the appropriate index file which references the exact record location of the data in the database file. The key information in the index file is sometimes stored as a hashed value.

Symbol Tables *e.g.* Fortran Variable Names

☞ It is very important in any language that the references to variables can be looked up quickly. This speeds up the execution of the program.

File and Directory Hashing in High Performance File Systems

☞ Two complementary techniques are often used to improve the performance of file access. One is caching which simply saves information in memory. The second is hashing. In large file systems that are typical of file servers, it is common to use hashing to improve performance. Looking up the file location in memory is much quicker using hashing than most other methods.

Example for Hashing

University student information often needs to be stored and retrieved. The data to be stored (student numbers) is normally in integer format or numeric string format which can easily be converted to integers. The length of the integers is normally uniform for all students (*e.g.* a 6-digit number). In this case the range of values would be from 100000 to 999999.

The first thing to do is to set up a hash table. If we set up a table with 999,999 positions, we will have a huge table with many positions that will never be used. The values from 0 to 99,999 will never be used, as there are values which have not yet been assigned to students. A better method would be to create a hash table whose size is the number of students.

Next, we must establish a hashing algorithm. A simple algorithm would be to simply subtract 100,000 from any student number. This will eliminate all of the values between 900,000 and 999,999, inclusive. The student number 100000 will be stored in position 0 in the hash table and so on. This still requires a very large hash table that will have many unused positions.

Let us assume that we are starting out as a fairly new university with a population of 100 students. Since a hash table with 100 positions does not require very much storage space, we will create a table of that size.

In order to store the student numbers in our hash table, we will use an algorithm that uses the modulus function to obtain a value from 0 to 99. 'y mod 100'. We will divide any student number by 100 and take the remainder as being the hash table position. If the students are assigned numbers sequentially beginning at 100000 and extending to 100099, we will have a 1 to 1 correspondence between student number and hash table position.

Suppose we start a new semester and 10 new students attend our university. These students will be assigned the numbers 100100 through 100109. When we use our hashing function, these numbers will correspond to positions 0 through 9 in our hash table. These positions are already in use by previously existing student numbers (*i.e.* 100000 to 100009).

We cannot store these numbers in the assigned positions because the positions are already in use. We have what is known as a conflict and now need a method of conflict resolution.

Let us suppose that in our university example, we have been operating for sometime in a non computerized environment. The students have been assigned numbers, but nothing has yet been stored on computer. It is decided that a computer system will be implemented and the student numbers will be stored in a hash table for quick retrieval.

The university has 90 students and their numbers range from 100000 to 100089. This will be a new term and the university anticipates that there will be 10 new students. The table size is set to 100 entries.

The hashing algorithm will use the modulus function to produce values between 0 and 100. 'y mod 100'.

All goes well as the first 10 new students register and are assigned student numbers ranging from 100090 to 100099. These values are stored in the hash table in the appropriate locations.

The university has a highly regarded Computer Sciences department and has attracted more students than anticipated. An extra 5 students want to register.

The student numbers assigned will continue sequentially from 100100 to 100104. When the hashing algorithm is applied to these values, the results are the integers 0 through 4. Since positions 0 through 4 in the hash table are already used by student numbers 100000 through 100004, there is no place to put these new numbers. A conflict has occurred and must be resolved.

Several methods exist for resolving conflicts of this type. We will review three in detail in the following sections.

Hashing Methods

There are seven essential methods of hashing, or ways to insert values into a key accessed table. Listed in no particular order they are the division method, multiplication method, folding method, length-dependent method, midsquare method, digit-analysis and the addition method. We should note that most of these methods have a timing complexity of O(1).

11.2.4 Division Method

Algorithm: H(x) = x mod m + 1

Where: *m* is some predetermined divisor integer (*i.e.,* the table size), x is the preconditioned key, and mod stands for modulo.

Note that adding 1 is only necessary if the table starts at key 1; if it starts at 0, the algorithm simplifies to

(H(x) = x mod m). Please note that in the applet, we did not add 1.

So, in other words: *given an item, divide the preconditioned key of that item by the table size (+1). The remainder is the hash key.*

Example :

Given a hash table with 10 buckets, what is the hash key for 'CAT'?

Since 'CAT' = 676584 when converted to ASCII, then x = 676584.

We are given the table size (*i.e.,* m = 10, starting at 0 and ending at 9).

H(x) = x mod m

H(676584) = 676584 mod 10
= 4 (Remainder is 4)
'CAT' is inserted into the table at address 4.
The Division method is distribution–independent.

11.2.5 The Multiplication Method

The method that is used in the applet is the multiplication method. It multiplies all the indiviudal digits in the key together, and takes the remainder after dividing the resulting number by the table size.

In functional notation, the algorithm is :

H(x) = (a * b * c * d *....) mod m

Where: m is the table size, a, b, c, d, etc. are the individual digits of the item, and mod stands for modulo.

Let's apply this algorithm to an example.

Example :

Given a hash table of ten buckets (0 through 9), what is the hash key for 'ZEE'?

Since 'ZEE' = 906969 when converted to ASCII, then x = 906969

We are given the table size (*i.e.,* m = 10).

H(x) = (a * b * c * d *....) mod m
H(906969) = (9 * 0 * 6 * 9 * 6 * 9) mod 10
= 0 mod 10
= 0

'ZEE' is inserted into the table at address 0.

Both of these Multiplication methods are distribution-independent.

11.2.6 The Folding Method

Algorithm : H(x) = (a + b + c) mod m

Where : a, b, and c represent the preconditioned key broken down into three parts, *m* is the table size, and mod stands for modulo.

In other words : *the sum of three parts of the preconditioned key is divided by the table size. The remainder is the hash key.*

Example :

Fold the key 123456789 into a hash table of ten spaces (0 through 9).

We are given x = 123456789 and the table size (*i.e.,* m = 10).

Since we can break x into three parts any way we want to, we will break it up evenly.

Thus a = 123, b = 456, and c = 789.

H(x) = (a + b + c) mod m
H(123456789) = (123+456+789) mod 10
= 1368 mod 10
= 8

123456789 is inserted into the table at address 8.

The Folding method is distribution–independent.

11.2.7 Other Hashing Methods

Now that we have shown, in detail, a few of the many hashing methods which you can use, we will briefly discuss the length-dependent method, midsquare method, digit-analysis and the addition method.

Midsquare

Multiply x by itself (*i.e.*, x^2) and select a number of digits from the middle of the result. How many digits you select will depend on your table size and the size of your hash key.

Digit Analysis

Certain digits of the preconditioned key are selected in a certain predetermined and consistent pattern.

Addition

The sum of the digits of the preconditioned key is divided by the table size. The remainder is the hash key.

COLLISION

11.3 INTRODUCTION

A failed attempt to insert an item in a table because there is already an item in the slot the new item has hashed to.

Once a space in the table is occupied, no other item can be placed there unless the existing item is deleted first. Think of a collision as *"interference."* A practical example might help solidify this idea.

> You have a class in a classroom that seats 20 (20 would thus be the 'table size'). Today is the day of your midterm, so everyone shows up. The first person to show up could choose a seat at random because they would all be empty. This random seating could be done for the first 12 people or so. Then, the free seats would gradually diminish. Out of the 20 people in the class, you are the last person to show up. Since you cannot sit in a seat that someone else is sitting in, you have to find the empty chair (it happens to be in the back row). So, you sequentially pass all the full seats until you get to the empty seat. By the time this happens, the test is over :

Collision-resolution techniques are used to compensate for the occurrence of collision.

Collision Resolution Techniques

Collision-resolution techniques are used to offset the effects of collision. If a collision occurs, these techniques look for another place in the table for an item to be stored (similar to your finding an empty chair). There are different methods of doing this : *linear probing, chaining, double hashing* and *open addressing.*

11.3.1 Linear Probing

After first being located to an already occupied table position, the item is sent sequentially down the table until an empty space is found. If m is the number of possible positions in the table, then the linear probe continues until either an empty spot is found, or until m-1 locations have been searched.

One thing that happens with linear probing however is clustering, or bunching together. Primary clustering occurs when items are always hashed to the same spot in the table, and the lookup requires searching through 4 or 5 buckets before finding the empty spot. A graphic might help explain this :

	X	X	X	X	X	X										X	X	X	X					
1				5															20					25

Fig. 11.26

The opposite of clustering is uniform distribution. Simply this is when the hash function uniformly distributes the items over the table.

11.3.2 Chaining

A collision has occurred. The position resolved by the resolution technique is already full, therefore the element you wish to insert into the hash table cannot go there without losing data. Separate chaining simply makes a backup list of elements that would have otherwise been inserted into a given position had that position been empty.

For example, let us assume that position x in the table has been previously filled by a hash insertion. Now, let us assume that the element we wish to insert into the hash table resolves to position x as well. We cannot simply overwrite the element already in position x. Each hash table entry requires a pointer to a linked list of records that can hold the element data. This list is only used when a collision occurs. The element that we are inserting, E, is then appended onto the list associated with the target position, x. The result is a linked list associated with each table position, each list containing only those elements that collided on that table position with an element already in that position.

11.3.3 Double Hashing

Double Hashing is another method of collision resolution, but unlike the linear collision resolution, double hashing uses a second hashing function which normally limits multiple collisions. The idea is that if two values hash to the same spot in the table, a constant can be calculated from the initial value using the second hashing function which can then be used to change the sequence of locations in the table, but still have access to the entire table.

11.3.4 Open Addressing

Using the open addressing technique, after a collision, new locations are examined until an empty one is found. The item to be inserted is placed here. If an item is deleted, then it is replaced with the word "DELETED". The sequence in which other locations are examined can be determined in many different ways. For example after collision, new locations could be searched from bottom to top, top to bottom, or by every 2 places.

CONCEPTUAL PROBLEMS

Problem 11.1 : *Write a C program to sort a list of 5 numbers (using bubble sorting).*

Solution :

```
#include<stdio.h>
#include<conio.h>
void bubble(int n[n],int count)
{
    int temp,i,k;
    for(i=count;i>0;i--)
    for(k=0;k<i-1;k++)
    {
    if(n[k]>n[k+1])
       {
          temp=n[k+1];
          n[k+1]=n[k];
          n[k]=temp;
       }
    }
}

void main()
{
    int num[5],i;
    printf("\n enter the numbers");
    for(i=0;i<5;i++)
    scanf("%d",&num[i]);
    bubble(num,5);
    clrscr();
    printf("\n sorted numbers are:");
    for(i=0;i<5;i++)
    printf("\n%d",num[i]);
}
```

Problem 11.2 : *Here are eight integers : 1, 7, 3, 2, 0, 5, 0, 8. Sort them using quick sort.*

(MCA December, 2001)

Solution :

STEP 1

Given array is

1 7 3 2 0 5 0 8

STEP 2

set pivot=array[0]

1 7 3 2 0 5 0 8

STEP 3 find first element larger than pivot (underlined) and the last element not larger than pivot(italicised).

1 7 3 2 0 5 *0* 8

STEP 4

Swap those elements.

1	0	3	2	0	5	7	8

STEP 5

Scan again in both directions.

1	0	**3**	2	***0***	5	7	8

STEP 6

Swap

1	0	0	2	3	5	7	8

STEP 7

Scan

1	0	***0***	**2**	3	5	7	8

STEP 8

The pointers have crossed : swamp pivot with italicised.

0	0	*1*	2	3	5	7	8

STEP 9

Pivoting is now complete : recursively sorts the subarrays on each side of pivot.

0	0	1	2	3	5	7	8

The array is now sorted.

EXERCISE

1. Write a nonrecursive version of quick sort.
2. Write an algorithm (recursive) to implement quicksort technique and discuss about its efficiencies.
3. The input to a sorting algorithm which sorts in increasing order : 1 2 3 4 5 6. What is that sorting algorithm which you do not prefer to use and why ?
4. Write an algorithm to implement Bubble sorting.
5. What is selection sort ?
6. What is Hashing ? Explain hash functions.

BIBLIOGRAPHY

1. Daniel F. Stubbs and Neil W. Webre, *Data Structure with Abstruct Data Types and Pascal.* Brooks/Cole Publishing Company, Monterey, Calif, 1985.

2. Hoare, Dahl, and Dijkstra (1972).
3. Kernighan and Plauger (1974).

4. Brian W. Kernighan and Dennis M. Ritche, *The C Programming Language,* Second Edition, Prentice Hall, Eaglewood Cliffs, N.J., 1988.
5. Samuel P. Harbison and Guy L. Steele Jr., C., *A Reference Manual,* Second Edition, Prentice Hall, Eaglewood Cliffs, N.J., 1987.

6. C.C. Gotlieb and L.R. Gotlieb, *"Data Types and Structures"*.
7. Lydia I. Kronsjo, *"Algorithms: Their Complexity and Efficiency",* John Wiley, New York, 1979.

8. Narain Gehani, *C : An Advanced Introduction.* Computer Science Press, RockvilleMaryland, 1985.
9. Allen I. Holub, *The C Companion,* Prentice Hall, Eaglewood Cliffs, N.J., 1987, 284.
10. Jim Welsh, John Elder, and David Bustard, *Sequential Program Structures,* Prentice Hall International, London, 1984.

11. Eric S. Roberts, *Thinking Recursively,* John Wiley and Sons, New York, 1986.
12. E. Horowitz and S. Sahni, *Fundamentals of Computer Algorithms.*

13. R.E. Tarjan, *Data Structure and Networks Algorithms,* Society for Industrial and Applied Mathematics, Philadelphia, 1983.
14. Shimon Even, *Graph Algorithms,* Computer Science Press.

15. R. Bayer and E. McCreight *"Organization and Maintenance of Large Ordered Indexes"* Acta Informatica 1 (1972), 1973-89.
16. D. Comer *"The Ubiquitous B-tree."*

17. D.L. Shell, *"A High-speed Sorting Procedure,"* Communication of the ACM2 (1959).
18. C.A.R. Hoare, *"Quicksort",* Computer Journal, 5.
19. Jonn L. Bentley, *"Programming Pearls: How to Sort,"* Communications of the ACM 27.

INDEX